"We sometimes forget that the real powers in this world are spiritual rather than physical. I'm thrilled that in *Unseen* Jack Graham reminds us of the hidden battles we face and instills hope and assurance that believers will emerge victorious. I highly recommend this insightful, biblical, and very personal book."

—Mark Batterson
New York Times bestselling author, *The Circle Maker*

"I was captivated by *Unseen* from start to finish. Dr. Graham has powerfully addressed some of the greatest questions and concerns of our day. We must all recognize that we are in a spiritual battle. This book will help you to not only understand what is going on, but how God has equipped each and every one of us to live a victorious, overcoming Christian life as light in the midst of darkness. This book is a must-read for every Christian."

—Christine Caine
founder, The A21 Campaign
bestselling author, *Undaunted*

"Good and evil, heaven and hell, God and Satan, angels and demons—the Bible says they are real. But what should we really do practically to live a Spirit-empowered life like Jesus? That is the very important theme of this timely book."

—Pastor Mark Driscoll
founding and preaching pastor, Mars Hill Church
founder, Resurgence and co-founder, Acts 29

"Jack Graham is a man of God who understands the spirit world. Our battle isn't against people. It's against Satan and demonic spirits. Jesus' conquest over those evil forces enables us to walk victoriously as we prayerfully put on God's armor and appropriate His Word. *Unseen* is a mandatory manual for every spiritual warrior!"

—Steve Gaines, PhD
senior pastor, Bellevue Baptist Church, Memphis, TN

"What you see is not all there is. Unfortunately, too many people are losing battles they don't even know are being fought. In his timely book, *Unseen*, Dr. Jack Graham equips and empowers us to fight and win spiritual battles God's way. If you are longing for more spiritual power and understanding, read this book."

—Craig Groeschel
senior pastor, LifeChurch.tv
author, *Altar Ego: Becoming Who God Says You Are*

"The key word that comes to mind concerning Jack Graham's new book *Unseen* is *needed*. There is a war in the heavenlies that touches this earth, but the good news is that we can win the war. Read, be instructed, embrace its truth, and win the battle."

—Johnny Hunt
pastor, First Baptist Church, Woodstock, GA

"Lift your eyes from the urgent and set your sights on eternity, where a hundred years from today you will be alive and fully aware. Jack Graham calls us not just to finish the race to eternity, but to break the tape accelerating, and his insightful book *Unseen* tells us why and how!"

—James MacDonald
senior pastor, Harvest Bible Chapel
author, *Vertical Church*

"The unseen aspects of the spiritual life are the most important and often most difficult to understand. But our lack of understanding doesn't negate the reality. Jack Graham's words in *Unseen* will open your eyes to the spiritual battle that surrounds us, and most important, a clear direction to our victory in Christ. Allow Dr. Graham to lead you on a life-changing journey into the unseen."

—Gregg Matte
pastor, Houston's First Baptist Church
author, *I AM Changes Who i Am*

"Pastor Jack Graham presents a tactical manual every Christ-follower needs for winning the spiritual conflict with unseen forces of evil."

—Kerry Shook
founding pastor, Woodlands Church

"There is a spiritual realm. It is real. I'm thankful that Jack Graham has given us a peek behind the curtain. His words and spiritual insights will challenge and encourage you to live this physical life with spiritual eyes."

—Pastor Dave Stone
Southeast Christian Church, Louisville, KY

"In a day when there is so much talk about heaven and hell, you may wonder, *What is fact and what is fiction?* In this marvelous book, my pastor, Jack Graham, takes us right to the source, to the Word of God, and brings us the truth with clarity and hope."

—Sheila Walsh
author, *God Loves Broken People*

UN SEEN

ANGELS, SATAN, HEAVEN, HELL,
AND WINNING THE BATTLE FOR ETERNITY

JACK GRAHAM

BETHANY HOUSE PUBLISHERS

a division of Baker Publishing Group
Minneapolis, Minnesota

Published by Bethany House Publishers
11400 Hampshire Avenue South
Bloomington, Minnesota 55438
www.bethanyhouse.com

Bethany House Publishers is a division of
Baker Publishing Group, Grand Rapids, Michigan

Printed in the United States of America

Library of Congress Cataloging-in-Publication Data is on file at the Library of Congress, Washington, DC.

ISBN 978-0-7642-1121-8 (cloth)
ISBN 978-0-7642-1222-2 (trade paper)

Author is represented by Wolgemuth and Associates.

Cover design by Lookout Design, Inc.

13 14 15 16 17 18 19   7 6 5 4 3 2 1

To David McKinley,
Mike Buster,
and Todd Bell,
three gifted, godly men
who have shared a lifetime
of ministry with me.
Your love and faithfulness
encourage me daily.

I thank my God in all my remembrance of you.
(Philippians 1:3)

CONTENTS

ACKNOWLEDGMENTS

Ashley Wiersma, thank you for enabling me to develop the message of this book—for shaping my words and working diligently to deliver the manuscript. Your love for God's truth inspires me.

Robert Wolgemuth and Associates, your encouragement challenged me to offer my best efforts and what I believe is my best book yet.

The privilege of publishing my messages in book form has been given to me by my friends at Bethany House. Thank you for the partnership and for believing in me.

Prestonwood, you are the most loving and supportive church imaginable. I am beyond blessed to be your pastor. Thank you for always believing the best is yet to come.

Thank you to my daughter, Kelly, and her husband, Jason Flores, and to my sons, Jason and Josh, and their wives, Toby and Kaytie. There really is no greater earthly joy than to know your children walk in truth.

What can I say about our grandchildren, Ian, Levi, and Dylan Claire? You are my living legacy; of such is the kingdom of heaven.

And to the love of my life, Deb Graham. God has melted our hearts together forever, in what truly is a marriage made in heaven.

INTRODUCTION

My fondness for baseball began when I was three years old. My dad placed a glove on the tiny fingers of one hand, a ball in the other, and effectively sealed the deal: I'd love the game all of my days.

In the small Arkansas town where I grew up, neighborhood kids would wake with the sun and immediately head over to the sandlot we'd configured with primitive bases and something approximating a pitcher's mound. We'd stop for ten minutes around lunchtime for a snowball cupcake and a carton of milk, but otherwise, from daybreak until nightfall, all we'd do is play ball. I learned the game by playing the game, and I *loved* playing that game.

Hall of Famer Ted Williams once said that hitting a baseball is the most difficult thing to do in sport, and I would have to agree. To hit a round ball with a rounded bat is one thing, but to do it when that ball happens to be careening toward you at ninety-five miles per hour is quite another. It's so difficult, in fact, that you hit it successfully even three times out of ten, and you just might land yourself right next to Ted in the Baseball Hall of Fame. For the twenty years I played ball, I was nearly addicted to the rush that comes from taking someone's fastball and turning it around. The suspense of being at the plate with runners on base—*Will it be a fastball or a curve ball? Will I strike out or drive in those runs? What's going to happen next?*—the windup of the guy on the mound, the *whoosh* of the ball as it speeds through the air, the crack of the bat as contact is gloriously made . . . what's not to love about this game?

Years ago, the late great comedian George Carlin used to spend part of his stand-up act poking a little fun at my beloved sport. "The Difference between Baseball and Football," it was called, and live audiences always went wild. He mocked the fact that in baseball, for instance, managers must wear the same uniform as the players. "Can you picture [then-head coach] Bill Parcels in his New York Giants uniform?" he asked.

He talked about how baseball is played on a *diamond* in a *park* in the *springtime*, when all is fresh and new, versus football, which is played on a *gridiron* (insert manly grunt), in a *stadium* (yet another grunt), in the season when everything *dies* (further grunting, coupled with snarled facial expression). Oh, and in football, you wear a *helmet*, while in baseball you wear a *cap*.

"In football," he continued, "you have unnecessary roughness, while in baseball, you have—get this!—*sacrifice*. In football, players endure all the elements, while in baseball, if it rains, well, then, 'We won't come out to play!'"

Carlin went on this way for four or five minutes before coming to his closing point, which was really the best part of the whole bit: "The objectives of the two games are totally different," he noted. "In football, the object is for the quarterback to be on target with his aerial assault, riddling the defense by hitting his receivers with deadly accuracy in spite of the blitz, even if he has to use the shotgun. With short bullet passes and long bombs, he marches his troops into enemy territory, balancing this aerial assault with a sustained ground attack, which punches holes in the forward wall of the enemy's defensive line. In baseball, the object is to go home—and to be *safe*."[1]

My baseball-playing days are long behind me now, but I still love watching others play. There is something especially gratifying about watching guys who are at the top of their game because I know what it took them to get there. I know how many thankless hours they spent lifting weights, running sprints, studying game film, talking through strategies, preparing for their next competitor, and getting their minds focused on the only thing that matters to a pro: *winning*.

The athletes who excel are those who are best prepared. The ones who take home the pennant are those who have persevered through setbacks, injuries, and loss after loss after loss, determining that *no matter what,* they are going to get that prize. They prepare to win. They play to win. They persevere so that they will *win*.

There is something very spiritual about all of this.

For many decades now, I've been of the mind that the apostle Paul was a baseball fan. Or at least a sports fan. How else do you explain all the athletic analogies he used—running the race and wrestling principalities and refusing to shadowbox evil? It was this same man who wrote:

> I do not consider that I have made it my own. But one thing I do: forgetting what lies behind and straining forward to what

lies ahead, I press on toward the goal for the prize of the upward call of God in Christ Jesus.

Philippians 3:13–14

"I've got my eye on the goal," another version says, "where God is beckoning us onward—to Jesus. I'm off and running, and I'm not turning back" (Philippians 3:14 THE MESSAGE).

For those who love God and have devoted themselves to his purposes in the world, the "prize" Paul refers to is not exactly a trophy or a pennant; no, the reason we prepare hard and play hard and persevere at every turn is that a *heavenly reward* awaits us—eternity spent at Christ's side.

In the same way that I love watching a player operating at the top of his game, I love seeing a Christ-follower at the top of his or hers, going ninety to nothing for the sake of the Lord Jesus, awake and alert, praying big prayers and taking big risks for God, just *pushing, pushing, pushing* toward that marvelous next-life prize.

This book is for people who want to live like that. It's for people who want to understand the "rules of the game" we're involved in here on earth. It's for people who want to learn about and prepare for a competitor they cannot see. It's for people who want to find out how to persevere, despite discouragements and defeats. It's for people who want to *win.*

There is nothing more exhilarating about playing baseball than that split second when you round third and start heading home. You see your coach going ballistic, waving you in with wild arms and a gigantic smile, and you know that you've got to give it everything you've got. And so, regardless of tired muscles and a heart that feels like it might thump its way right out of your chest, you turn on the afterburners and sprint to score. Billy Graham, one of my pastoral heroes, talks about this very concept in his terrific book *Nearing Home.* As a young boy, he used to imagine himself standing in the batter's box with bat in hand, "hitting a big-league grand slam into the stadium seats and hearing the crowd roar with thunder as I ran the bases—*nearing home.*"[2]

Granted, it's probably easier for someone in his nineties to envision going home than it is for someone in his twenties, forties, or sixties. But the fact is that each day that you and I live puts us one day nearer to home. My prayer in putting down the thoughts in these pages is that you would make the choices during this present life that will set you up for future success. My hope is that you'll head for a home where you'll be *eternally* safe.

Millions of spiritual creatures walk
the earth unseen, both when we sleep
and when we awake.

–John Milton

ONE
PRESSING QUESTIONS WE CAN'T HELP BUT ASK

W hen I was twenty years old, I got the phone call nobody wants to receive. Actually, it was a message to return a phone call, handed to me on a small slip of paper at a youth revival where I was preaching, in the tiny Texas town of Crowell. This was 1970—long before cell phones arrived on the scene—and the only way someone could reach me was by leaving word with the secretary of the little church in Wichita Falls that was hosting the event. A volunteer at the conference placed the message in my hand, and as I read it, my heart sank low in my chest. "Please call your brother," it read. "It's an emergency."

As I made my way to a pay phone, my mind swirled with morbid supposition. . . . Had someone been injured? Someone in my family? A close friend? Had something happened to *Deb*? My wife and I had only been married for three months. Our lives were just beginning. Surely she was okay.

I dialed slowly, trying to subdue the nervousness that fumbled my fingers over the keys. My brother, Bob, picked up immediately. "Jack," he said, "it's Dad. He's been hit."

Hit? Hit with *what?* My incredulity betrayed the fear I felt deep in my bones.

My father managed a hardware store that was connected to a grocery store in downtown Fort Worth, Texas, and took great pride in his work. He loved people and loved working with his hands, so he was a natural for the job. At fifty-six, he was vibrant, strong, in shape. He'd always been that way; in fact, during his growing-up years he was something of a street fighter, a rough-and-tumble guy who knew how to defend himself. But on this day, he would be caught off guard. On this day, he'd lose the fight.

Local merchants all over Fort Worth evidently had been put on high alert because of recent shoplifting activity in the area. The morning I was to begin my preaching duties at the revival two hours south of there—it was a Friday morning, I remember—Dad stepped outside into the parking lot of the hardware store to nail a "sale" banner to one of the posts that flanked the front door.

He was partway through the task when a man darted through the grocery store's front door and raced right past my dad, a carton of cigarettes tucked under his arm. Moments later, the grocery manager flew out of the store behind the man, yelling, "Shoplifter! Stop him! *Stop him!*"

Seeing the manager's panicked countenance and wanting desperately to be of help, my dad did the only thing he could think to do: He flung the hammer he was holding at the shoplifter, who was a good twenty yards away by now and gaining distance. Dad had hoped to arrest the man's progress and at least impair him long enough for police to arrive on the scene. But instead of hitting the shoplifter, the hammer whizzed right past his ear and tumbled to the asphalt, claw over handle twice. The mere fact that my dad had thrown a hammer at the man so enraged the crook that he stopped dead in his tracks, walked over to where the hammer was, reached down and picked it up, then turned toward my father and charged at him like a man possessed.

As I say, Dad was well-versed in the art of self-defense, but that day as he threw his fists up in front of his face to brace for attack, his street shoes gave way. He lost his balance and fell backward, hitting his head on the concrete. Seconds later, the man reached my father, who was probably already knocked out cold, raised the hammer into the air and brought it down on my father's skull. And then he did it again. And again. And again.

By now a crowd had gathered, everyone fear-stricken and unsure what to do. Several people tried to distract the attacker, in an effort to get him to stop striking my dad, but each time someone took the risk to encroach on the small space where evil was having its way, the man hit my dad again. Onlookers said it was as if he had become an animal, as if he were actually deriving *pleasure* from bludgeoning my father nearly to death.

The bloody attack went on for several minutes before the man's accomplice arrived in a get-away car. The shoplifter jumped into the passenger seat and with his friend quickly fled the scene, while my father, a man who had done nothing wrong, lay there dying.

Dad Was Always There

When I was in grade school, my dad owned and operated a drive-in called the Dan-Dee-Dog, and as a little tyke of six or seven years old, I remember dipping corn dogs and scooping ice cream for customers, being proud that I could do it "just like Dad." This was during our country's days of innocence; it was the 1950s in Conway, Arkansas, and life was simple and sweet. Husbands and wives stayed married—even happily so. Kids were respectful. Churches were packed. Spirits were high. Stress was low. Baseball and apple pie and long summer days in the sun—these are the things I remember most from those blissful growing-up years.

Admittedly, my dad was a big part of the sense of security I felt. He was my hero, my idol, my biggest fan. He was a man's man, yes, but he also had a gigantic heart. He loved his family. He loved God. He was moral and upright and funny and strong . . . and, as far as I could tell, invincible. Every kid thinks his dad is invincible, I guess. I sure felt that way about mine.

My father coached my baseball teams when I was a kid, and he never missed a single game. This perfect attendance fueled a belief in me that Dad would always be there. As a twenty-year-old, I still held this belief.

The Most Difficult Good-bye

Back in front of the hardware store, one of the city's fire marshals happened upon the shocked crowd and immediately radioed for backup help. Authorities arrived, and within minutes of the two criminals' departure, they had been apprehended. They'd made it only three blocks.

My dad was rushed to a nearby hospital as my brother hurried to get word to me that I needed to come home—fast. I hung up with my brother and called Deb, who had stayed home that weekend. We were living in Abilene at the time, both still in school at Hardin-Simmons University. The drive would take her three hours.

As soon as she pulled into Crowell, I took the driver's seat, and we headed north to Fort Worth. I was on pins and needles that entire trip: Would Dad pull through? Would he live to tell about this terrible tragedy? If he *did* live, would he ever be the same? His head injuries sounded so severe that I honestly didn't know what to hope for, what to expect.

Life unfolded at an achingly slow pace, in suspended animation, even as we raced across the state to get to Dad. In my heart, I was preparing for the most difficult good-bye of my life. Hopefully my instincts would prove themselves wrong. But somehow, I knew they were right.

When Deb and I reached the hospital, we found my mom and my brother already there, loving sentinels guarding my unconscious dad, willing him to recover, to talk, to blink, to show any sign that he knew they were there. But there would be no signs. For ten days, there was only the angry *whir-clink-thunk* of the high-tech machinery tasked with keeping my father alive.

Day after day, I'd crouch beside Dad, take one of his big, strong hands into my grip, and say, "Dad, if you know it's me, give me a squeeze." And day after day, there was nothing. No squeeze. No acknowledgment that I was there. No "Dad," as I knew the man.

On the ninth day of the ritual that had until this point been futile, I took my father's hands into mine, asked him to squeeze if he knew it was me, and then bowed my head as if resigning myself to one more letdown amid this colossally discouraging week. But then, just as I was ready to release Dad's limp hand, I felt a gentle squeeze. It was subtle. It was weak. But it was there. Tears sprang to my eyes as God whispered to my soul: *This will be the last interaction you'll have with him. That squeeze will be his last.*

And it was.

Thomas Benjamin Graham would survive for ten days in that "barely there" state, and then God would take him home.

So Many Questions

During that grueling week while Dad was hanging on for dear life, the exhaustion and despair caught up with me, and I needed a few minutes to think, pray, and sit in silence alone. I headed downstairs to the hospital chapel, which, thankfully, was totally deserted. I found a pew near the back, slipped in and sat down, and let pent-up tears finally flow. I was angry—angry that someone had stolen my dad's life from him . . . and also confused: Why would God take my one and only father in such a violent way?

I felt rudderless in the way that only the loss of your hero can make you feel.

With my head in my hands, I began to talk to God. Among skeptics there is a long-held assumption regarding the odd dynamic of bad things happening to good people that goes something like this: Either God cares about our painful circumstances and personal tragedies down here on planet Earth but is powerless to intervene, or else he possesses the requisite power to intervene but simply does not care. But in my heart, there in the chapel that day, neither of these options sat right with me. I knew enough of God to know that he is caring, he is powerful . . . he is both of these things at the same time. But what to make of Dad's gruesome death? Where was that third option I knew simply had to exist? And what was I to do with all my unanswered whys?

Why this? Why now? Why me? Why my dad? Why this tragedy, for a family that loves the Lord?

Was anyone really "up there"? And was he really in control? This is how it goes, I think, when hard events stop us short. Questions outweigh answers, and we find ourselves dismayed and perplexed. A spouse calls it quits. A boss says he's sorry, but your services are no longer needed. A wayward teen only digs in her heels further. A check bounces . . . and another, and another. A friend delivers a verbal blow.

A parent is ruthlessly murdered.

Even the most devoted Christ-followers can't help but wonder sometimes if God really has their backs. Great faith still asks tough questions; great faith still sometimes doubts. Or *often* doubts, according to Madeleine L'Engle, who once wrote, "Those who believe they believe in God but without passion in the heart, without anguish of mind, without uncertainty, without doubt, and even at times without despair, believe only in the idea of God, and not in God himself."[1]

I "believed I believed in God," and in his goodness, in his rule and reign over both the things I could see, as well as those things I couldn't. I had committed my life, my mind, my soul, my career to this set of beliefs, and had never once looked back. And while I didn't look back even then, there in the chapel that day, I spent a significant amount of time looking up, shaking my head in wobbly belief.

You're sufficient for this confusion I'm feeling, right, Father? You're enough for me, even in the loss of my dad? You'll help me interpret all this someday, won't you? You'll do something about this anger, this pain?

Of Supernatural Things

Growing up in a traditional Southern Baptist church in Arkansas meant that from a very early age I learned a lot about the plan of salvation and personal evangelism and the perils of rebellion and sin. It also meant I learned almost nothing about "spiritual forces," about the tension between good and evil, about the afterlife and heaven and hell—except to be told that one place was desirable and the other place definitely was not. I also knew next to nothing about the power and presence of the Holy Spirit in believers' lives. To that last point, I understood that God's Spirit was the third person of the Trinity. But as far as I could tell, he was MIA and had been for quite some time. "Spirit-led" *anything* was relegated to the snake handlers at the church down the street, and I wasn't about to darken that doorstep. No, my family, my community, my church—we stayed away from all that "hype," preferring to deal exclusively in the "natural" realm. Sure, supernatural stuff had happened during biblical times. But hadn't God come to his senses since then?

Still today, many self-proclaimed Christians are confounded by what really goes on—if anything—outside of the world we can touch and see. Yes, we believe in gravity. We even believe in love. We believe in photosynthesis, in electricity, and in oxygen, as well as in that nebulous thing called a *soul*. But when it comes to angels, demons, and the good-versus-evil spirit world, we're really not so sure.

Popular culture doesn't do much to help us here. There is an influx today of television shows, movies, books, video games, and news magazines obsessed with the paranormal, with what may be "out there." And certainly, not all the perspectives are valid. What began building decades ago with *Touched by an*

Angel, Angels in the Outfield, Michael, The Preacher's Wife, Teen Angel, City of Angels, Fallen, and more is culminating today with an onslaught of supernatural-themed media: *Ghost Hunters, Walking Dead, True Blood, Paranormal Activity,* and the *Twilight* trilogy. The list goes on, and the danger is this: To some degree, we rightly categorize these shows as "fantasy," as nothing more than an entertaining way to decompress over a giant bowl of buttered popcorn after a long, hard week at school or work. And yet the messages they deliver stick. If we're not on our guard, we'll start dismissing as mere fantasy *all* that is unseen, including that which God says is real.

Well-known cultural researchers The Barna Group conducted a survey centered on adults' spiritual beliefs and found that nearly 60 percent of professing Christians do not believe that Satan is a living being, but merely a *symbol* of evil. Likewise, 58 percent believe the Holy Spirit is a symbol of God's power or presence, but not a living entity with whom a person could relate. Perhaps more interesting still is that in the same survey, nearly half (47 percent) of Christians who said Satan was only a symbol of evil nevertheless agreed that a person can be under the influence of spiritual forces, such as demons; and almost half (49 percent) of those who agreed that the Holy Spirit is not a living entity but rather a symbol of God's presence, conceded that the Bible is "completely accurate in all the principles it teaches."[2]

The contradictions are impossible to ignore: I think you'd agree that a person cannot be demonically possessed by a mere symbol; equally true, the Bible teaches that the Holy Spirit is a living entity who literally takes up residence in the life of a person surrendered to Christ and guides and directs that person throughout his days and years, serving as a comforter in times of need.

Indeed, we are perplexed by all that is contained in the untouchable, invisible realm.

George Barna, head of the research group that conducted the study, summed up his team's findings this way:

> Most Americans, even those who say they are Christian, have doubts about the intrusion of the supernatural into the natural world. Hollywood has made evil accessible and tame, making Satan and demons less worrisome than the Bible suggests they really are. It's hard for achievement-driven, self-reliant, independent people to believe that their lives can be impacted by unseen forces. At the same time, through sheer force of repetition, many Americans intellectually accept some ideas—such as the fact that you either side with God or Satan, there's no in-between—that do not get translated into practice.[3]

Barna's remarks strike at the core reason I decided to write this book—I wish I'd had important spiritual truths explained to me even earlier than they were. I wish I'd been given answers to questions that at the time I didn't know to ask. Fortunately, God would place people in my path who would enlighten and educate me; but oh, the angst I could have avoided had I known the truth of how the world—both seen *and* unseen—works.

The Battle Is Real

My ignorance about the prevalence and relevance of all things supernatural would start to be allayed in the early 1970s, when a revival swept through Southern Baptist circles, led by Bible teachers such as Ron Dunn, Jack Taylor, and Manley Beasley. They were men from our own (rather traditional, rather skeptical) denomination who possessed an uncommon boldness for talking about Things We Didn't Talk About—angels and demons, good and evil, the Holy Spirit as alive and accessible and eager to help Christians live their lives. I was in seminary at the time and remember being more captivated by what I was learning outside than inside of class. I began to add taboo volumes to my library, including Barnhouse's *The Invisible War* and Spurgeon's writings on spiritual warfare; what's more, I had accepted preaching responsibilities for a church in Abilene on the weekends and even began to—gasp!—teach on these subjects. My theology surrounding the supernatural was being turned on its head, which, in hindsight, was a useful thing.

Life experience was bearing out what my newfound book knowledge had told me was true: There was a very active unseen realm at work all around me, and to deny its existence would be akin to denying gravity. And yet a quick leap from a tall building was probably all it would take to remind me of that reality.

Equally true, this invisible realm is *inhabited*—both by God and angels and spiritual forces fighting for good, but also by other forces, dark forces, satanic forces, forces that seek to do God's people harm. How else could I explain my father being beaten to death, than to acknowledge such a battle in my midst? Scriptures I'd never really paid attention to now seemed to leap off the page: "Though we walk in the flesh," Paul says in 2 Corinthians 10:3–4, "we are not waging war according to the flesh. For the weapons of our warfare are not of the flesh but have divine power to destroy strongholds."

In 2 Timothy 2:3–4, the "war" references continue. Paul refers to his young apprentice as a "good soldier of Christ Jesus" and reminds him that good soldiers do not get themselves entangled in civilian pursuits, since his aim is to "please the one who enlisted him."

In Philippians 2:25 and again in Philemon 2, Paul calls his friends and colleagues Epaphroditus and Archippus his "fellow soldiers."

Peter continues this sort of talk: "Beloved, I urge you as sojourners and exiles to abstain from the passions of the flesh, which wage war against your soul" (1 Peter 2:11).

The more I read of God's Word, the more I realized there was little room for a "whistle while you work" mentality as it related to my ministry and life. My feet had been planted not on a playground, but on a battleground, and the battle was for my faith, for my family, for my purity, for my fidelity to Christ, for my very soul. How had I missed this before?

In his bestselling book, *A Grief Observed,* C. S. Lewis wrote, "You never know how much you really believe anything until its truth or falsehood becomes a matter of life and death to you." Watching my father fade from this earthly life at the hands of a hammer-wielding madman forced me to come down on one side or the other: Either there was an invisible war being waged all around me, complete with forces both angelic and demonic vying for allegiance from every soul (including mine), or there wasn't.

I knew in my heart there was. And because there was, I wanted to be sure I was on the good guys' side of the fight. I wanted my life to be a candle that illuminated the darkness, an idea first planted in my mind and heart when I was a boy of seven years old. My favorite television program back then was *Life Is Worth Living* with Bishop Fulton J. Sheen, an American archbishop of the Catholic Church, who is widely considered to be the world's first televangelist. Each week, I'd sit on the greenish-brown carpet in our living room and stare wide-eyed at the chunky box with thick knobs that broadcast in black-and-white the bishop in all his "bishopness"—the dark suit, the priest's collar, the flowing, official-looking robes. And I'd watch with rapt attention all the way from the opening scene to his persuasive parting words.

Bishop Sheen's show always began the same way—a perfectly black screen, perfect silence. Then the sound of a match being struck, followed by a flame chasing across the screen, leaving a trail of light that brightened what had once been black. The hand that struck the match would then carry it over to a candle, reach toward the wick, and offer up its light. Just then, by dramatic voice-over, you'd hear, "It is far better to light a candle than to curse the darkness!" It may have been a very bad voice-over, but instinctively I knew the message was good.

Back in the hospital chapel, as I gathered up the pieces of my broken heart, that line came to mind. That simple phrase—*it's far better to light a candle than to curse the darkness*—had served as the spine of my life philosophy through the years. From a tender age, it had prepared me to deal with the bad things that invariably happen in life: Yes, we should pound our fists over persisting ills we see, but unless we also put our hands to work in providing workable solutions to those problems, what are we left with in the end but bruised fists and a bitter heart?

Not only was I beginning to understand that there are spiritual forces at work all around me, all the time—forces for good and for evil as well—it also occurred to me that I actually could choose which forces to align myself with. Focusing my attention on these simple truths that day served to shift my focus from anger and confusion to peace and strength . . . even joy. *Joy,* even as my father lay dying? It was proof that God was still at his post, reshaping the awfulness of the week that had passed into something useful, instructive, and good.

I thought about the man who had taken my dad's life. And I wondered what would have happened if he hadn't demanded to go his own way in life but had gone God's way instead. My thoughts gained steam: What if I made it my life's mission to reach as many people as possible with the good news of God's grace, so that nobody else had to lose their dad because of a vicious, senseless crime?

Yes, the world was broken and fallen and in a desperate state of sin. Bad things happened to good people—this was and always would be true. But if my efforts could help even *one* self-focused person surrender himself to faith in Jesus Christ, *one* would-be murderer about to take the life of an innocent man, wouldn't it be worth it to devote my life to this cause?

Seeing the unmistakable ravages of darkness shroud my family gave me fresh resolve to use whatever light I'd been given to push back that darkness all the remaining days of my life.

Admittedly, the notion was lofty. Who has time to "push back the darkness" when there is a lawn to mow, bills to pay, a job to hold down, errands to run, taxes to file, kids to raise, meals to prepare, and baseball games to watch? "The world is too much with us," William Wordsworth once famously wrote. And was he ever right. We're often too much "of this world" to focus on any other world that may (or may not) exist.

But my plea to you—and also to me—is this: We mustn't brush this stuff aside, thinking that what we don't know won't hurt us. What we don't know *absolutely* will hurt us, and hurt us in meaningful ways. I don't know a single person who wants to sign up for any more pain. I don't know a single person who wants to fail at life. We only get one shot at this thing, and most level-headed people want to succeed. We want to get it right.

We want to spend our time and energies on things that matter, not fritter them away on useless pursuits.

If you fall into that well-populated camp, then I have very good news for you: There is a clear-cut way to succeed at this thing called life. There is a way to *get it right*. Learning how to discern and respond to the presence of God and his angels, how to avert the attacks of Satan, how to thrive during our time on earth and prepare for everlasting life in heaven—developing some spiritual muscle in these areas will usher in peace and provision and the fulfillment of unparalleled promise, all of which will serve us well for all of our days.

Years ago, *The New Yorker* ran an article about a Midwestern man named Virgil[4] who had a hereditary condition called retinitis pigmentosa, which slowly but relentlessly eats away at the retina—the rods-and-cones part of the eye. Virgil had been virtually blind since childhood, only able to discern light from dark or the shadow of a hand moving in front of his face.

After visits to more than half a dozen specialists, Virgil—now nearly fifty years old—finally happened upon an ophthalmologist who promised complete restoration of the man's sight. The day of the surgery came, and after the doctor worked his magic, Virgil's bandages were removed. A small posse of staff and family members had gathered in the clinic's recovery room, eager to see Virgil finally see. But to their surprise, once Virgil's new eyes were exposed, there was no exclamation, no cheer, no enthusiasm whatsoever from the now-seeing man. Wasn't he excited that at last he had his sight?

As it turns out, the reason for Virgil's subdued post-surgery state was that while he could now discern colors and shapes and fine movement and depth, he had absolutely no idea what he was looking at. None of these images had any meaning to Virgil; after being blind for more than forty-five years, he had no visual memories to support his newfound perception. Yes, he now could see the world. But it was a world that made no sense to him.

Over time, Virgil would learn to enjoy clear vision. He would come to appreciate the beauty of rolling hills, blooming flowers, and the sun as it makes its descent. He would begin to grasp the wonder of a shifting shadow, stepping over a curbside puddle, and succeeding at reading an eye chart. But it took time, experience, and discernment before this sense of cohesion could take hold.

Mark 8 tells the story of a man born blind whose friends brought him to Jesus for healing. As was the case every single time someone asked Jesus to heal him, the Great Healer instantly agreed:

> He took the blind man by the hand and led him out of the village, and when he had spit on his eyes and laid his hands on him, he asked him, "Do you see anything?" And he looked up and said, "I see people, but they look like trees, walking."
>
> vv. 23–24

The text goes on to say that Jesus laid his hands on the man a second time, and when the blind man opened his eyes, his sight was perfectly restored. "He saw everything clearly," says verse 25. In other words, *no more trees.*

This is a fascinating story to me, because the process of my own spiritual eyes being opened to the unseen world that surrounds us unfolded in much the same way. My understanding *developed.* It *evolved.* It came into focus, slowly but surely. I was once just like Virgil, who could make no sense of what he was seeing. I was like the man who mistook people for trees. But over time, as I racked up life experience and divinely issued discernment, I started to see the world for what it really was—the good, the evil, the powers that be, the forces pushing and pulling and positioning and angling for a hold on my mind, my soul, my life. Still, I find myself learning, asking God to bring into focus all that blurs. But I'm getting better. I'm seeing what I did not see before.

I suppose this is what I want to say to you, as you consider concerning yourself with the invisible realm: If you truly desire spiritual eyesight—if you crave eyes that *really see*—then God will answer that desire with keen vision and will also show you things you've not seen. He will help you make sense of the life you're living. He will lend wisdom to your questioning heart.

Jeremiah 33:3 contains one of the most powerful promises in all of the Bible: "Call to me and I will answer you," God says through his prophet Jeremiah, "and will tell you great and hidden things that you have not known." God has revealed truth that can disentangle our confusion and direct our every step. But we have to *ask* him for wisdom if we want this sort of life. We ask; he answers—this is the way this deal works.

But what a deal it is! God is not afraid of our questions; he *welcomes* them, in fact. We can bring him our curiosity, our anger, our confusion, our whys, and know that he'll offer heartfelt answers in reply. He alone holds the keys to our understanding—about life that is both seen and unseen.

Discussion Questions

1. What are one or two memorable life experiences that have caused you to question the existence of a "supernatural" realm?

2. What questions, specifically, did these experiences conjure for you?

3. What cultural inputs—TV shows, movies, and the like— have influenced your understanding of the supernatural realm? In what ways have they been helpful in guiding you to truth? Have any been harmful?

4. How did George Barna's words strike you: "Many Americans intellectually accept some ideas—such as the fact that you either side with God or Satan, there's no in-between—that do not get translated into practice"?

5. "The more I read of God's Word, the more I realized there was little room for a 'whistle while you work' mentality, as it related to my ministry and life. My feet had been planted not on a playground, but on a battleground, and the battle was for my faith, for my family, for my purity, for my fidelity to Christ, for my very soul." What thoughts does this sentiment spur in you?

There is no neutral ground
in the universe; every square inch,
every split second, is claimed by God
and counter-claimed by Satan.

—C. S. Lewis

TWO
THE DARK ANGEL

In the late 1980s, *Saturday Night Live* funnyman Dana Carvey sent ripples of laughter through millions of American homes every weekend with his portrayal of uptight, pious, holier-than-thou Enid Strict, better known as "The Church Lady." According to Carvey, the character was based on the actual uptight, pious, holier-than-thou women in the church he attended as a kid, who busied themselves with religiously tracking his and others' attendance. No wonder he nailed the role.

The Church Lady hosted a faux talk show called *Church Chat*, during which she interviewed various celebrities or other

SNL characters. She'd patronize them for a few minutes before homing in on some well-publicized sin streak in their lives and launching into a sanctimonious tirade. Then the real fun would begin. She'd ask them to justify their errant ways, and after they stumbled and bumbled a bit and came up with no plausible reason for their immorality, iniquity, or general wrongdoing, The Church Lady would purse her lips, cock her head, and in a perfected know-it-all tone, say, "Hmmm . . . could it be . . . *Satan?*"

It was all in good fun, this weekly mocking of the notion that there could be some evil being roaming about the earth, pulling the strings on people's every idiotic move. Because, of course, there isn't an evil being roaming about the earth, promoting dishonesty, depravity, and decadence, right? Surely Satan is just a funny little caricature, reserved for things like late-night TV, hockey-team logos, harmless Halloween costumes, and canned deviled ham.

Down through the ages, Satan has been depicted as something of a man-goat with tail, horns, and a wicked grin, clad in red tights and holding a pitchfork, which he ostensibly uses to shovel coal all day long in hell. It is commonly held that this caricature originated in the days when Greek gods were thought to rule the heavens, the world, and the underworld. And the belief might actually hold water; if you throw the gods Pan and Neptune in a blender, you really are left with something that looks an awful lot like our modern-day depictions of Satan. Further perpetuating this particular representation of evil were the "miracle plays"[1] of the Middle Ages. In those days, actors would put on good-versus-evil stage dramas as a means of exposing the illiterate serfs in the audience to concepts such as morality and virtue.

But to showcase morality, they needed a depiction of immorality; to herald the goodness of good, they needed a way to show all that was bad. So they went back to the commonplace version of Satan—the red tights, the horns and tail, the whole bit. And the getup sort of stuck: Even in today's contemporary world, our collective minds chase back to the caricature when we hear "Satan" or "the devil" named. As a society, we've long believed that if we can keep the devil relegated to his silly red tights and pitchfork-carrying ways (who carries a pitchfork around, anyway?), he won't seem so malevolent. He won't seem so nasty. He won't seem so . . . real.

And that's a central goal of Satan's, to make Christians doubt his existence, his power, his prowess in causing destruction in our lives.

In *The Screwtape Letters*—C. S. Lewis's ingeniously imagined account of the ongoing correspondence between junior demon Wormwood and his senior-level-demon uncle Screwtape—we find one letter in particular from uncle to nephew that captures this precise idea. Wormwood has asked his uncle if he should reveal himself to the person he has been assigned to tempt, or remain hidden and invisible. In response, Uncle Screwtape says:

> The fact that "devils" are predominantly comic figures in the modern imagination will help you. If any faint suspicion of your existence begins to arise in his mind, suggest to him a picture of something in red tights, and persuade him that since he cannot believe in that (it is an old textbook method of confusing them) he therefore cannot believe in you.[2]

On more occasions than we like to admit, we fall prey to this very ploy. Unable to get that image of the red tights, the cloven hooves, the heartless cackle out of our mind, we put forth *suspicion* instead of *certainty* regarding Satan's enthusiasms, strategies, and schemes. Or worse yet, we race to the other end of the spectrum, looking for a demon behind every bush: We frivolously surf the Web all day at work and claim not negligence or lack of performance, but "spiritual warfare" when we finally get fired. We stay up too late watching worthless shows on TV and blame the fact that we can't get out of bed in the morning not on laziness, but on "Satan's opposition to my spending time with God." We wind up having to pay double for new brakes on our car because they should have been replaced three months ago, but instead of admitting procrastination, say, "This must be another of Satan's attacks."

So where is the balance between acknowledging a very real force for evil in the world and still owning up to our own junk? It's a critical question to answer if we hope to thrive in life. (Ephesians 6:12 describes the unseen realm as comprising forces "not against flesh and blood"—things that are tangibly, visibly evident—but rather against "rulers, authorities, cosmic powers, and spiritual forces of evil"—the stuff we *can't* touch or hear or see.) For starters, let's abandon all cultural references to Satan, the myriad caricatures, exaggerations, and theatrical depictions that undoubtedly coast lazily through our brains. Let's instead learn something of the real-deal Satan—who he is, what he looks like, and how he typically behaves.

Assessing Our Adversary

A friend of mine, Scott Turner, played in the NFL for nearly a decade, and recently we had a discussion about how his team scouted opponents each week before they met them on the playing field. He played for three different teams, and all of them followed the same practice: For a full seven days they'd dissect the tactics, techniques, and tendencies of their next opponent by watching game film and taking note of various formations, play-calling, and receivers or running backs the other team tended to favor. They picked apart the opponent's special teams, paying attention to kick coverages, return-blocking, and trick plays they gravitated toward, and then they factored all this knowledge and insight into their plan of attack for that week's game.

Those involved in leading troops into military conflicts will tell you they practice a similar approach. In Robert Greene's *The 33 Strategies of War,* which consolidates winning strategies from the likes of Napoleon Bonaparte, Alexander the Great, and Lawrence of Arabia, the first key piece of advice offered is "know your opponent."

Whether we're talking about a sports team, a military offensive, or everyday life for a Christ-follower, it's absolutely critical to assess one's adversary before charging off into battle.

Throughout Scripture, we are given plentiful descriptions of who we're dealing with when it comes to the leader of the demonic realm. In 1 Peter 5:8 we find that "adversary" reference, meaning one who opposes the things of God and who will do anything to thwart God's kingdom rule and purposes. Our adversary is also called

- the *devil,* a slanderer who disparages anything God finds valuable, anything that is holy and pure (Matthew 4:1)
- the "serpent" from Genesis 3 who "leads the whole world astray" (Revelation 12:9 NIV)

- *Beelzebub*—literally, "lord of the flies" (Matthew 10:25 and 12:24, 27 KJV)
- *Belial* (2 Corinthians 6), meaning a false god who has exactly nothing in common with the loving, just God we serve.

He is named

- the evil one (1 John 5:19)
- the tempter (1 Thessalonians 3:5; James 1:13)
- the prince of this world (John 12:31 KJV)
- the accuser of the brethren (Revelation 12:10 KJV)
- a hungry, roaring lion (1 Peter 5:8)
- a thief and a robber (John 10:10)
- the originator of sin (1 John 3:8)
- a murderer and a liar—even the *father* of lies (John 8:44).

But perhaps most telling is the name he is given in Job 38:32 (in some translations) and again in Isaiah 14:12: "Lucifer," Latin for *the one who bears bright light*. To fully appreciate our enemy's evil machinations, we must understand this name. Indeed, if Satan manifested himself in the room where you are sitting, you would sooner be tempted to fall to the floor, bow down before his beauty, and worship him as an angel of light, than you would be to flee from his presence as though you'd seen evil incarnate, quivering in terror with each step you took. Yes, he may be *disgusting* in motive and action, but he appears *desirable* in manner and sight.

God's Fallen Angel of Light

Today Satan may be the tempter, the accuser, the evil lord of the flies, but it wasn't always this way; there was a time when he was perfect and beautiful, when he represented all that was good. Ezekiel 28:14 says (referring to Lucifer, as he was known in the beginning), "You were an anointed guardian cherub. I placed you; you were on the holy mountain of God; in the midst of the stones of fire you walked."

Among the angelic hierarchy, there was none more important than Lucifer. Cherubs are the highest class of angelic beings; in fact, when Adam and Eve were expelled from the garden, God placed "cherubim" there to guard the Tree of Life (see Genesis 3:24). Lucifer was the highest of high, in terms of position— second only to God himself. No created being was closer to God than Satan, before his fall. Ezekiel 28:15 says he was "blameless in [his] ways from the day [he was] created." He walked in the very presence of God, existing as near to him as one could get. He occupied the role of prime minister for God, ruling over this world on God's behalf. He had vast authority given by the mighty hand of God and delivered an entire universe of angelic beings' praise into God's hands. Sometimes referred to as the first worship leader, Lucifer dispensed God's power to the universe and in exchange returned the universe's praise.[3]

But that would all change drastically the day Lucifer decided he would turn his back on his Creator and try to keep some of God's praise for himself. (*Note to self*: Don't ever try this at home.)

Rebellion From God, Rebellion From Good

There came a time when the spirit-being known as Lucifer allowed his blossoming pride to get the better of him. He *was* beautiful. He *was* perfect. He *was* positioned in close proximity to God. But instead of allowing these truths to knit him more tightly to the bosom of his Creator, he chose instead to rebel. We don't know from Scripture precisely how Satan's sales pitch to the rest of the angels unfolded, but God's Word is clear that when the rebel puffed out his chest and knowingly defied the authority of the Father, he took one-third of the heavenly host with him, in a massive revolt against the one true God.[4]

This large-scale disobedient departure would thrust the earth into chaotic darkness, and there the world would remain until God chose to one day say, "Let there be light." This ought to be instructive to us: With Satan, all is dark.

Let's return to Ezekiel 28. The first part of the chapter is a rebuke from God to the Prince of Tyre, delivered by the righteous prophet Ezekiel. But soon the tone shifts. Beginning in verse 11 (below), it is clear that we're no longer talking about an earthly prince, but about Lucifer—Satan—himself.

God's Message came to me: "Son of man, raise a funeral song over the king of Tyre. Tell him, A Message from God, the Master: 'You had everything going for you. You were in Eden, God's garden. You were dressed in splendor, your robe studded with jewels: Carnelian, peridot, and moonstone, beryl, onyx, and jasper, sapphire, turquoise, and emerald, all in settings of engraved gold. A robe was prepared for you the same day you were created. You were the anointed cherub. I placed you on the mountain of God. You strolled in magnificence among the stones of fire.

"'From the day of your creation you were sheer perfection . . . and then imperfection—evil!—was detected in you. In much buying and selling you turned violent, you sinned! I threw you, disgraced, off the mountain of God. I threw you out—you, the anointed angel-cherub. No more strolling among the gems of fire for you! Your beauty went to your head. You corrupted wisdom by using it to get worldly fame. I threw you to the ground, sent you sprawling before an audience of kings and let them gloat over your demise. By sin after sin after sin, by your corrupt ways of doing business, you defiled your holy places of worship.

"'So I set a fire around and within you. It burned you up. I reduced you to ashes. All anyone sees now when they look for you is ashes, a pitiful mound of ashes. All who once knew you now throw up their hands: 'This can't have happened! This has happened!'"

EZEKIEL 28:11–19 THE MESSAGE

Satan had all that a created being could ask for, but with ungrateful hands he crumpled it all up and promptly threw it away. He went from leading the universe in the worship of God to being absolutely allergic to that praise. He went from being just a little lower than Jesus to turning and running at the sound of the Messiah's name. He went from holding the highest of positions to haughtily rebelling against the One whom he served. And it all started with the simplest of statements. It started with the words *I will.*

Isaiah 14:12–14 bears this out:

How you are fallen from heaven, O Day Star, son of Dawn! How you are cut down to the ground, you who laid the nations low! You said in your heart, "*I will* ascend to heaven; above the stars of God *I will* set my throne on high; *I will* sit on the mount of assembly in the far reaches of the north; *I will* ascend above the heights of the clouds; *I will* make myself like the Most High."[5]

As a result of that astounding haughtiness, God cast out Lucifer altogether—out of heaven, out of power, out of the right standing he once enjoyed. From there, Satan's reign of wrath began.

There is a lesson here for you and me: Pride really does go before a fall, and it has been rightly said that the shortest definition of *any* sin—pride included—is "I will":

I *will* go my own way.
I *will* do my own thing.
I *will* prize my own thoughts.
I *will* chart my own course.
I *will* be my own source of truth.
I *will* build my own kingdom.
I *will* be my own god.

From the moment Lucifer sneered "I will," he was doomed to hellish disappointment, and the same is always true for us. It is when we think we can navigate life apart from God that we too are doomed—to disappointment and discomfort and despair, to an eternity marked by pain. We'll explore this concept further in chapter 6.

Satan's Singular Goal, Then and Now

We see from the passages in Ezekiel and Isaiah that Satan's demise was birthed in rebellion; in fact, rebellion is what he still seeks today. Throughout all the centuries that have passed, his method of operation has not changed a bit: *The thing our adversary most desires is for human hearts to rebel against God.*

Satan wants lovers of God to detach their allegiance from God and attach it to him instead.[6] For most of us who have a deeply ingrained sense of right and wrong, it's not all that likely that we'll spend our lives worshiping Satan. What happens instead is that we detach from God and attach to *ourselves*. It's only a partial victory for Satan; he would much prefer we help him build his kingdom instead of our own. But it is a step in the

44

right direction, in his view. Because as long as we're consumed by *our* interests, *our* needs, *our* desires, *our* six steps toward sure success, at least we're not focused on God. And that is very good news for the enemy of our souls.

Satan speaks only three times in Scripture, but the three occasions tell us much about how he works toward his detachment/ attachment goal.

First, in the book of Genesis, Satan—who shows up in the form of a serpent—approaches Eve and convinces her that her God is holding out on her, that he obviously doesn't want what is best for her, given he has forbidden her from eating the fruit of the garden's one and only "hands-off" tree. He slanders the character and nature of God and tempts the unsuspecting Eve to rebel against the Lover of her soul (Genesis 3:1–5).

The second time Satan speaks is in the book of Job. Job is living a righteous life for God when Satan requests permission to test Job's real allegiance. Satan appears before God's throne and says, "Of *course* Job loves and serves you! You've given him a great family, a great house, and he's making lots of money. The guy's got the world by the tail! But take all that stuff away, and he'll drop you faster than a hot potato."

God knew what Satan was fishing for, and he chose to take the bait. "All right," he said to the evil one. "Have it your way. You may do whatever you want to my servant Job, but you may *not* take his life."

And from there the fabric of Job's favored life came undone until it was just a pile of tangled thread. First, Satan attacked Job's property, including all of his livestock. Then he took the man's children—and finally his health. Again, the goal was to get Job to rebel—from his faith, his foundation, his God. In the end, Job didn't succumb to outright rebellion, but he asked his fair

45

share of questions. Such as why he'd been forsaken when he'd lived a perfectly righteous life. And why God wasn't protecting him from this hellish attack. Even Job's deep-seated frustration and anger must have given Satan great hope. He loves to make us doubt whether our caring God *really* cares (Job 1–2).

There was a third occasion when Satan spoke, and it was directly to Jesus Christ. Matthew 4 reveals the account of Jesus being tempted three times by the devil after fasting and praying in the wilderness for the forty days before his earthly ministry began. The third test was especially revealing when it comes to understanding Satan's goal: "If you will bow down and worship me," Satan said to God incarnate, "I will give you all these things." (See v. 9 NCV.)

Ah, there it is again: "Detach yourself from God, and then attach yourself to me." Jesus wasn't swayed, and we need not be swayed either. We can know Satan's plans. We can prepare to thwart them. And we can rest in sure victory, despite *any* attack.

Satan's Plan of Attack

In 2 Corinthians 2:10–11, the apostle Paul encourages believers to forgive the people who harm them, who hurt their feelings and do them wrong. He says that by extending forgiveness to someone—even if that person doesn't request it—we keep ourselves from being "outwitted by Satan." Paul then says an interesting thing, which is why I bring up these verses in the first place. At the end of his exhortation, he tacks on this reminder, referring to Satan: *"for we are not ignorant of his designs."*

It's another way of saying, "As believers, we know *exactly* how Satan attacks." Which admittedly is both discouraging and encouraging—yes, Satan *will* try to strike us; but we can guard ourselves against the blow.

We are not ignorant of our enemy's designs. We are not ignorant of his plans. For instance, we know from Scripture that part of Satan's *modus operandi* is to stand against all that is good. When Satan rejected God, he rejected all good things as well, because God is the purest manifestation of good. He is the Creator and Sustainer of good. Where God promotes light, Satan promotes darkness; where God promotes truth, Satan promotes lies; where God promotes love, Satan promotes apathy; where God promotes freedom, Satan loves to see us bound up. The enemy of our souls seeks to divide, to divert, to deny, twist and mislead, destroy and kill. He specializes in subversion, perversion, and digression, and he is prepared to use every tactic in his arsenal toward these undeniably sordid ends.

Interestingly, you and I probably nod our heads in agreement that this is how Satan works. And yet *still* we struggle to see his attacks for what they are, in the dailiness of our lives. We see situations and relationships and dynamics all around us that clearly are not lovely, joyful, truthful, or good, but we tend to pin those realities on human targets instead of understanding where the evil *really* comes from. Pastor and author Chip Ingram writes,

> Our sophisticated worldview can actually hinder us in the situations we confront. We start thinking the problem is a spouse, a child, a boss, a policy, an illness, or a circumstance. These symptoms are easy to see, and I certainly wouldn't imply that they are never relevant. But they are often just symptoms, not the source of the problem. Behind many of the things we see on the surface is an archenemy who wants to destroy our lives.[7]

So while we may not experience Satan himself firsthand, (in fact, very few people ever have), we certainly encounter the effects of his evil activity throughout our lives: unwillingness to forgive, bitterness, anger, deceit, depression, and anything else that causes fear, anger, mistrust, split relationships, ulcers, and anxiety. What we fail to do in those moments, however, is to look just beneath the surface of the wretched dynamics, to see two beady eyes staring back at us. That's the face of Satan we're staring at, just *daring* us to stay planted on holy ground.

Satan's gaze is set on terrorizing us, on making us impotent, unstable, and weak. He will strategize and scheme at our expense until we're worthless to the cause of Christ. He will stop at *simply nothing* to make our lives miserable and marked by defeat. Simply put, he seeks nothing more and nothing less than to steal the glory of God, and he accomplishes this twisted goal by tempting us to sin, by crossing his bony fingers in hopes that we'll defiantly say, "I will . . ."

I will go my own way.

I will do my own thing.

I will lead my own life.

I will . . . I will . . . I will.

This is why sin is so tragic—because ultimately what our sin is shouting is precisely what Satan himself once said: "God, I want my will, not yours. I want my way, not yours. I want my glory, not yours."

But take heart! Really: *Take heart*. You and I possess the spiritual authority to triumph over the "I will" of our failing heart.

Our Authority

My friend Tony Evans, who pastors another congregation in the Dallas area, came to speak to a group of men in our church recently, and one of the distinctions he drew during his talk centered on the difference between power and authority. "Anytime you watch a football game," he said, "you probably notice two groups of people at work. The first group is made up of a bunch of strong, powerful men in protective pads who run up and down the field, plowing into each other and knocking each other down. The second group is made up of much smaller, weaker guys, each wearing a whistle around his neck and carrying a bunch of yellow flags. And while the second group may not look as strong as the athletes—and may not have as much raw power at their disposal—they possess far more *authority* than those men. All they have to do to control the action on the field or to make adjustments to the game is to throw that yellow flag or blow a puff of air into that whistle. At their cue, the *whole deal stops.*"

Satan and his elaborate ranks of demonic beings are known for wreaking havoc in our world, but we must remember that they possess only *limited power*. God is the only one who is omnipotent, and Satan is not coequal with God. To run further along this theme, Satan is present, but only God is omnipresent; Satan knows things, but only God is omniscient; Satan is creative, but there is only one Creator—and his name alone is God. In one scholar's words, "We deal with the only being in the universe that has never made a mistake, who has never been astonished, who has never been caught at a disadvantage, who has never been surprised at a superior force or stratagem."[8] Just as the referees in a football game possess authority that trumps the players' power, all we have to do as believers to thwart Satan's actions is to remember our authority in Christ. We don't have to be influenced by the enemy of our souls. We can whistle his every play dead.

I love how *The Message* renders this idea of our authority in Christ Jesus, in Colossians 2:11–15:

Entering into this fullness is not something you figure out or achieve. It's not a matter of being circumcised or keeping a long list of laws. No, you're already *in*—insiders—not through some secretive initiation rite but rather through what Christ has already gone through for you, destroying the power of sin. If it's an initiation ritual you're after, you've already been through it by submitting to baptism. Going under the water was a burial of your old life; coming up out of it was a resurrection, God raising you from the dead as he did Christ. When you were stuck in your old sin-dead life, you were incapable of responding to God. God brought you alive—right along with Christ! Think of it! All sins forgiven, the slate wiped clean, that old arrest warrant canceled and nailed to Christ's cross. He stripped all the spiritual tyrants in the universe of their sham authority at the Cross and marched them naked through the streets.

Did you catch that last part? Once you and I accept Christ, from that moment forward, we can rest in the knowledge that at the cross, Jesus exposed Beelzebub and his bullies for the frauds they are. Revelation 12:11 says that Satan is defeated "by the blood of the Lamb and by the word of [our] testimony." And our testimony is this: In Jesus is our victory over the schemes and shams of Satan. In Jesus is our peace, that we may not be overcome. In Jesus is our confidence, that we no longer have any obligation to sin. Satan can never win any victory over the Christian who holds fast to the Word of God.

My friend, this is very good news!

Yes, Satan roams about the earth as a roaring lion, but he is a lion on a leash . . . little more than "God's monkey," in the words of first-century Christian author Tertullian.[9] This ought to serve as an instructive reminder for those believers who have somehow bought in to the notion that God is on one side of the cosmic battle, Satan is on the other, and the two of them are duking it out as they desperately vie for control of the earth. Nothing could be further from the truth! We'll take a longer look in chapter 4 at the specifics of how to equip ourselves to defeat Satan's attacks, but for now, let us remember that evil had a clear beginning and evil will one day come to an end. In all manner of life, the creation is subject to its Creator; therefore, Satan is subject to God.

What comfort there is for us believers when evil knocks at our front door, threatening our family, our friends, our career, our possessions, our hopes, our dreams, and our plans. We may not be touched without God's permission. Unlike those outside the family of God, *we are not subject to Satan's whims* (see 2 Timothy 2:25–26).

Acknowledging Our Victory in Christ

One spring when I was a little boy, I decided I wanted some Easter chicks, the brightly dyed blue and red and green ones sold at the Montgomery Ward in our town. I asked my grandfather if I could have a few of them, and to my heart's delight, he agreed. (Good grandfathers never say no to charming six-year-olds, so I made sure to pour on extra charm.)

My father drove me down to the department store, and as soon as we got those chicks back to Grandpa's house, where my family also lived, I immediately made them my pets. I played with them, fed them, and chased them around the yard. But over time, the bright colors wore off those feathers, and we were left with a bunch of big, white chickens running all over the place. We didn't live on a farm; we lived in a typical neighborhood, and my grandfather didn't especially like the idea of unruly chickens ruling the roost.

One afternoon, Grandpa announced with a wry grin that he was in the mood for chicken and dumplings for dinner. Even a six-year-old could sort out what that meant. Moments later, my eyes grew to the size of saucers as I watched my typically loving, gentle grandfather take a chicken in his left hand, a chicken in his right hand, and begin to rotate his wrists in fast, little circles until those chickens' heads popped right off. I'd never really considered how Mom's chicken and dumplings got made, but clearly, I didn't think headless chickens were part of the deal.

More shocking still was what I saw transpire next: Even without their heads attached, those chickens bobbed and weaved and flipped and flopped, all over Grandpa's yard. And as they bounced, blood from their headless bodies squirted all over the place, which, I'll admit, was pretty cool.

It would be years before the spiritual lesson of that rather grotesque experience dawned on me: Despite their frenetic activity, *the chickens were already dead.* (Remember the Colossians 2 quote? The part about being marched naked through the streets?) When I think about our adversary and the authority we have in Jesus Christ, I realize that Satan is just like those poor chickens, flopping around, raising a ruckus, seemingly oblivious to their imminent demise. My point here is this: As believers in the Lord Jesus, you and I fight this spiritual battle not *for* victory but *from* it. Because of Jesus' redemptive work on the cross, we fight from a position of certain success. Clearly, we are not as strong as Satan; in fact, left on our own, we'd be consumed. But because of Christ's empowerment, we stand in the winner's circle every day.

Certainly I'm not suggesting swagger in the face of Satan; he remains a formidable foe. But don't hesitate to stand strong and steady, or to confidently tell him to take a hike. Depend heavily on God. Claim his promises for your life. Pray with all sincerity. And know that your victory is assured. The enemy has no right to you, no authority over you, no claim on you, and no hope in the face of your God. "Be strong in the Lord and in the strength of his might," the words of Ephesians 6:10 suggest. Yes, yes, and yes. *This* is what it looks like to acknowledge our victory in Christ.

Recently I was in Jerusalem with a team of pastors from our church, and as I do each time I visit that marvelous land, I stood just outside the city gates at the place of the cross, the historic site of Jesus' death. Golgotha, or "Skull Hill," as it's called, is so named because of the eerily realistic eye sockets, nasal passages, and skeletal teeth seemingly etched in the side of the mount.

I took in the scene, letting my imagination chase back two thousand years to the day of Jesus' crucifixion—the chanting crowds, the abusive Roman soldiers, the God-man crying out in agony, "My God, my God, why have you forsaken me?" (Matthew 27:46). I thought about his pain. About his agony. About his death.

Then I thought about the eternal victory that his suffering yielded, victory over sin and sorrow, over death and judgment and hell. The Bible says that when Jesus died on that cross, on that mount called Skull Hill, Satan himself fell from heaven like lightning, in utter defeat. As our Savior declared, "It is finished" (John 19:30), I imagine every last demon shrieked in evil delight:

"He is finished! He is finished!" they must have cheered. But in fact, *he* was not finished at all; what was finished was his beautiful mission—of love, of mercy, of grace. He had come from heaven to earth; he had died a common criminal's death; he had taken on the full burden of our sin—for the sake of our souls.

Yes, he died. Yes, he was buried. Yes, some may have thought that was the end. But on the third day, the long-awaited Messiah miraculously rose again. And there clutched in his firm grip were the keys to life and death, to heaven and hell, to *victory* over all. Hebrews 2:14–18 reminds us that he did all of this for *us*. Not for the angels, which admittedly are important to God, as we'll see in chapter 3, but for *us*. Take a look:

> Since the children are made of flesh and blood, it's logical that the Savior took on flesh and blood in order to rescue them by his death. By embracing death, taking it into himself, he destroyed the Devil's hold on death and freed all who cower through life, scared to death of death.
>
> It's obvious, of course, that he didn't go to all this trouble for angels. It was for people like us, children of Abraham. That's why he had to enter into every detail of human life. Then, when he came before God as high priest to get rid of the people's sins, he would have already experienced it all himself—all the pain, all the testing—and would be able to help where help was needed.
>
> THE MESSAGE

Indeed, he has helped us greatly. And he remains immensely helpful today. Thanks be to God—the One who ensured that no weapon formed against us shall prosper[10] in our lives! This is the eternal covenant of peace for our souls, forged between a loving God and us. Whatever Satan's plans for us may be, God's plan for us is *peace*.

Discussion Questions

1. How do you "picture" Satan and his minions? A red-suited caricature with a pitchfork in hand? A snarling, slimy, otherworldly being? A seemingly upstanding business-man, complete with tailored suit and tie? Something else entirely? What influences have most significantly shaped your view?

2. Several names for Satan are cited, including:
   • the evil one
   • the tempter
   • the prince of this world
   • the accuser of the brethren
   • a hungry, roaring lion
   • a wolf who appears in sheep's clothing
   • the originator of sin
   • a murderer and a liar.

   Which of these roles most resonates with you, and why?

3. How do you respond to the assertion that "Pride really does go before the fall, and it has been rightly said that the shortest definition of any sin—pride included—is 'I will'"?

4. In what ways have you seen the idea that Satan wants lovers of God to detach their allegiance from God and attach it to him instead play out in your own life?

5. What comfort does it afford you to consider Satan not as omnipresent or omnipotent, but rather as a "lion on a leash"?

THREE
HEAVEN'S (MOSTLY)
UNSEEN WARRIORS

My wife, Deb, and I have a carved wooden angel that sits on our bedside table and serves as a reminder that there are spiritual forces all around us, and that as people who love God and do our best to walk in his will for our lives, his divine protection surrounds us every moment of every day. I'd never really noticed the angel's specific features until our grandson Ian began coming for frequent sleepovers. As is typical of a young child, he doesn't particularly like sleeping in an unfamiliar place all alone, and so most times during those trips to Grandma and Grandpa's house, the only way the kid gets any rest is by being wedged right between us, in our comfy, king-size bed. It was during one of these sleepovers that Ian drew my attention to the angel, explaining that in spite of my wife's and my fondness for the statue, it was "creepy" through and through.

Upon closer inspection, I had to agree that the angel looked a little . . . angry. As though the dimwit he had been charged with guarding had blown it for the umpteenth time. And then there were the muscles. In Ian's view, angels should look more like gentle fairies than the Incredible Hulk on a stressful day. The wings were okay, Ian conceded, but *four* wings instead of two? He wasn't so sure.

One night recently, after Ian had brushed his teeth and was ready to climb into bed, he rushed back into the bathroom and returned clutching a hand towel and wearing a grin. "What's that for?" I asked, to which he draped the towel over the top of the statue and with all the confidence of a seven-year-old said, "There. Problem solved."

If there is one thing I'm coming to understand, after immersing myself in research for this book for the past few years, it is that Ian is not alone in his struggle to sort out what an angel ought to look like. Or act like. Or be like. Or say. Ideas about angels are rampant, but what's the truth about who, or what, they are?

Certainly there is much we don't know about angels. For my part, I've never actually seen one. I've never spoken to one—at least not that I know of.

Just as there is a renewed fascination with the demonic realm these days, angels too are making plentiful appearances in movies, television series, books—even, allegedly, during the course of everyday life. And while some of what we are being fed is grounded in actual truth, far too much of it is simply rehashed folklore being passed off as bona fide fact.

A few staff members from our church took to the streets of downtown Dallas recently for the sole purpose of discovering what people think about angels: Do they exist? And if so, what are they like? The answers were interesting, to say the least.

"I believe babies can see angels," one woman said, "but then it's different, you know, as you get older."

"The Bible talks about angels and God and all that," came another reply, "so, yeah. I guess I believe it's all real."

A businessman said, "There's a god-thing up there, whether it's Muslim or whatever you want to call it—Allah or some other name. There's some supernatural power up there that will take care of you, but you gotta lose your pride and say, 'Help me!'"

"Sure!" said one young man. "Angels and ghosts and all that? Sure, it's real!"

Another young man: "I know I've seen my dead grandfather a couple of times. . . ."

And another: "I have an angel over my head right now."

A mom of two kids said, "Something occurs and you just get this unexpected strength from somewhere. I believe it's angels. Specifically, your angel. I believe everybody is assigned an angel and that angel works to help him or her out. God places all of those angels here on earth for us human beings."

"Well, you can't see them," one woman offered, "so, no. If you can't see it, it ain't real."

Then came this response: "I believe in the idea that there's some force greater than us that watches out for us, and I guess

I'm optimistic in that I think a higher power is working for my good. . . ."

And finally: "There are angels out there, brother. Let me tell you, there are angels out there!"

In short, our impromptu research confirmed what we'd suspected all along: People don't really know what to believe about angels—who they are or what they do. Certainly we like the *idea* of them, with their halos and fairies' wings. They seem so *nice*, so good, so helpful . . . sort of a way to get our arms around the idea of divinity, of *transcendence*, when God seems distant at best.

But how many of our ideas about angels are actually grounded in truth?

The answer to that simple question is as close as the Word of God, where it seems with every page turned the rustling of angel wings can be heard.

Angels in the Bible

In Genesis 3:24, as we've discovered, after Adam was expelled from the garden of Eden, God placed mighty angels and a flaming sword just east of Eden, to guard the way to the Tree of Life.

In Exodus 3:2, an angel of the Lord appeared to Moses in "a flame of fire out of the midst of a bush," and yet it was not consumed.

Numbers 22:22 features an angel of the Lord standing in the road to obstruct the way of the prophet Balaam. Nine verses later, after the Lord opened his eyes, the prophet saw the angel for who he was, a mighty force of God with sword drawn, and Balaam bowed down and fell on his face.

In Judges 6:11–12, an angel of the Lord came to Gideon and delivered an encouraging message: "The Lord is with you," he said, "O mighty man of valor."

An angel stretched out his hand to destroy the city of Jerusalem in 2 Samuel 24:16, only to be rebuked by God, who at the last minute relented concerning the disaster. "It is enough," God said to the angel. "Now stay your hand."

When the young Israelite Daniel refused to worship a golden idol and was tossed into the lions' den as punishment, it was an angel who shut the mouths of those lions, protecting him from certain death (Daniel 6:22).

Certainly we find angels in the book of Isaiah. During Isaiah's prophetic vision, he sees seraphim, angels thought to be especially devoted to the uninterrupted worship of God the Father, each possessing six wings—two to cover the face, two to cover the feet, and two with which to fly (6:2).

The text also mentions that these seraphs had audible voices, and that their calls of "Holy, holy, holy is the Lord of hosts!" made the foundations of the thresholds shake and the temple fill with smoke (6:3–4). The Bible isn't clear about whether all angels have literal wings and loud voices, but Isaiah seems sure about what he saw.

In Luke 1:26–31, God sent the angel Gabriel to Nazareth to tell Mary that she would be the mother of Jesus. And in Psalm 91, we read that *all* believers are protected by the sure presence of angels all around them. "He will command his angels concerning you," we are promised, "to guard you in all your ways" (v. 11).

Hebrews 12:22 and Revelation 5:11 reveal that "innumerable angels" exist—more than 100 million, at least—and that they are organized into ranks and offices, a massive army marching at God's command.

✝ angels·

Indeed, there *are* angels out there. Even as you read the words on this page, angels may be superintending the space around you. They exist. They are real. And they are active in the here and now, certainly not because I say it is so, but because God's Word reveals it to be true. Legendary preacher Billy Graham once put it this way:

> I do not believe in angels because someone has told me about a dramatic visitation from an angel, impressive as some rare testimonies may be; I do not believe in angels because UFOs are astonishingly angel-like in some of their reported appearances; I do not believe in angels because ESP experts are making the realm of the spirit world seem more plausible; I do not believe in angels because of the sudden worldwide emphasis on the reality of Satan and demons; I do not believe in angels because I've ever seen one . . . because I haven't. I believe in angels because the Bible says there are angels, and I believe the Bible is the true word of God.[1]

Yes, Christ-followers believe in angels, but only because God himself believes in angels. He created angels. He purposed angels. He *values* angels, and therefore so should we.

Throughout Scripture, we learn much about the nature of angels. For instance, they are created beings of God who possess intelligence, personality, power, and emotion but not physical bodies, physical features, or physical hearts, except when God chooses to let us physically see them.[2]

Angels existed even before heaven and earth were made and will exist after time is long gone.[3] They do not reproduce, and they cannot die.[4] They are distinct one from another in appearance (when they do, in fact, appear), in temperament,[5] and in rank.[6] A halo is never mentioned, but they are often described as having bright light around them.[7] And while they may be surrounding us at this very moment, they can't be everywhere at once.[8]

A key role angels play throughout Scripture is that of messengers for God.[9] Serving at God's divine beckoning, angels most notably glorified the Father when the Messiah, the Christ-child, was born; they ministered to Jesus as he sweat drops of blood at Gethsemane; and it was an angel at the empty tomb who declared, "He is not here, for he has risen" (Matthew 28:6). We don't know precisely what these angels looked like—did they inhabit physical bodies? Did they appear as shafts of light? Was their presence "seen" at all? These are unanswered questions as of now. But Hebrews 13:2 provides rationale for keeping our eyes peeled, just in case. "Do not neglect to show hospitality to strangers," the verse reads, "for thereby some have entertained angels unawares." Angels were present as God formed the land and the sea, the stars and the skies, the animals and, ultimately, humankind, and angels will play an important role in this earth's final days. The Bible says that when believers are taken up into the forever-presence of the Lord, raised with the dead in Christ, translated into the presence of Christ, we will be attended by angels along the way and will be led by the shouting voice of the archangel of God.[10]

Equally true is that angels will weave their way through the entire experience of the tribulation period, caring for the earth and the natural elements while announcing the everlasting gospel of Jesus Christ. Here's how Revelation 7:2–3 reads:

> Then I saw another angel ascending from the rising of the sun, with the seal of the living God, and he called with a loud voice to the four angels who had been given power to harm earth and sea, saying, "Do not harm the earth or the sea or the trees, until we have sealed the servants of our God on their foreheads."

angels - worship God & to accomplish His will

Finally, when Christ returns in glory to the Mount of Olives, angels will accompany him (see Acts 1:9–11). Verse 11 says, "This Jesus, who was taken up from you into heaven, will come in the same way as you saw him go into heaven."[11]

The Mission of Angels

Attending, encouraging, submitting, advocating, speaking, guarding, protecting, ministering, accompanying—we learn much of the nature of angels from even a cursory journey through God's inspired Word. They are preachers and they are proclaimers. They are recruiters and they are rescuers. They are explorers and they are executors. They are comforters and they are communicators. They are birth attenders, lion tamers, and more. But primarily, their mission can be summed up thus: to worship God and to accomplish his will.

Angels Are Worshipers

While it is true that angels do not spend the entirety of their existence standing before God's throne—we know they are messengers moving between the realms of heaven and earth and that they can only inhabit one place at a time—we can be sure that when they *are* in heaven, they *are*, in fact, worshiping God.[12] Certainly the day will dawn when their earthly ministry will be complete and they will remain before God's throne at all times, sounding their praises in honor of the One who is alone worthy to receive it. I envision us as fellow lovers of God taking our cue from them—our angelic worship leaders—and quickly joining the heavenly chorus, offering praise and glory to him.[13]

Even now, as we recognize angelic activity in our midst, we understand more of who God is and what he is like. They are his emissaries, his messengers, his representatives here in the earth, and to see the effects of their involvement is to see something of God himself. They are fearsome, as is God. They are strong, as is God. They are pure, as is God. They are caring, as is God. We grasp more deeply why the angels say, "Holy, holy, holy is the Lord All-Powerful."[14] The One the angels announced at birth remains the One their worship points to still. We must never direct our worship to angels, but instead let it flow to the God they adore.[15] He is their magnificent obsession; he must be our magnificent obsession too.

Angels Are Warriors

We learn in Psalm 103:20–21 that in addition to worshipers, angels also are warriors, mighty beings fighting for the will of God to unfold in the world. "You who are his angels, praise the Lord. You are the mighty warriors who do what he says and who obey his voice. You, his armies, praise the Lord; you are his servants who do what he wants" (NCV). Yes, angels are mighty. But equally true, they are *obedient*, committed to fulfilling God's every request. In this way they possess the righteousness that Christ-followers seek.

Angels are described in Scripture as an army, complete with levels, ranks, and serial numbers, if you will. They are powerful warriors who exist solely for the purpose of advancing the kingdom of God. They work around the clock to give glory to God and to guard God's most precious possession, his people.[16] But even as they may wish to come to our aid at our beckoning, they cannot deploy themselves in a volitional way unless they first were to rebel against God. Case in point: It would have taken only one renegade angel for our Savior to have been rescued from the agony of the cross. Truly, angels who wish to remain in their holy estate act *only* when God directs them; his is the voice they obey.

Despite the many ministries angels offer—three of which we'll explore in the next section—they do *not* give revelation apart from the revelation of God.[17] God alone reveals himself, and while angels may facilitate revelation, they never offer fresh revelation apart from him.

The Ministry of Angels

We already saw that Psalm 91 contains a powerful promise for the lover of God: "For he [God] will command his angels concerning you," it says, "to guard you in all your ways. On their [the angels'] hands they will bear you up, lest you strike your foot against a stone" (vv. 11–12). When you and I surrender our will and our ways to the lordship of Christ, we are guarded in *all our ways,* those verses declare. I don't know about you, but I desire this type of guardianship. I crave it. I long for it. I *need* it. And when I rest in the shadow of my heavenly Father's wings, that protection is absolutely mine. When I choose to live in his strength instead of mine, when I choose to follow his plan instead of my own, at his perfect timing and in his perfect way, he may choose to send angels to comfort me, to bless me, to support me, to sustain me. And if you are a follower of the Lord Jesus, then the same is magnificently true for you.

The Ministry of Observation

The first angelic ministry in the life of the believer is the *ministry of observation.* In 1 Corinthians 4:9, we as God's children are

66

referred to as spectacles in the eyes of angels. Angels are watching over us, viewing our actions and reactions, taking in the nuances of our everyday lives. They watch us as we talk with our spouse, as we parent our children, as we work diligently at our jobs, and even as we worship God, which is an astounding thought to me. An old hymn says that angels must fold their wings in amazement as they witness the worship of God's saints. And why are they amazed? Because they've never needed to experience grace for themselves and I imagine they are captivated by our thankful hearts.[18]

Angels have never needed forgiveness, never needed resurrection power in their lives, but also have never enjoyed the personal relationship with Jesus Christ that we're afforded as those whom he has redeemed. And so, as the song goes:

> Then the angels stand and listen, for they cannot join
> the song,
> Like the sound of many waters, by the happy, blood-
> washed throng,
> For they sing about great trials, battles fought and
> vict'ries won,
> And they praise their great Redeemer, who hath said to
> them,
> "Well done."[19]

Yes, they're watching us and witnessing with great delight every godward move we make.

The Ministry of Guidance

Angels also offer a *ministry of guidance* in our lives. In Scripture, this guidance most often shows up as supernatural direction or as aid in passing from this temporal, time-bound life to eternity at Jesus' side. Testifying to the former, in Acts 12, we find the apostle Peter chained to armed guards in a dingy prison cell. An angel had already facilitated Peter's miraculous release from prison the first time around, so this time, King Herod said, "Let's chain not one, but fourteen Roman guards to the guy. Maybe that will keep him here."

I can just hear God briefing the angel assigned to Peter's second escape. *We'll do a middle-of-the-night exit,* he whispers with a conspiratorial grin. *Wait until Peter is fast asleep, and then quickly unlock the cell, make your way inside, tap Peter on the shoulder, and quietly lead him out. I'll make sure every door is opened for you, as you take each faith-fueled step.*

The angel did just as he was told, and Peter was a free man once again.

I love the story told in Acts 8 (THE MESSAGE) about Philip, a godly man who was led into the wilderness by an angel of God. The angel said, "At noon today I want you to walk over to that desolate road that goes from Jerusalem down to Gaza" (v. 26). Wisely, Philip obeyed the angel's command, knowing this was instruction straight from God.

On his way, the text says that Philip met an Ethiopian man who was coming down the road. He was a man of high position, the minister of finance for the queen of Ethiopia, and was riding in a chariot, reading the book of Isaiah as he traveled. The Spirit of God said to Philip, "Climb into the chariot," and in a bold stroke of obedience, Philip immediately started running alongside the chariot, asking, "Do you understand what you're reading?"

The Ethiopian man was seemingly unfazed by the spectacle of a random guy running alongside his chariot, hurling comprehension questions his way. In response, he simply said, "How can I without some help?" and then invited Philip to join him in the chariot. "Philip grabbed his chance. Using this passage as his text, he preached Jesus to him" (v. 35). But the story gets better still.

They kept going down the road, eventually coming to a stream of water. The Ethiopian leader eyed Philip and said, "Here's water. Why can't I be baptized?" and then ordered the chariot to stop. Both men went down to the water, and Philip baptized him there on the spot. When the freshly redeemed man emerged from the waters of baptism, Philip was suddenly gone, taken evidently by the Spirit of God, never to return again. "But [the Ethiopian] didn't mind," the text tells us. "He had what he'd come for and went on down the road as happy as he could be" (v. 39).

Certainly we are never promised this sort of radical angelic rescue. Nor are we ever promised a specific "guardian angel," assigned solely to ensure our everyday care. I don't have an angel named Joe hanging around my life 24/7. At least, not as far as I know.

We *do* know, however, that angels will guide us when we pass from this life to the next.[20] During the hours of Jesus' crucifixion, a thief hanging on the cross by his side asked Jesus to "remember him" during Jesus' kingdom reign. And because that thief believed, the text says that very day he was carried from loneliness to fellowship, from emptiness to abundance, from powerlessness to the eternal presence of God.

For all who believe, then, death need not be a final or fear-filled tragedy. Instead, it is a *triumph*, the culmination of our faith. "I will come again," Jesus promises us in John 14:3, "and will take you to myself, that where I am you may be also." Death means life to the devoted follower of Christ. And when that final appointment shows up, we can be sure that angels will be the ones ushering us into God's forever embrace.

We don't have to fear death. To live is Christ, yes, but to die? That is *gain*, as Philippians 1:21 assures us. "Precious in the sight of the Lord is the death of his saints," Psalm 116:15 says, which sounds like a morbid sentiment from a cruel God until you understand fully that in death, we as saints are comforted. In death, we as saints are strengthened. In death, we as saints are accompanied into the very presence of God.

When my grandfather lay on his deathbed many decades ago, he reported seeing my grandmother, who had passed away years before. Was it an angel, taking on appearance as my deceased grandmother? Was it nothing more than the hallucination of an elderly mind? To this day, my family does not know. But of this much, we are sure: If he was passing to the other side right then and there, then death was being swallowed up in victory, and he was entering eternal life. And angels were flanking him on either side, translating him from this world to the majestic and mysterious life beyond.

3. The Ministry of Protection

A third ministry afforded to believers by angels is the *ministry of protection*.

One example of this is the story of the young dream-interpreter Daniel, who refused to follow the king's decree that no prayers would be prayed to anyone but him for a period of thirty days. As punishment, Daniel was tossed into the lions' den and left for dead. But God had a different plan in mind. He deployed an angel to Daniel's den, where he shut the lions' mouths and saved Daniel from certain death (Daniel 6).

Angelic protection occurred in Scripture, but does it still occur today?

In his book *Angels*, Billy Graham wrote of a missionary named John Paton who served in the New Hebrides Islands, a remote island chain near Fiji that is now the nation of Vanuatu. One evening, Paton and his family were distressed to find hostile native warriors surrounding their mission headquarters apparently determined to kill them all. Paton and his wife committed themselves to prayer throughout the night and were astonished to wake the next morning to find the hostiles had fled the scene.

A year later, the chief of that hostile tribe surrendered his life to Jesus Christ and befriended Paton, his one-time foe. Paton, recalling the terror-filled night, asked the chief why his men had aborted their mission to carry out their evil deeds. The chief was obviously surprised. He explained that all of the men standing guard on the premises convinced them not to attack.

Now Paton was the one to register surprise. "There were no men there, just my wife and I."

Reverend Paton listened as the chief described all he had seen that night: hundreds of big men in shining garments with drawn swords in their hands, circling the mission station, protectors of God's servants huddling inside.[21]

We know that angelic protection of this sort occurred in biblical times. Elisha was a great prophet of God and a force to be reckoned with in battle. During one particular fight, Elisha and his servant woke one morning to find the Syrian army poised for attack. The servant was so frightened that he trembled, saying to Elisha, "What shall we do?" But Elisha simply prayed, "O Lord, please open his eyes that he may see." And immediately, God did just that. The servant saw, for the first time, not sure devastation and destruction, but rather a mountain covered with horses and chariots of fire positioned on every side (2 Kings 6:15–17).

Angels were in their midst, and yet the servant didn't have eyes to see them.

But back to the key question: *Does this happen today?*

When I was three years old, I may not have known much, but I did know one thing for sure: Bread crusts were for the birds. I hated the crust. And guess what I was made to eat, nearly every day of my life? "That's where all the vitamins are!" my mother insisted, even as I scrunched up my nose and frowned at what had to be my six-hundredth sandwich.

One day, I rode along in the car while my mom picked up my brother from school. I was sitting in the backseat of our old Dodge sedan, trying to enjoy my afternoon snack, when a bright idea occurred to me regarding what to do with my crust.

In those days, if you wanted to roll down the window, you actually had to *roll the window down*. I decided that I would slowly, quietly let down my window and let my crusts go the way of the wind.

In hindsight, it wasn't the best of ideas.

As the car rumbled down the road at fifty miles an hour, I reached for the crank to roll down the window but grabbed the door handle instead. As if in slow motion, that door flew open, exposing me to the wind and elements. I tried with all my might to pull the door shut, but for a three-year-old with spaghetti-thin arms, the weight was too much to bear. And as the reality of my feeble body overshadowed my hopes for supernatural strength, time stood painfully still.

This happened fifty-nine years ago, and I remember it like it was yesterday. I tumbled out of the car, thinking to myself, "Uh-oh. This is it." Within nanoseconds, my head met the cold, hard concrete, coming to an abrupt and ugly stop. But here's where the story gets interesting, because if there is one thing I remember from that unfortunate incident, it is a *soft landing* as I fell. Something—or someone—simply laid me down, before I slowly came to rest. Still today, I bear a few scars from that fall, and each time I catch sight of them I wonder, *Was that an angel protecting me that day?*

I'll likely never know the answer to that question—on this side of heaven, anyway. But here is what I do know: God's hand of protection is on his children, and angels remain at his beck and call. And for the record, I believe that I'm alive here and now because an angel saved my life.

It's an intriguing thing to think about, how many times we have been rescued by angel wings.

How many times have you been saved from certain peril that was headed your way? Indeed, God has placed a hedge of protection around each of his daughters and sons, and I believe that often, that beautiful encirclement is accomplished by angels who stand ready to serve.

Observation, guidance, protection—power and safety at every turn. These are the resources available to every person who surrenders to Christ. What comfort this is for the believer! And what conviction for those far from God. Angels are "ministering spirits sent out to serve," Hebrews 1:14 says, "for the sake of those who are to inherit salvation." And it is to this final form of angelic ministry that I want to draw your attention now.

If there is a fourth ministry that angels provide, it is to faithfully announce the good news of Christ.[22] Even now, God could use his heavenly host to proclaim the power of gospel truth, but instead, he chooses us—human ambassadors working for his divine will. And based on how frail, frightened, and faithless we sometimes are, I often find myself wondering if members of that mighty angelic realm run to God sixteen times a day saying, "Those humans just aren't getting it done! We're ready! Let us intervene!"

It's time for those of us who have given our hearts to God to be motivated by the faithfulness of the invisible angels in our midst to be worshipers and warriors like them. The stakes are high, and the time is now to point people to the only faith that saves. There is a vast, invisible battle raging, and we have a prime opportunity to join the noble work of God's heavenly host and leave a legacy of truth, transformation, and strength.

Discussion Questions

1. Based on the Scriptures that feature the presence of angels, what do you think God wants us to know about who they are and what they do?

2. Psalm 91 promises that God commands his angels concerning you. What concerns do you hope are falling under an angel's purview?

3. The first of the angels' ministries is that of *observation*. How might knowledge of this ministry affect how you worship, lead, serve, and go about the business of your daily life?

4. Have you ever experienced what you would call an angel's ministry of guidance? Has there been a time in your life when you needed this kind of help?

5. In what area would you say you typically need divine protection?

We don't want to think that
something as ugly and brutal
as combat could be involved in any way
with the spiritual. However, would any
practicing Christian say that
Calvary Hill was not a sacred space?

–Karl Marlantes

FOUR
BATTLE GEAR

Over the years I have taken groups to Israel twenty times or so, and these last five or six trips, we've enjoyed the same guide, a dear man named Yuval Shemesh. Yuval is fifty-one years old and had a decorated career in the Israeli army before becoming a guide for the country he knows and loves. In his homeland, immediately after graduating from high school, teens are funneled right into the military system, young men and young women alike, no exceptions. As an eighteen-year-old, Yuval began working in covert operations for the government, a role that launched him into more than a decade of military service before becoming a reservist. Most servicemen and servicewomen are listed as in "reserve" for twenty years or so; once they hit age fifty, evidently they're no longer called to duty.

Yuval and I got to talking one morning, and I said, "So, Yuval, you're fifty-one years old now. You've served your time, both in active duty and in the reserves. What happens next?"

The Middle East can be a hot spot for military activity, and as we know, the Israeli army must always be on guard in order to defend their country effectively. In all my travels there, I've never felt ill at ease, even for a moment. But there are armed guards everywhere you look—on the streets, in the airport, in local cafes—and there is a detectable tension in the air, a sense that when you stand on Jerusalem soil, you're standing on ground zero of all the problems of the world.

Yuval kind of chuckled at my question. I could tell that he had been wondering the same thing. What does happen, after the thing your life has been about for more than three decades abruptly comes to a halt?

Before he could respond further, I painted a scenario for Yuval. "Suppose there is a war here," I said. "You're over the age limit for serving, but you care deeply about your country's success. Would you go back into battle?"

He didn't flinch. "Absolutely," he said. "Here in Israel, we are fighting not only for our families today but also for our collective futures tomorrow. We stay on guard. We stay vigilant at all times. And we stay committed to the cause, regardless of our age."

Yuval's passion and devotion blew me away. Here was a man who had a wife, children, grandchildren, interests and obligations and responsibilities to tend to each day, who essentially said, "No matter what it takes, I am ready, and I will fight."

It's with that same sense of preparedness and determination that you and I are to engage in the invisible war that is waged all around us, every day.

We Don't Wrestle Against Flesh and Blood

In the last two chapters, we looked both at Satan's role—to distract, to divide, to dissuade us from believing God—and at the role of the angelic host—to observe, guide, and protect believers—in the unseen battle. Now we turn our attention to *our* role in the fight. As appealing as it may sound on some days to simply take a defensive posture or live life as innocent bystanders, there is an offensive position we're expected to hold. And the stakes are incredibly high for our involvement: Our faith, our families, our future—the success or failure of these things all ride on what you and I choose to do with that role.

Scripture is clear that in these "last days" here on planet Earth, we are to shake off our lethargy, put away all forms of darkness, and engage in the good fight of faith. We don't wrestle against flesh and blood, Ephesians says, but against spiritual wickedness in high places (6:12). Ours is a *spiritual struggle*, and the devil's purpose is to get a stranglehold upon us spiritually, to neutralize our testimony for Christ. I've always thought that one of his most clever strategies is getting lovers of God to fight against flesh-and-blood opponents, forgetting entirely that our real issue is with him.

Case in point: Remember when Jesus pulled together his disciples one day and told them about how in a few short days he was going to have to go to Jerusalem and suffer at the hands of the leaders there and ultimately die in order to fulfill the prophecies of Scripture? He looked into the eyes of his closest followers and told them these things, promising them that while he would indeed have to be killed, on the third day he would rise again. But this resurrection detail was not good enough in Simon Peter's mind. He couldn't imagine his Messiah being killed. He couldn't stand for such injustice and pain. The text says that Peter "took him [Jesus] aside and began to rebuke him, saying, 'Far be it from you, Lord! This shall never happen to you'" (Matthew 16:22).

Here's what Jesus said in reply: "Get behind me, Satan! You are a hindrance to me. For you are not setting your mind on the things of God, but on the things of man" (v. 23).

Later, after Jesus prayed agonizing prayers in the garden of Gethsemane—even to the point of sweating drops of blood— Peter struck one of Jesus' accusers and actually cut off the man's ear. He was probably looking to chop the guy's head off entirely, but he was a fisherman, not a swordsman. Jesus must have shaken his head, thinking, "*Still,* these guys don't get it."

"Put your sword back into its place," he said to Peter (Matthew 26:52). In other words: Our struggle is not with these people. Our struggle exists in the unseen realm.

But how are we supposed to engage in a battle that we can't even see going on? The answer is as close as Ephesians chapter 6.

Standing Up to Satan

If you were to assess the book of Ephesians from a thirty-thousand-foot view, you'd notice three major divisions for the six brief chapters it holds: Chapters 1 through 3 cover the abundant life that is in store for the believer—our riches in Christ,

Stand against satan.

our blessings in Christ, our exalted and high position that is ours as joint heirs with the King.

In chapters 4 and 5, we shift gears to a discussion of the believer's behavior—how to promote unity, how to avoid sin, how to succeed in marriage, how to love as Christ loved, and so forth.

And then there is chapter 6. The *wealth* of the believer, the *walk* of the believer, and now, the *warfare* every believer endures. In something of a call to arms, this chapter of Scripture includes helpful hints on both defensive and offensive moves guaranteed to take our enemy down.

By way of context, the apostle Paul likely wrote the book of Ephesians while chained to a Roman officer. The officer may not have been heavily armed or especially fit for battle, but it is clear from the text that the imagery of a Roman soldier played heavily into Paul's depiction of the "soldiers" we're to be for Christ. Verses 10 through 18 read this way:

Finally, be strong in the Lord and in the strength of his might. Put on the whole armor of God, that you may be able to stand against the schemes of the devil. For we do not wrestle against flesh and blood, but against the rulers, against the authorities, against the cosmic powers over this present darkness, against the spiritual forces of evil in the heavenly places.

Therefore take up the whole armor of God, that you may be able to withstand in the evil day, and having done all, to stand firm. Stand therefore, having fastened on the belt of truth, and having put on the breastplate of righteousness, and, as shoes for your feet, having put on the readiness given by the gospel of peace. In all circumstances take up the shield of faith, with which you can extinguish all the flaming darts of the evil one; and take the helmet of salvation, and the sword of the Spirit, which is the word of God, praying at all times in the Spirit, with all prayer and supplication.

As it turns out, we engage in the invisible war by putting on invisible armor, a shell, a shield, a suit of protective clothing that keeps us safe from harm. This is how we stand up to Satan and his evil domain. In fact, in four places the text says it exactly that way: "*Stand* against the schemes of the devil"; "*withstand* the evil day"; "*stand* firm"; "*stand* therefore . . . having put on the readiness given by the gospel of peace."

Stand. There is something powerful about that posture, isn't there? We stand to say the Pledge of Allegiance. We stand when we are meeting someone or introducing ourselves to someone new. We stand when we are fired up at a ball game. We stand when someone important enters a room—a bride on her wedding day, a judge in her courtroom, a revered speaker.

Standing communicates deference, honor, appreciation, respect. In the case of Ephesians 6, standing conveys the idea that those of us who follow Jesus are not going to cut and run when the going gets tough and the battle gets fierce. Quite the opposite! Devoted followers of Christ stand their ground. They prepare for battle ahead of time and *engage* when Satan provokes. Even when they don't understand the circumstances involved in the fight—and certainly, there are many mysteries in the invisible realm that confound us, anger us, and leave us grasping for answers—they plant their feet on God's unchanging promises, on his assurance that he is present and he cares.

Clearly, Paul would not encourage us to "stand firm" if he wasn't convinced we would win the war that has been waged. The reason he can tell us to stand, and then tell us again and again, is that he knows beyond the shadow of a doubt that this battle we engage in has already been won in Christ. Satan, the roaring lion, has already been declawed and defanged. All he can do is roar. And while that roar can get quite loud sometimes, it's harmless to us in the end.

Exodus 14 tells the story of the people of Israel escaping from Egypt just after they saw God allow ten plagues to ravage the land and even destroy Pharaoh's own son. They had seen this magnificent display of power, and yet a few days into their wilderness experience, upon realizing that Pharaoh's army had trailed them and now was encroaching on their locale, they began to worry. Would God protect them? Would he provide for them? Would he give them a way of escape? Sure, he had done these things before. But would he be inclined to do them again?

Although Pharaoh had released the Israelites from their enslavement, unbeknownst to the Israelites, he'd had second thoughts. So he gathered six hundred of the fastest chariots in the region, which were that day's battle tanks, and they pursued the children of Israel with all their might. In the ancient world, chariots were virtually unstoppable on open terrain; when the Israelites saw this massive army approaching, they figured that with or without God, they were toast.

They didn't know what else to do but launch into a fear-fueled tirade to Moses, their leader. They whined. They worried. They complained. They panicked. And in response, Moses said in essence, "Relax! The Lord will fight for you; you need only to be still" (see Exodus 14:13–14).

It's good advice for us still today. *Relax!* Yes, a battle rages. But equally true is that our good and gracious God has our back. He is our Soldier. He is our Warrior. He is our Victory and our Relief. The Israelites were a ragtag mob of former slaves with nothing but pitchforks and shepherd staffs. But their God was heavily armed and oh, so able to take down any enemy around. And *this* God had promised to save his people. He extends the same promise to us today.

When we feel helpless, standing in the face of too-big, too-daunting circumstances, we must remember that it is actually God who does our fighting for us.

Back to the story. After God delivered the Israelites from Pharaoh and parted the Red Sea on their behalf, the once worrisome children sang, "The Lord is my strength and my song; he has become my salvation; this is my God, and I will praise him, my father's God, and I will exalt him. The Lord is a man of war; the Lord is his name" (Exodus 15:2–3).

So yes, our God is a warrior, and yes, we are assured victory in the end. But still, while we continue to live in this fallen world, in this now, and yet not-yet version of eternity, Satan's schemes can wreak serious havoc in our lives. This is why Paul says, essentially, in Ephesians 6, "Don't fear Satan in the long run. He's *done* when this world is done. But stay on your guard between now and then, recognizing that he is powerful and prevalent today."

"Stand firm," he says. "Be prepared. Watch yourselves while you live on this earth. Don't run heedlessly into battle, and DO NOT give up your God-given ground." This is an important point to note: Any influence Satan has in a believer's life is granted to Satan by that believer's surrendering territory Christ has already given to that one. We must take the ground—stand firm on the ground—that God has already given us. And he has already given us the victory.

May the devil always find us standing—standing firm and standing strong.

How do we stand firm? By putting on the seven pieces of spiritual armor Paul says we must wear. The key here is that we put on *all* seven pieces; picking and choosing in this regard is the spiritual equivalent of rushing headlong into battle with a butter knife when the enemy has an AK-47. No thank you! I'll take all seven pieces, please, and first up is the *belt of truth.* "Stand therefore," Ephesians 6:14 says, "having fastened on the belt of truth. . . ."

The Belt of Truth

In Paul's day and age, people wore belts to keep their flowing garments from dragging on the ground. Similarly, we wear belts to keep our pants up, to keep everything cinched in. For a Roman soldier, the belt was absolutely central to his suit of armor, because all of his weaponry hung off that belt. His life support was on that belt! So is ours.

We are to approach Satan's schemes with strong reliance on the truth of God—who he is, what he has said, and what he promises to do for those who have devoted their lives to him. Listen, I would be terrified for the future of my children and grandchildren if not for the truth of God. It is truth alone that strengthens me, that keeps me sane in an insane world.

Living a life bound up in God's truth means living sincerely, living honestly, living candidly before God and before others. It is a life devoid of secrets, of duplicity, of ongoing sin. It is a life that pursues wholeness and holiness, regardless of what the rest of the world says about life.

In chapter 2 we described Satan as being a liar, even the "father of lies." John 8:44 says it this way: "He [Satan] was a murderer from the beginning and does not stand in the truth, because *there is no truth in him*. When he lies, he speaks out of his own character, for he is a liar and the father of lies" (emphasis mine).

Refute Satan with God's truth.

As we think about what it means to live with a belt of truth fastened around our waists, we need only to do the exact opposite of what Satan would do. When he lies to us, we must refute him with God's truth. Where he prompts us to make bad choices, we must make wise choices instead. Where he tempts, we must stand firm. Where he promotes immediate gratification, we must rest on the timeless truth of God's Word.

It is truth that keeps our eyes trained on Christ instead of on the ever-shifting highs and lows of life. It is truth that helps us detect falsehood that leads to nothing but ruin and destruction. It is truth that keeps our feet on the path of holiness and that keeps us from being led astray by Satan's schemes.

Truth prompts us to own up to our sin. Truth invites us to bring that which is dark into the brightness of Christ's penetrating life. Truth washes us clean—our hands, our hearts, our lives. And this truth always points us to Jesus, who is "*the way,* and *the truth,* and the life" (John 14:6, emphasis mine).

The Breastplate of Righteousness

Ephesians 6:14 continues with the second piece of armor we are to wear: "and having put on the breastplate of righteousness . . ."

In Paul's day, unlike today, most combat was of the face-to-face, hand-to-hand variety. Think fewer air strikes and more wrestling matches, which meant that if an enemy could get to your chest—and thus your vital organs—with his sword, more than likely, he would win. For this reason, the chest of a warrior had to be protected at all costs, which typically involved a sleeveless piece of armor made of bronze, chain mail, or heavy leather.

Battle Gear

Paul is saying, "In the same way a soldier protects himself with a breastplate, protect your vitality at all costs!" "*Guard your heart*," Proverbs 4:23 says, "for it is the wellspring of life" (NIV 1984). Guard it with what? *Righteousness.* Not self-righteousness, but the righteousness of Christ. Second Corinthians 5:21 says, "For our sake he made him to be sin who knew no sin, so that in him we might become the righteousness of God." We don't fight with carnal, worldly weapons that rely on our own strength; no, we fight with the strength found only in Christ, the righteousness that is ours in him. Another way to think of righteousness is "right living," living that is possible only in Christ.

As we fasten on the breastplate of righteousness, we put on purity to protect us from defilement. And purity is what we need in this dirty, filthy day and age. Sin is a seductive power. And the devil needs only a tiny crack to get a foothold in our lives.

> "Who is that who knocks so loud?"
> The answer came, "Just a little sin."
> So I opened the door and all hell was in."

Nobody starts out an addict. There's always a first sip, a first click of the computer, a first "innocent" flirtation, a first moment of anxiety . . . and then one day, all hell is in. One day, with fearsome force, bondage has us all wrapped up.

I often talk with believers about why they don't share their faith with people who don't yet know God, and interestingly, their answers often come down to sin. They neglect sharing their faith not because of fear or intimidation or lack of knowledge of the gospel message; they neglect sharing their faith because,

87

while they love God and long to follow God, truthfully, they love their sin more. They're not pursuing righteousness—right living—themselves and therefore find it difficult to encourage others to live this way. Their friends know of their struggles with sin; their family members know of the struggles too. "What kind of hypocritical phony would I have to be, to tell somebody to live like I myself can't live?" they say. And Satan scores a victory by neutralizing yet another believer's impact in a world so desperately in need of God.

Again, please read carefully that I'm *not* endorsing legalism or self-righteousness. I'm simply encouraging those of us who follow the Lord Jesus to put on the power that is ours in him. This is no Mickey Mouse power we're talking about! In 1 John 4:4, we read, "He who is in you is greater than he who is in the world." In Ephesians 1:19–20, referring to the "immeasurable greatness" of God's power toward us who believe, Paul explains that it is the very same power that God worked in Christ when he raised him from the dead and seated him at his right hand in the heavenly places. This power is ours! This righteousness is ours! Integrity and morality and being above reproach in all things—*all* of this is ours, if only we'll live out practically who we are positionally, in Christ.

Truly, the most powerful, joyful believers I have known are those whose beliefs and behavior line up with each another. Likewise, the most impotent, miserable believers I have come in contact with are those whose position has been changed by the power of the gospel and yet their practical living does not match up. In short, it is the breastplate of righteousness that makes all the difference here. When there is integrity in our lives, we live in victory. When there is a lack of integrity, we live in defeat. It all comes down to whether or not we are willing to wear the vest.

③ Feet Shod With the Gospel of Peace

Verse 15 of Ephesians 6 presents the third part of the armor: "As shoes for your feet," Paul's list continues, "having put on the readiness given by the gospel of peace."

A Roman soldier knew that to be effective in battle, he had to take care of his feet. There were mountains to climb, obstacles to overcome, territory to take from the enemy. It wasn't uncommon for opposing armies to plunge spear-like sticks into the ground they knew you'd be traversing, which, if happened upon, could pierce the foot. Bare feet wouldn't do; they needed cleated sandals, hobnail boots, or some other strong, sturdy footwear in order to stay mobile day by day.

The late John Wooden, UCLA's famed men's basketball coach, was known to reinforce the simplest of lessons for his players, knowing that mastering the fundamentals often meant the difference between victory and defeat. For example, he spent an inordinate amount of time each year reminding his players how to properly put on socks and shoes. If a player's sock had a wrinkle in it, it could cause a blister that would bench even the most proficient seven-footer. The same was true for shoes: A shoe that caused the toes to rub together or be jammed during jumping or abrupt stops could cost the team their star player.[2]

In my day, there was basically one type of athletic shoe available. And there wasn't much better in life than a new pair of Converse All-Stars. Today, you can walk into any Sports Authority or Dick's Sporting Goods store across the nation and find literally *hundreds* of options. Depending on your sport, your foot, and your price range, there are scores of shoes to choose from. Why all this variety? Because serious athletes are serious about their *shoes*. Competitors know that to be effective, they have to be stabilized, they have to be able to move; they have to stay strong throughout the entirety of the game.

The same is true for us.

We need footwear that stabilizes us, mobilizes us, and keeps us strong as we take back ground from the enemy of our souls. And according to the apostle Paul, we accomplish these goals by slipping our feet into the *gospel of peace.* This gospel—the "good news" that by grace, through Christ, we can be saved from the consequences of our sin—stabilizes us by assuring us that when we surrender our lives to Jesus, our future is secure. We live at peace with God, both now and for all of eternity. We aren't exempt from challenging circumstances, but we know God's presence and power as we walk through them. We aren't necessarily strong all the time, but in our weakness we're able to stand firm. In the power of Jesus, we stand.

In addition to being stabilized by the gospel of peace, we also are *mobilized* to share this gospel with others. Romans 10:15 says that the feet of those who preach the gospel are "beautiful" . . . and indeed they are. Think back on your own faith journey; who first introduced *you* to God's message of hope and love? You'd probably agree that having that person take courageous steps toward you, even as you were hip-deep in your sinful ways, or at least oblivious to your need of a Savior—was a beautiful, life-changing act. I certainly feel that way. I absolutely treasure the steps taken toward me by mentors and Bible teachers along the way, men of God who set aside their own interests long enough to disciple and correct and instruct me in the ways of Christ.

God's hope for every believer is that we'd have beautiful feet, that we'd be a living testimony, a powerful witness to the world of his goodness and grace. He wants you and me to mobilize our feet each day to carry hope to those who are hopeless, to carry community to those who are ostracized, to carry healing to those struggling with disease, to carry love to those who have long ago given up on knowing anything but hatred in this life. I assure you, Satan will do anything in his power to point our feet in any direction but *this* one. We must be intentional about shodding our feet with the preparation of the gospel of peace.

④ The Shield of Faith

So we fasten on the belt of truth, which is our purity. We put on the breastplate of righteousness, which is our integrity. We outfit our feet with the gospel of peace, which is our stability as well as our mobility. And, next, we hold up the shield of faith.

Ephesians 6:16 says, "In all circumstances take up the shield of faith, with which you can extinguish all the flaming darts of the evil one."

In Paul's day, a Roman shield typically was made of leather and metal or wood and was large in size, around two feet by four feet, such that you could hide behind the frame. Essentially, this shield would cover you from shoulder to knee and would curve toward you on both sides, which provided protection for at least 75 percent of your body. And if you think about the way battles were fought back then—with soldiers advancing on enemy territory in a forward direction—there really was no need to protect one's back.

There's a spiritual lesson for us here. As we move forward, advancing, progressing, taking territory for God, we need coverage not for our back, but for our front, for our sides. Paul basically says, "All the coverage you need is found in strong, unyielding *faith*."

By some estimates, there are eight thousand promises listed in Scripture, promises given by a loving God to his children.[3]

Promises of God

He will bless the righteous, for example (Psalm 5:12). He will be a refuge for the oppressed (Psalm 9:9). He will bless his people with peace (Psalm 29:11). Those who wait upon God will run and not be weary (Isaiah 40:31). If we believe on the Lord Jesus Christ, we will have everlasting life (John 3:36). The peace of God, which surpasses all understanding, will guard our hearts and minds in Christ Jesus (Philippians 4:7). We'll be delivered from our troubles when we call upon God (Psalm 50:15). We will seek God and find him, when we seek him with all our heart (Jeremiah 29:13). The list goes on and on. Faith says, "I take God at his word, that he will do what he says he will do."

This utter reliance on God's Word as *truth* is how we protect ourselves in battle. This is how we fend off Satan's fiery darts. We'll talk more in chapter 5 about what these darts look like, when we are most vulnerable to being hit, and the sheer devastation usually left in the wake of a fiery-dart attack. But for now, let me draw your attention to a more uplifting discussion: the *communal* value of raising a shield of faith.

Within a Roman troop, soldiers quickly learned how to cover their entire company as they traversed enemy territory, using only their shields as defense. Even as they were under attack, by connecting their shields together, they assured themselves fast, safe progression from one plot of land to the next. It's an important concept to keep in mind, this power of connecting our shields. Sometimes when our faith is flagging, we need to link our shield with another whose faith is flying high. It is often only in the context of such unity that we find protection from the enemy's assault. When our shields are linked together, we form a strong wall to fend off attack. When as one organism we raise our shields overhead, we disallow destruction and despair.

5 The Helmet of Salvation

The fifth piece of armor is described as a "helmet of salvation," which I will discuss further in chapter 5. "Take the helmet of salvation," Ephesians 6:17 says—the "helmet of deliverance," the "helmet of health," according to some translations. I devote an entire chapter to the importance of protecting our heads—our minds—because if Satan can capture our thoughts, he can capture our lives.

6 The Sword of the Spirit

The Bible says that when Christ returns to the earth, he will come with one weapon and one weapon alone: the Word of God. "From his mouth comes a sharp sword with which to strike down the nations," Revelation 19:15 says. And what is that sharp sword? It is the Word—the living, active Word of God. We will further explore this Spirit and his sword in chapter 6 as a means of better understanding the latent power of God's Word for defending us in battle.

7 Prayer, Prayer, Prayer

Finally, there is prayer. Constant prayer. Spirit-directed prayer. Prayer that actually *wins wars*. Following his rundown of physical "armor" all believers must wear, Paul says that the way we get the armor onto our bodies, the way we are to approach the spiritual battle each day, is through devoted, heartfelt prayer. We will pick up this subject in chapter 7, "Warfare Prayer."

I saw a guy in a restaurant one time wearing a T-shirt with a picture of a soldier on the front. Below the picture, it said, "Don't fight naked." I think it's a pretty good summary of the Christian life. When we fight naked, all we've got is our flesh. And our flesh will get us into trouble every time. But when we *put on* the spiritual armor, *put on* things like truth and faith and righteousness, *put on* the Lord Jesus . . . when we consistently, intentionally clothe ourselves with the protection, provision, and power afforded to us by God, we fight smart. We fight savvy. We fight to win. And "win" we've already done, remember? In Jesus there is nothing but victory.

In his letter to the church at Rome, the apostle Paul said these words: "The night is far gone; the day is at hand. So then let us cast off the works of darkness and put on the armor of light" (Romans 13:12). Let us—you and me and everyone who believes on the name of Christ—take responsibility for belting ourselves with truth, for covering ourselves with righteousness, for shielding ourselves with faith, and so forth, knowing that nobody else can do it for us. Not our well-meaning parents, not our well-educated pastor, not our right-living neighbors, not our deeply caring friends. Only we can prepare ourselves for battle, and this particular preparation cannot help but save our lives, as we take a stand against Satan and his schemes.

Discussion Questions

1. This chapter's epigraph contains a pretty powerful sentiment. Do you agree that Calvary Hill—albeit horribly violent—was in fact a "sacred space"?

2. How does the metaphor of being "warriors" in an invisible battle, clad in spiritual "battle gear" mesh with your life experience, or with your expectations of following Christ?

3. The importance of the term *stand* in Ephesians 6 is mentioned. When have you taken a stand for something important, and what were the results?

4. Which pieces of the armor of God has been most necessary in your walk with Christ thus far?
   - truth — *belt*
   - righteousness — *brestplate*
   - peace — *feet w Gospel Peace*
   - faith *sheild*
   - salvation *helmet*
   - activity of the Spirit — *sword*
   - prayer

5. Which piece of armor would you like to wear more faithfully from this point forward, and why?

It is the nature of thought
to find its way into action.

–Christian Nevell Bovee

FIVE
MIND MATTERS

Those who know me well know that I'm a die-hard Texas Rangers baseball fan. Between the months of April and October each year, if I'm not at the ballpark, I'm watching as many games as possible on TV, and although I try not to let the losses get to me, a win sure does make my day. Over the years, I've had the privilege of meeting many Rangers—some of whom are now members of our fellowship and others who have shared their faith with our men's ministry or with various business groups that meet on our campus. One of the players I developed a real affinity for is outfielder Josh Hamilton, a guy whose personal struggles and professional victories alike have been well documented since 1999, when he was Major League Baseball's first overall draft pick.

Josh moved through several minor-league systems for his first five years in baseball and hoped by 2004 to start with Tampa Bay's major league team. But that was not to be. Instead, he spent the next several years battling injury and, more devastating still, drug and alcohol addiction. He attempted rehab but relapsed, and it seemed his major league dream was all but gone. But then came 2007.

In April of that year, Josh debuted with the Cincinnati Reds; then, in 2008, he was traded to the Rangers and was ready to put his demons behind him. He has recently been traded again, this time to the Anaheim Angels, but while he was with us in Texas, he quickly racked up a slew of admirable achievements: five-time All-Star, several-time American League Player of the Month, American League MVP (2010), and more. At one point, Hamilton was hitting .402 with an .877 slugging percentage. Not too bad, I'd say. In fact, frenzied sports writers unabashedly likened him to the Sultan of Swat, Babe Ruth.

But the path to greatness wasn't an easy one. In his former life, he describes himself as a "dead man walking."[1] Booze and drugs have so shrouded various seasons of Josh's life that it really *is* amazing he's still here. This is how addiction goes, I suppose: moments of strength and steadiness, followed by deep, dark pits of despair.

Josh's journey with drugs and alcohol began during a month-long absence from baseball that happened early in his career. He and his parents were traveling home together from Josh's spring training when they were hit by a dump truck that ran a red light. Josh's body would take many months to recover, and even then, his back didn't seem quite right.

Bored and aimless, Josh began hanging out at a tattoo parlor, adding to his own personal collection of tattoos. As it happened, his new friends at the parlor were into drugs; in time, Josh would be too. What started as just "dabbling" eventually thrust Josh into a life-threatening habit. He says of that dark era:

> There were nights I went to sleep in strange places, praying I wouldn't wake up. After another night of bad decisions, I'd lie down with my heart speeding inside my chest like it was about to burst through the skin. My thinking was clouded, and my talent was one day closer to being totally wasted. I prayed to be spared another day of guilt and depression and addiction. I couldn't continue living the life of a crack addict, and I couldn't stop, either. It was a horrible downward spiral that I had to pull out of, or die. I lay there—in a hot and dirty trailer in the North Carolina countryside, in a stranger's house, in the cab of my pickup—and prayed the Lord would take me away from the nightmare my life had become.[2]

Later, during a meaningful moment of reflection, Josh said this of the entire experience: "I thought I was better than that. . . . I didn't have Jesus first in my life. . . . I didn't think I needed help from anybody."[3]

I nodded my head when I read those words, realizing that for Josh Hamilton—and also for you and me—every sin we'll ever know can be traced back to a single, errant thought.

Where Satan's Attacks Always Begin

I decided to devote an entire chapter to this issue of "minding our mind," because I firmly believe that all ground given to Satan is given first and foremost between our ears. It really is true:

99

What we *think* ultimately becomes what we *do*. The attitudes we hold, the actions we take, the patterns we establish, the vices we indulge—all of these things and many more are the result of how we think. Whether we follow the path to righteousness or the one that leads us astray, we always will be slaves to that which our minds crave.

For the next several pages, we will look at when we're most vulnerable to Satan's attack; then we'll turn our attention to what it looks like to fend off the enemy's assaults by taking "every thought captive to obey Christ" (2 Corinthians 10:5).

Satan Attacks After Spiritual Victory

In my experience, there are five key danger zones where Satan and his evil minions are prone to attack unsuspecting believers, and the first is *on the heels of spiritual victory.*

Now, this may seem incredible to you: Just after a spiritual victory, shouldn't we be riding high, experiencing great strength in God? In fact, the opposite is true. After the high often comes the low; we enjoy the view from a spiritual mountaintop and walk away feeling a little puffed up, a little independent, a little self-reliant, a little proud of what we have done. Sure, we toss a bone of gratitude God's way, but we can't help but think how the victory wouldn't have occurred had we not been faithful/obedient/selfless/dependable/helpful/capable/strong.

We unwittingly slip out from under God's protective covering on our lives, and *bam!* Satan strikes.

This happened even to Jesus. Well, not the gloating, self-aggrandizing part, but the part about experiencing his greatest temptation just after his greatest success. In Matthew 3 and 4, we see that right after the great and glorious moment when

Jesus was baptized in the Jordan River, just after he'd received his heavenly Father's blessing—"This is my beloved Son, with whom I am well pleased" (Matthew 3:13–17)—just after the inauguration of what would be his magnificent earthly ministry, Jesus was driven by the Spirit of God into the desert, where he had a triply tough encounter with the devil.

I see this same trend play out in countless people's lives. A man with a sin-stuffed background finally surrenders his life to Jesus Christ, he enters the waters of baptism, and he emerges on top of the world. Something inside of him relaxes a little: *Whew!* he thinks. *I'm headed to heaven when I die. At last! I've got it made.*

He lets down his guard ever so slightly, and within moments, he's vulnerable to attack.

Or a woman returns home after spending a week in Africa helping others from her church to build an orphanage for kids who have no place to live. She's filled to overflowing with joy and peace after seeing such fruit borne by her own two hands. But within days of her return, she's weary and disheartened. Her relationship with her husband feels strained, her children seem distant, she feels isolated from social circles, and her boss is frustrated because she has been out of the office for so many days. She lies awake in bed one night thinking, *Where is all this opposition coming from?*

Certainly I'm not suggesting that we neglect the pursuit of spiritual victory. On the contrary! What I am saying is that we stay on guard, recognizing that those who stand really must take heed, lest they fall (1 Corinthians 10:12).

Satan Strikes When We're Alone

I have been a pastor for more than four decades, and a trend I've seen consistently is that people step off the path of righteousness with greater frequency when they're walking that path alone. There is a reason God extols the benefits of community throughout Scripture. We are built for togetherness, not isolation. ✗

It always concerns me when followers of Christ start pulling away from meeting regularly with a local church. They miss a Sunday or two because of vacation or illness or inclement weather, and the exception becomes the norm; eventually, months have elapsed since they last worshiped with other believers, and they're vulnerable to attack. I always tell the congregation at Prestonwood, the church I pastor, that _to pull away_ is to _pull Satan in,_ and he always leaves a mess in his wake.

For you, isolation may look like traveling for work and finding yourself on far too many occasions all alone in a hotel room, with nobody there to hold you accountable to what you say you believe. Or maybe for you, isolation looks like being new to your neighborhood, where nobody knows your name, nobody knows you're a believer, nobody has any expectations of you, and nobody will tell if you happen to do something wrong.

Or maybe for you, isolation looks like some other set of circumstances entirely. My point is the same: When you and I are either circumstantially or willfully separated from Christian community, we are _always_ vulnerable to attack.

(3) Satan Strikes When We're Tired

Another common source of vulnerability in believers' lives is physical and emotional exhaustion. Even Jesus' disciples found this to be true. Just before his arrest and crucifixion, Jesus gathered his disciples together in the garden of Gethsemane and asked them all to wait and pray. But the hour was late and their resolve was weak, and they couldn't help but fall asleep. Peter's plight was far worse; he ran away and denied he even knew Jesus Christ, the Messiah to whom he had committed himself! (Matthew 26:69–75).

But their behavior—Peter's and the others—adds up, doesn't it? When we're exhausted, we tend to fall prey to attack. When we're drained, our resistance is low.

Satan Strikes When We're in Church

A fourth danger zone, believe it or not, is right in the midst of your church. I have come to believe that Satan delights in hurling missiles at our heads while we're sitting in a roomful of believers, worshiping the one true God. In fact, if you've got eyes to see his schemes, you'll notice them all over the place.

Over the course of my forty-plus years in the pulpit, I've noticed that whenever the gospel is preached, there comes a tender moment when people are ready to respond. I liken it to a heart patient who is about to go under the knife. A fifty-five-year-old man complains of chest pains, for example. He pays his cardiologist a visit and has an EKG, which reveals, not surprisingly, clogged arteries. Bypass surgery is ordered.

During surgery, the doc puts the man to sleep and begins to cut open his chest cavity. Once this is accomplished, the surgeon takes the man's heart in his hand—literally, he's holding his life.

At that precise moment, life hangs in the balance. The chest is wide open, the heart is separated from the rest of the body, and germs are champing at the bit to invade. This is what vulnerability looks like, and it's precisely what occurs in the spiritual realm. When the Word of God penetrates a person's heart, the devil likes to come alongside that holy advancement and refute it every step of the way. I've seen his attempts to thwart progress take a thousand forms: A Sunday school teacher makes a benign comment just before her student's parent walks down the hall to attend the worship service. The parent misinterprets the comment and can't pay attention to what's being said from the pulpit. Someone gets distracted by a worship leader's "too puffy" hair and lets his mind wander away from God. Just ten minutes after singing her gratitude to God for his great gift of grace, a woman is cut off trying to exit the parking lot and mutters curses under her breath.

I know you know what I'm talking about. And this stuff happens right there in *church*. It shouldn't happen, but it does. We must be wise to Satan's attacks.

⑤ *Satan Strikes When We're Attempting Something Great for God*

A final danger zone to watch out for is when you're investing your time and energies to build the kingdom of God. The writer of Hebrews reminds us that Jesus suffered the ultimate rejection—the death penalty for sins he did not commit—and that rejection took place on the other side of the tracks, as it were, from the city's trash heap. "So Jesus also suffered outside the gate," says Hebrews 13:12, "in order to sanctify the people through his own blood."

Then, verse 13: "Therefore let us go to him outside the camp and bear the reproach he endured."

Here's another way of reading this text: "When you fight for the same cause Jesus Christ fought for and lay down your life as he did, you can expect to be treated the way he was treated, and the way he was treated wasn't good."

When you finally muster the courage to share your faith with a cynical co-worker, and that co-worker is transferred to another city, making your interactions dwindle to nil, you shouldn't be surprised.

When you insist on purity in your relationship with your girlfriend and then are disparaged by guys you consider friends, you shouldn't be surprised.

When you work tirelessly for weeks on end to organize an anti-trafficking event at your church and then watch helplessly as an ice storm cancels the evening, you shouldn't be surprised.

When you invest yourself in a dozen noble ways and see Satan sucker-punch you each and every time . . . You. Should. Not. Be. Surprised.

Satan's Primary Objective

Satan doesn't know how to do much besides spend his days reloading his bow and firing flaming arrows our way. But whether he actually takes us out of the game is secondary to him; his primary objective, which harkens back to the garden of Eden, is to *plant a single idea in our minds*, namely, "You cannot trust your God."

His empty accusations are hissed straight from the depths of hell: "God won't provide for you. He won't protect you. He won't comfort you when you're in despair. He won't bring you satisfaction. He won't bring you livelihood. He won't bring you love, or hope, or peace. He's never been there for you, and he'll never be there for you now. You're better off taking matters into your own hands."

Just after my dad died, a strong feeling of foreboding overtook my thoughts, that sense that another tragedy was surely headed my way; it was only a matter of time. Interestingly, I thought everyone experienced that other-shoe-about-to-drop sensation; I thought everyone lived that way. It would take many years and many hours of therapy before I'd come to realize I had been plagued by a spirit of fear.

Fear was a dark, lurking shadow in my life. When our kids were born, I worried about something happening to them. Years later, when they started driving, I thought for sure they'd have a wreck. When they left home to go on trips or to head off to college, I just knew I'd get the middle-of-the-night phone call every parent dreads. In my own life, I feared even routine doctor visits, knowing in the depths of my being that the report was going to come back bad, the test was going to be positive, and the worry was going to prove to be justifiable in the end.[4]

This is how Satan wages war against us, isn't it? He loves to break in on our thoughts. He introduces doubt, which leads to fear, which leads to confusion, which leads to pain. He is a terrorist, in every sense of the word, seeking to oppress us and then to occupy us, seeking to make us slaves to our very own sin.[5] Chip Ingram writes:

> Most of the [spiritual] battle is in our thought life—that's where Satan can manipulate people toward his ends discreetly and invisibly. If he can distort our thoughts, our emotions, and our knowledge, then our behaviors and relationships will fall the way he wants them to. And even if he doesn't manage to turn us to overt evil, a little bit of distorted thinking can neutralize us and render us practically ineffective.[6]

A bit of distorted thinking . . . isn't that where all waywardness begins?

Choosing Hope When Hopelessness Reigns

When I was a baseball player, I never went to bat without a helmet. Nobody in a right mind wants to face a ninety-five-mile-an-hour fastball without something protecting that noggin. And this is what Paul was advising when he in essence said, "Protect your *head*. Protect your *mind*. Protect your *every thought*. Your wholeness and holiness depend on these things; please don't leave them to chance. Put on your helmet each day!"

But it wasn't just that we should protect our minds that mattered; it was *what we should protect our minds with*. Let's revisit the verse. "Take the helmet of salvation," Ephesians 6:17 says, meaning it is with salvation that we guard our minds—salvation, which ultimately translates to hope. For whenever you or I or any other sin-scarred person at last lays down a heart, lays down a life, to the lordship of Jesus Christ, hope is what we gain.

The book of 2 Timothy is one of Paul's three "pastoral epistles," this one addressed from mentor (Paul) to mentee (Timothy) as something of a swan song when Paul faced imminent death. Throughout the letter, Paul encouraged Timothy to live without a spirit of timidity and to boldly testify to the Lord's goodness and grace. In 2 Timothy 4:8, he says these words to his protégé on the eve of his departure: "You take over. I'm about to die, my life an offering on God's altar. This is the only race worth running. I've run hard right to the finish, believed all the way. All that's left now is the shouting—God's applause! Depend on it, he's an honest judge. He'll do right not only by me, but by everyone eager for his coming" (THE MESSAGE).

The applause of God for a race well run—isn't that what you and I both yearn for, the words, "Well done, my child. Well done"? For the believer, there is a future crown of righteousness, which eclipses every earthly gain. And as we pursue proper thinking in our lives day by day, we "hope for" that ultimate reward. When our thoughts try to convince us that soul-level hope can be found anywhere else—in a secure job, in a set of tight abs, in a checked-off to-do list, in a healthy bank account, in a thriving marriage, in accomplished children, in a local sports team finally taking the title—we do well to remember this encouragement from Paul, which basically says, "Our hope is in Christ alone." This truth is what helps us keep our thought lives pure. This truth protects our minds.

A few years ago, a group of research doctors joined forces to assess 194 breast-cancer patients in hopes of discovering what variables contributed to their quality of life. More specifically, they wanted to know whether the concept and practice of hope played a role. There is fancy language to describe the study's approach and findings, but I'll sum it up this way: They asked a bunch of questions, evaluated a bunch of surveys, examined a bunch of women, and then published their conclusions for all to see. Want to know what they discovered? Here it is, in their exact words: "Hope may be an important coping mechanism that clinicians need to consider when they try to help patients reduce the psychological distress associated with cancer and its treatment."[7]

I'm no medical doctor, but I could have saved that team a wad of cash and told them that news from the start. *Of course* hope helps us cope. Hope helps us do *everything* better in life. Surely you have found this to be true. Perhaps you've noticed along the way that when the status of your marriage, your relationship with a close friend, your bank account, or your job has you in the doldrums, all it takes is a microscopic amount of hope for you to feel revived once more. Your spouse invites you out on a romantic date; your best friend calls to say "sorry"; an unexpected Christmas bonus comes your way; your boss stops by your office to deliver a quick but meaningful "well done." Suddenly, your emotional universe starts spinning again. Your breathing returns to normal. Your shoulders relax. And all of this, for the simple reason that your *hope* has been restored.

When you and I put on the helmet of salvation each day, we're essentially strapping *ultimate hope* to our heads. When our minds and our outlook are focused on Jesus and on him alone, we are protected against the despair and discouragement that inevitably come in this life. Salvation reminds us that even the most unfortunate circumstances can't change the fact that our lives are eternally secure in Christ.

Training Our Brains

In 2006 I got a bad report from my doctor. (See, I knew it would happen!) I had gone through a normal checkup, and he noticed on my blood test results that my PSA levels were running high. He ordered a biopsy, which came back clear. Predictably, I was thrilled. But my doc was unconvinced. Six months later, he ordered another biopsy. That one came back clear too. Again, I was thrilled; again, my doc was not. "Something is causing these spikes in your PSA levels, Jack," he said.

I thought about getting a new doctor.

In 2009, after continuing to be concerned about my PSA level, which had become even more elevated than before, he ordered a third biopsy. I was less than thrilled. For starters, this particular biopsy doesn't make for a pleasant experience. But I kept hearing my doctor's voice in my head, saying, "I know something is going on, Jack. For some reason, our first two biopsies missed it."

The last thing I wanted to do was naively stick my head in the sand, when my doctor—who is, in fact, a long-time trusted friend of mine—believed something in my body was going awry.

The third biopsy came back positive. "Just as I suspected, Jack," he said, with tenderness in his eyes. What he had known that I couldn't fathom was that cancer had been lurking all along. Surgery was on the horizon for me, but I'd have to wait six weeks for it to occur.

I remember that six-week period from early April until mid-May being an intense mental battle for me. My mind was obsessed with the diagnosis, the surgery, the lifestyle that would result from all of this. It was like having an annoying song stuck in your head; try as I did, I couldn't get my brain to skip to the next tune. I am a get-it-done guy. Get it done, and get it done now. Being asked to wait for six weeks before enduring what would be the most severe medical procedure of my life was sheer torture.

The words of Philippians 4:8 became my shelter in a time of storm: "Finally, brothers," it says, "whatever is honorable, whatever is just, whatever is pure, whatever is lovely, whatever is commendable, if there is any excellence, if there is anything worthy of praise, think about these things." If I were to show you my journals from those dark days, you'd find those sentiments on nearly every page. I breathed in the words like oxygen, realizing that the only hope to be had was in the truth of God. I had to fix my gaze above my circumstances, as dire and consuming as they were.

The surgery was successful, and since 2009, I have enjoyed a cancer-free life. But certainly I was not unchanged by the experience, and one of the greatest lessons I learned centers on this idea of taking captive my thoughts. I discovered firsthand that it is never enough to just try harder not to think the wrong things; you and I also must intentionally work to think thoughts that are right. It wasn't enough for me to merely try to avoid thinking dark things—*My surgery isn't going to be successful. The surgeon isn't going to be able to get the entire tumor. My best days are behind me.* I also had to pour in positive thoughts: *With God, all things are possible. God is my refuge and my strength. Because I am God's and he is mine, hope is where I make my home.*

We have to train our brains to think pure thoughts. Admittedly, it's not an easy task, but there is a simple way to begin.

For starters, you may have noticed that it is only humanly possible to think one thought at a time. It's an amazing design feature we possess, courtesy of a loving God: If we are thinking a pure thought, we can't simultaneously think an impure one. I find that whenever I face a tough situation, it helps to slow down and take things one single thought at a time. You might try it too. Surrender the very next thought you'll think to the lordship of Jesus Christ, asking him to purify it, to make it holy, to align it to the way *he* thinks. Believe it or not, you do this a few times in a row, and you'll find you've got a whole string of helpful thoughts rushing their way through your brain. Do it for a few *days* in a row, and you'll experience a spiritually prosperous week.

As I say, every sin can be traced back to one errant thought, but equally true is that every victory over temptation can be traced back to one righteous thought. Every thought we think, then, will either positively or negatively dictate the future we enjoy. In other words, thinking is not for wimps!

So what are we to do if we want to retrain our brains to think good thoughts? There are two steps we must take.

The Prerequisite of Salvation

For every action you take, your brain creates a neurological pathway that paves the way for familiarity, so that the next time you take that action, your mind already knows what to do. As you'd imagine, as you repeat behaviors over and over, those pathways become increasingly more stable. Think of it this way: A single behavior maps out a dirt road in your brain, creating a basic pathway on which your thoughts travel. But as you repeat behaviors, your brain builds a concrete highway, which allows for increased volume and frequency of thoughts to move about more effectively and more efficiently.

These consistent "default" thoughts then dictate your actions, for good or for ill, in the same way that you tend to shift into autopilot when you're taking your typical route home. You don't even have to think about driving, you've driven those turns so many times. The same is true with your thinking. Think a thought enough times and, eventually, you're not really thinking anymore; your mind is just doing what it has been trained to do. In order to change our thoughts, then, we must deconstruct existing highways and make way for new pathways to be built.

When we arrived here on planet Earth, we arrived enslaved to sin. Before we were born, our mind was predisposed to selfish thoughts, errant thoughts, running along dead-end paths. If you have children, you know this to be true. After all, how much effort did you have to put into teaching your kids to say, "Mine!"? How long did it take to teach them to lie? Deceive? Manipulate people and situations to get their own way? If your kids are anything like my kids, they showed up on day one with these skills already in place. At the outset, the ways we think, dream, reason, and act are limited to the flawed, failed ways of the world.

It was for this reason that Jesus clothed himself in human flesh, left heaven for the pain of earth, died a criminal's death, bore our sin—past, present, and future—and paid a ransom we can never repay. When we surrender our lives to his leadership, assenting to the idea that in him alone is redemption, we essentially get a brain transplant. We get to trade old ways of thinking for new ways. When we accept the helmet of salvation from our Commander in Chief, we are serving notice to Satan that our lives are "under construction," a project financed by God himself.

Every day during my morning commute to my office at the church, I go through a massive construction zone on the North Dallas Tollway. An old part of the expressway is being deconstructed so that a superhighway can be built, and at the moment it looks like a war zone. It's a disaster to drive through, but I try to remember the overall objective here, and how smooth and seamless my commute will be someday when the stunning new road is complete. Similarly, it can feel rather messy to allow God to deconstruct old thought patterns for the sake of constructing something new. But the roads our Father longs to build for us lead to life that is *truly* life. They lead to our fulfillment. They lead to our protection. They lead to our purpose. They lead always to our peace.

This is what salvation is all about: restoring us—mind, body, soul, spirit—to the original intent God had in mind for our lives. It is about reconstructing the way we think, which as I've said, affects everything else. The Bible uses terminology such as "taking every thought captive" (2 Corinthians 10:5) and committing daily to the "renewing of your mind" (Romans 12:2) through the power of God's Word. In time, entirely new neurological road maps emerge, leading you to the life you were meant to live.

The Principle of Sanctification

But there's a second step we also must take if we're serious about being reconstructed in our thinking. After surrendering our lives to Jesus, we must *sanctify* our lives day by day.

Here is how this works: Let's say you are outside the family of God, but one day you hear the gospel proclaimed. You become aware of your sinfulness and your need for a Savior; you see the goodness and kindness of God toward you, and you decide to turn from your own will and your old ways, and you surrender your life to Christ. This is the "personal salvation" I spoke of a few pages ago, or *repentance*, to use a theological term.

However, because you were born with a sin nature, and because the devil continues to tempt you and lure you away from God, while your one-time repentance led you to salvation, it is only by *daily repentance* that your fellowship is maintained with God. This is also known as *sanctification,* which basically means "becoming more Christlike."

Certainly when we sin against God, it does not stop us from being his children. It doesn't put our eternal future in jeopardy. It doesn't cause us to lose our salvation. But it *does* hinder our fellowship with God. In order to restore that fellowship, in order to clear the lines of communication between us and God and therefore foster intimacy once again, we must confess our sin, repent of it, and turn back toward God. Again, this type of repentance—sanctification—is not repentance leading to salvation, but rather repentance leading to fellowship.

We learn from 1 Thessalonians 5:23 that it is actually God himself who does the sanctifying in our lives, but he will not force it on us; we must surrender willingly to the process.

Let me show you what this looks like in daily life.

I'm sixty-two now, and one of the challenges of aging is not to become hypercritical. The issue can be trivial: *Why is this moron cutting me off in traffic? Why are my Rangers playing so terribly?* Or it can be significant: *Why is everyone out to get me? Nobody has my back.*

I don't know if it's the physical aches and pains inherent in getting older, or that your friends start dying off, or that the young world passes you by, but for several years now, I've noticed the trend that as people grow old, they also grow cold. It was a bad day when I saw this coldness surfacing in my own life. I looked in the mirror and saw glimpses of Walter Matthau from the movie *Grumpy Old Men* staring back at me! Do you remember that movie from the early 1990s? I don't want to be a grumpy old man! I don't want to be cynical. I don't want to be cold.

It's a tough mental battle to fight, though. By the time you get to be my age, you've seen a lot of heavy stuff in life. You've seen people doing stupid things, hurtful things, ungodly things, and you start thinking everyone is a blooming fool. You see angry people, malicious people, abusive people, and you come away believing all people are awful all the time. You won't want to think like this, but left to your own devices, your thoughts will veer this way.

Part of my practical sanctification work lately has centered on arresting curmudgeonly thoughts and inviting Jesus to change my ways. A handful of times each day, I have to stop what I'm doing, physically shut my mouth, and whisper, "Jesus, may my thoughts be praiseworthy, positive, and productive." This has become my constant prayer. As you'd guess, laying down my natural-man thinking and picking up God's thoughts instead has dramatically changed my outlook. And it has made me a far more pleasant guy to be around.

Destroying Strongholds

In my estimation, this process of stopping in the midst of an errant string of thoughts, asking Jesus to come into the situation and correct our thinking, and then walking forward in grace and power, provides an adequate way of escape for 90 percent of the temptations we face. But then there's that pesky other 10 percent.

Second Corinthians 10:3–5 raises the issue of "strongholds," or besetting vulnerabilities or obsessions or weak areas that seem to require special attention if they're ever to be overcome.

> For though we walk in the flesh, we are not waging war according to the flesh. For the weapons of our warfare are not of the flesh but have divine power to destroy strongholds. We destroy arguments and every lofty opinion raised against the knowledge of God, and take every thought captive to obey Christ.

These weapons of warfare we're discussing, especially the helmet of salvation, which you'll recall is our helmet of hope, are more than sufficient to tear down every streak of sinfulness we'll ever know.

A stronghold is a mental fortress, something that gets stuck in our heads. It can be an unhealthy fixation, a phobia, an anxiety that shows up day by day. It can be a root of bitterness that we never can seem to pull up. It can be seemingly uncontrollable anger, greed, pride, or lust. It can look like a businessman who calls on prostitutes, and also like a woman who consistently cares more about what her girlfriends think than about what God says is true. We're not talking here about passing temptations, but about captivating ideas that control you and stand in direct opposition to God.

In C. S. Lewis's 1940s fantasy *The Great Divorce*, a man who is a resident in the "grey town" is trying to decide whether to leave the home he has known and inhabit the "heavenly country" instead. Factoring into his decision is a lizard that lives on his shoulder. The lizard, which symbolizes lust, is clearly hurting the man, but still, the man allows the lizard to stay. After all, he knows the lizard. He's used to the lizard. He likes having the lizard around.

An angel of God comes to the man and asks, "Shall I kill it?" to which the man replies, "Maybe later."

The man wants the lizard killed. Or rather, he *wants* to want the lizard killed. But he just can't bring himself to do it. Realizing the man is tempted to rid himself of this lizard, the lizard speaks to the man. (I did mention this was a work of fantasy, right?) The talking lizard says (referring to the angel of God):

> Be careful. He can do what he says. He can kill me. One fatal word from you, and he will! Then you'll be without me forever and ever. It's not natural. How could you live? You'd be only a sort of ghost, not a real man as you are now. He doesn't understand. He's only a cold, bloodless, abstract thing. It may be natural for him, but it isn't for us. Yes, yes. I know there are no real pleasures now, only dreams. But aren't they better than nothing? And I'll be so good. I admit I've sometimes gone too far in the past, but I promise I won't do it again. I'll give you nothing but really nice dreams—all sweet and fresh and almost innocent. You might say, quite innocent.[8]

I've talked to countless people who are stuck in a stronghold—even in this particular stronghold of lust—and sincerely do not know how to get freed. They are swept up in the devastating habit of using drugs or drinking alcohol or visiting porn sites or acting on homosexual tendencies or insisting on perfection in every corner of their life or gambling away their paycheck . . . and they just don't know how to get out. The apostle Paul warned against this very type of thing when he wrote in Romans 6:12: "Let not sin therefore reign in your mortal body, to make you obey its passions."

Egotism and arrogance, violence and contentiousness, stubbornness and faithlessness, addictions, compulsions, and doubt—these well-traveled pathways can be deconstructed. My friend, we can be set free. Let's back up for a moment. Our thoughts lead to our actions, and it is our actions that ultimately form habits. It is by wielding the weapons of warfare, then, that we fight the beginnings of our battle and *win*.

I should say here that I believe Christian counseling programs can be wildly effective, that medication is sometimes necessary, that one-time deliverance indeed can happen, and also that positive self-talk has its place. Yes, positive thinking beats negative thinking, every single time. But pasting on a smile, popping a pill, or merely *hoping* problems will get resolved just encourages Satan's schemes in our lives. No, this battle requires far more of us. It demands that we get ruthless in the area of our thoughts. It demands that we plant our feet, square our shoulders, and speak a bold, unwavering "No!" to the devil, to the one whom, when resisted, has no other recourse but to flee (see James 4:7).

It demands that we dig in, that we invite God to deconstruct the dead-end paths we've been walking, that we repent of all known sin in our lives, and that we surrender to being discipled by the only true Lover of our souls. It demands that we turn toward Jesus again and again, until the most natural response in our daily lives is to walk intimately with him.

When my granddaughter, Dylan, was born, I remember seeing how content the child was whenever she was resting in my daughter-in-law's arms. Dylan could be totally out of sorts—hungry or tired or in need of a diaper change—but as soon as Kaytie reached down, picked up the child, and cradled her close, all was right in Dylan's world once more. Spiritually, that same sense of comfort is available to you and me.

Paul wrote that it is, in fact, possible for God's peace to guard our hearts and minds (see Philippians 4:7). Satan's schemes can be encroaching on us from every side, and yet you and I can rest as peacefully as a newborn in her mother's capable arms. We really can. We can let our minds be settled with the knowledge that God's peace is close at hand.

Discussion Questions

1. How have you seen the concept play out in your life that what we *think* is ultimately what we *do*?

2. Satan commonly attacks a follower of Christ on the heels of spiritual victory. Describe a time when this was true for you.

3. Why is isolationism in the life of a believer such a powerful tool in the enemy's arsenal?

4. How does our weariness play into Satan's strategies for our demise?

5. When have you experienced firsthand especially negative thoughts or actions while participating in corporate worship in the context of your local church?

6. Why do you suppose following Jesus Christ requires us to lay down our lives in the same way that he did? Is there an easier approach to the Christ-following life?

7. Fear can rule various seasons of life. What entanglement have *you* known throughout your life?

8. What does the phrase *choose hope* mean for you? What broken strongholds in your life bear testimony to the fact that God really can set prisoners free?

How can a young man keep his way pure?
By guarding it according to your word.

−Psalm 119:9

SIX
MORE THAN CONQUERORS

For more than three centuries, John Bunyan's book, *The Pilgrim's Progress*, has been considered one of the most important religious works of English literature, and for good reason. It is an allegory that paints the picture of the Christ-following journey perhaps better than any other book, with the exception of the Bible. The protagonist, an average man named Christian, faces temptation, sin, regret, salvation, hope, worldliness, restoration, ups, downs, mountains, valleys, both intimacy and distance from God, as he makes his way from his homeland, the "City of Destruction," to the "Celestial City," where his hoped-for salvation awaits. This is what life looks like, isn't it? We try and we fail and we try again, realizing that it is only by God's grace that we are sustained.

There comes a point in Christian's journey where he faces intense spiritual warfare and goes toe-to-toe with the enemy of his soul. Christian's enemy, Apollyon, appears as a dragon-like creature with scales, bat wings, and a full quiver of arrows he uses liberally as he works to take his opponents down.

As Christian makes his way along the road, a wild scene unfolds. Apollyon, clearly representing the devil, springs across the highway in front of Christian and says, "I am without fear in this matter! Prepare yourself to die, for I swear by all the infernal powers that you shall go no farther. I will take your soul right here!" Then he hurls a flaming dart at Christian's heart.

But Christian holds out his shield and blocks the arrow from making contact. Christian draws his sword and braces himself for battle. Apollyon then comes at him with a fury of darts as thick as hail. Some fly above and some below Christian's shield, wounding him painfully in spite of all that he is doing to defend himself. Then he falls back a little, staggering and swaying to keep his footing amid the onslaught. Seeing this, Apollyon comes on with all his might.

Suddenly our hero remembers an effectual prayer and takes courage by reciting it aloud. But still, the fighting persists. Apollyon and Christian brawl up and down the highway for over half an hour, and Christian's strength is almost spent from loss of blood and sheer exhaustion. Apollyon perceives that Christian is gradually growing weaker; leveraging this advantage, he takes hold of Christian and throws him to the ground, causing Christian's sword to fly from his grasp. "Now," said Apollyon, "I am sure I have you!" And he beats the man nearly to death.

But as God would have it, just as Apollyon pounds his final punches against Christian's person, the man's hand touches his sword, infusing his spirit with a fresh jolt of energy. Gripping the sword with all his might, he says, "Rejoice not against me, O my enemy! When I fall, I shall rise again!"

And giving Apollyon a deadly thrust that causes him to fall back as if mortally wounded, with all the strength Christian can summon, he rises to his feet and advances toward him, crying, "In all these things we are more than conquerors through Him who loves us!"

Having no recourse against the power of Christian's words, Apollyon then spreads his wings and flies away.[1]

The Power of the Word of God

It's easy to write off a book such as *Pilgrim's Progress* as nothing more than ancient allegory, to assume that it has nothing relevant to say to the modern trials and tribulations we face. Granted, it's not every day that you and I find ourselves walking along a highway armed with shields when a scaly dragon with the wings of a bat starts firing arrows our way. But let me caution you against so quickly tossing it aside: Bunyan's classic work—and especially this particular scene—carries with it a truth so fundamental, so useful to believers, that to miss it is to miss the essence of the Christian life.

If I told you that it was possible to live the rest of your life without falling prey to temptation as often as you do, would you be interested in knowing more? Think of it: less heartache, less regret, fewer relational chasms, less confusion, chaos, and sin.

Is a life like this even *possible*? Is this really an option for broken and sin-scarred people such as us?

To answer these questions, we need look no further than to the person and example of Jesus Christ. After all, this was the track record *he* enjoyed in life, and because of his great sacrifice on Calvary's cross, you and I can live this way too. Let's revisit a trio of scriptural scenes you're likely familiar with.

In Matthew 4:1–11, the passage we first looked at in chapter 2, you'll recall that Jesus is on the tail end of a forty-day fast. Understandably, the Messiah is hungry. Satan, here called "the tempter," comes to Christ and says, "If you are the Son of God, command these stones to become loaves of bread," to which Jesus replies, quoting Deuteronomy 8:3, "It is written: 'Man shall not live by bread alone, but by every word that comes from the mouth of God.'"

Moments later, scene two: The devil escorts Jesus to a holy city and has him stand on the highest point of the temple, where he says, "If you are the Son of God, throw yourself down, for it is written, 'He will command his angels concerning you, and on their hands they will bear you up, lest you strike your foot against a stone.'"

This was a direct reference to Psalm 91; if you think Satan isn't familiar with the Bible, think again.

Jesus also knows God's Word. He eyes his opponent and quotes Deuteronomy 6:16 in reply, "Again it is written, 'You shall not put the Lord your God to the test.'"

And finally, scene three: The devil takes Jesus to a very high mountain and shows him all the kingdoms of the world and their splendor. "All these I will give you," Satan says, "if you will fall down and worship me."

Pretty attractive offer, don't you think? You and I might easily be swayed. *All* the kingdoms of the world? Just think what we could do with all that money, all that power, all that prestige, all that renown! Not surprisingly, Jesus is not impressed. He knows better than to negotiate with Satan. Some deals are never worth doing, regardless of how promising they seem.

"Be gone, Satan!" Jesus bellows. "For it is written: 'You shall worship the Lord your God and him only shall you serve.'" Again Jesus quotes Scripture, this time Deuteronomy 6:13. At last, the text says, the devil left him, and angels came and ministered to him.

Three times Jesus is tempted by none other than Satan himself, and three times Jesus refutes him with one simple weapon: the powerful, immutable, inspired Word of God.

Taking Up the Sword of the Spirit

In Ephesians 6:17 the apostle Paul tells believers to "take the helmet of salvation, *and the sword of the Spirit, which is the word of God*" (emphasis mine). This is the only place in Scripture that we find the phrase *sword of the Spirit* used, but Hebrews 4:12 also uses *sword* to refer to God's Word. "For the word of God is living and active," that verse says, "sharper than any two-edged sword, piercing to the division of soul and of spirit, of joints and of marrow, and discerning the thoughts and intentions of the heart."

Paul's exhortation to "pick up the sword" should be read as a reminder that because of the Holy Spirit dwelling within us as believers, we have *access* to God's Word, we have spiritual eyes that are able to *appreciate* God's Word, and we have the ability to *apply* God's Word in our everyday lives. We have the sharpness and swiftness of a two-edged sword at our disposal, the ever-sharp Word of God.

Swords have two edges, which makes it easier to cut through an opponent, regardless of which way the blade is swung. In early Roman days, swords were used to protect people from harm, from an enemy seeking to overtake and ultimately destroy them, making Paul's analogy a fitting one; possessing and knowing how to rightly appropriate the Word of God serves as an effective weapon in spiritual warfare, both defensively and offensively. It should be noted here that nearly every weapon Paul encourages believers to wield during spiritual battles is a defensive one, which is further substantiation of a point I made previously: Because Christ secured our ultimate victory when he bled and died on the cross and then rose from the grave three days later, you and I fight not for victory (offensively) but rather from it (defensively). Yes, we can use a sword to push forward and gain ground if need be, but more often the case is our need to simply stand and protect the ground Christ has already secured.

So this sword—this double-edged sword Paul describes—should be considered useful for gaining strength, gaining maturity, gaining ground, but also for emboldening us to withstand our enemy's evil onslaughts and live to tell of the attack. Psalm 119 bears testimony three separate times to this truth: In verse 11, we read, "I have stored up your word in my heart, that I might not sin against you." Later, in verses 33 through 40, we read,

Psm 119

Teach me, O Lord, the way of your statutes; and I will keep it to the end. Give me understanding, that I may keep your law and observe it with my whole heart. Lead me in the path of your commandments, for I delight in it. Incline my heart to your testimonies, and not to selfish gain! Turn my eyes from looking at worthless things; and give me life in your ways. Confirm to your servant your promise, that you may be feared. Turn away the reproach that I dread, for your rules are good. Behold, I long for your precepts; in your righteousness give me life!

And finally, verses 99 through 104 offer these sage words:

I have more understanding than all my teachers, for your testimonies are my meditation. I understand more than the aged, for I keep your precepts. I hold back my feet from every evil way, in order to keep your word. I do not turn aside from your rules, for you have taught me. How sweet are your words to my taste, sweeter than honey to my mouth! Through your precepts I get understanding; therefore I hate every false way.

It is God's Word that leads us to righteousness. It is God's Word that leads us to understanding. It is God's Word that keeps us from sinning, from taking the "evil way." The Holy Spirit uses the power of God's Word to *rescue* us through salvation and then to *resource* us with spiritual strength to be mature soldiers for the Lord in fighting corruption that runs rampant in our world. The more we know and understand the Word of God, the more useful we will be in doing the will of God and the more effective we will be in standing firm against the myriad ways Satan hopes to trip us up.

To Know and Understand God's Word

The only challenge that remains, then, is coming to "know and understand"—or *appreciate*—God's Word. The words of Deuteronomy 6:6–9 are known in the Jewish tradition as the *Shema*, one of their centerpiece prayers. In it, God instructs the nation of Israel regarding the importance of keeping his Word foremost in their lives.

> These words that I command you today shall be on your heart. You shall teach them diligently to your children, and shall talk of them when you sit in your house, and when you walk by the way, and when you lie down, and when you rise. You shall bind them as a sign on your hand, and they shall be as frontlets between your eyes. You shall write them on the doorposts of your house and on your gates.

You might take from this text that God is pretty serious about our honoring his Word in our lives. Indeed he is! And for good reason: Imagine how many children's lives could be improved if their parents made a point of reading and explaining the primary principles of the Bible to them. Imagine how many families would grow stronger and more unified if they took a few minutes each evening to talk about their understanding of a particular psalm or a proverb or a well-known Bible story. Imagine how drastically incidents of road rage would decrease if every person on the road had begun his or her day meditating on a verse of Scripture before getting out of bed. Imagine *all* the good that could occur in this world if God's Word were allowed to direct our lives!

God knows that in his Word we find hope and peace and promise, rest for our weary souls, and strength for the journey ahead. He knows that here we find direction when we're confused, comfort when we feel forsaken, inclusion when we feel alone. And for these reasons and a thousand more, he says, "Come. Drink deeply of my deeply satisfying Word."[2]

When I was a young pastor preaching youth revivals across the southwest region, a mentor of mine was like a walking Bible. He couldn't complete a sentence, it seemed, without referencing a little piece of God's Word. He was the wisest, most encouraging man I'd ever met because his language was bolstered by divine ideas. There was *power* in his words. Cohesion. Thoughtfulness. Depth. I wanted my words to carry weight like that, but honestly, I didn't know where to begin.

In the same way that it was necessary in ancient days for a Roman soldier to receive rigid training on the proper use of the sword for maximum protection or defense, I knew that I needed to be trained on how to properly handle the Word of God. Only then would it be an effective defense against evil, a viable means for me to "destroy strongholds" of error and falsehood, as 2 Corinthians 10:4–5 promises. Somewhere along the way, I came across a little structure that walked me through how to internalize what I was reading in God's Word. It goes like this:

- Read it through
- Think it clear
- Write it down
- Pray it in
- Live it out
- Give it away

Let's look at each point in turn.

131

Read It Through

First, to rightly pick up the sword of the Spirit, we must *read God's Word through*. In his tremendous work, *Eat This Book: A Conversation in the Art of Spiritual Reading,* pastor and author Eugene Peterson writes, "Language, spoken and written, is the primary means for getting us in on what is, on what God is and is doing. But it is language of a certain stripe, not words external to our lives, the sort used in grocery lists, computer manuals, French grammars, and basketball rulebooks."[3] The sort of writing we find in the Bible—"Spirit-sourced writing," Peterson calls it, "requires spiritual reading, a reading that honors words as holy, words as a basic means of forming an intricate web of relationships between God and the human, between all things visible and invisible."[4]

To "read it through" is to approach God's Word with spiritual eyes, recognizing that it is through the holy Scriptures that we are instructed, reproved, corrected, and trained in righteousness (2 Timothy 3:16–17). It is by God's Word that we find the model for the life we are to lead, and it is by God's Word that we relate intimately with that role model, Jesus Christ.

Think It Clear

Next, we *think it clear*. As you take in God's Word with spiritual eyes, step back from the text for a moment and think through what you've read. What is happening in the passage, and to whom? What is the point being made? What lesson can you take from the verses and begin to apply in your daily life? Consider carefully the text, the context, and the application regarding *every* verse you read. Assess what you're reading.

Analyze it with a careful eye. Study the passage as though you'll be quizzed on it. In fact, life will see to it that you are.

③ Write It Down

Third, we *write it down*. Whenever I'm reading my Bible, I find it useful to keep a journal handy for answering the questions in the above point, and also for capturing prayer requests that surface while I'm reading. Which brings me to point 4.

④ Pray It In

Fourth, we *pray it in*. One of the best ways to personalize the Word of God is to insert your name and the names of those in your circle of influence into various texts. For example, while the words of Psalm 34 are powerful on their own, they can become personal when you pray them on behalf of someone in your life who is having trouble overcoming fear:

> *Father, I know that if Sue will simply seek you, you will answer her. I know you have promised to deliver her from all her fears, and on her behalf, I claim that promise today. May her face be radiant as she looks to you. May her face never be ashamed. When she cries out to you, I know you'll hear her. I know you will save her out of all her troubles. Please remove all fear she faces, except for holy fear toward you. Protect her, Father, by sending your angels to encamp around her. Please deliver her from this valley of despair.*

Praying various Scriptures over your own life and over the circumstances of those you love not only will cause you to pray with increased specificity but also will increase your knowledge of God's Word. You'll begin "writing" those words on your heart, on your behalf, and on behalf of your friends and loved ones. You'll begin effectively *wielding the sword.*

⑤ *Live It Out*

Fifth, *live it out.* The more Scriptures you read, the more relevance you'll unearth for daily life. Especially if you are faithful in making Bible reading a daily practice, you'll discover that your anxiety is replaced by peace, your fear is replaced by confidence, your weariness is replaced by strength, and your stress is replaced by solace, in nothing short of supernatural ways. God's Word is finally getting "in you," and transformation is having its way.

The word for *word* in Ephesians 6:17—"and the sword of the Spirit, which is the *word* of God"—does not refer to the general Word of God, but rather to a specific, strategic word used to counteract the temptations of the enemy. (If you're a Greek-language guru, then you'll appreciate this tidbit: The original text uses the word *rama*, not the word *logos*.)

For example, say Satan comes at you with the accusation that you're a loser, that you're worthless, that you'll never add up to anything meaningful. Picking up the sword of the Spirit means you have the wits about you to recall Romans 8:1 in response: "There is therefore now no condemnation for those who are in Christ Jesus."

Satan says, "The mess you've made of your life is beyond anything even God can repair." And in response, you boldly state the words "He who began a good work in [me] will bring it to completion at the day of Jesus Christ" (Philippians 1:6).

Satan says, "You've racked up so many sins that there is no way you'll ever get into heaven," to which you whisper the words of Isaiah 1:18: "Though [my] sins are like scarlet, they shall be as white as snow."

You get the idea. The Bible can speak into any situation, if only we will let it. But therein lies the problem; most believers readily nod at the idea that they should read God's Word, know God's Word, and rely on God's Word like oxygen for their souls. And yet they don't. They don't spend time reading it. They don't invest any effort in knowing it. They rely on their own self-focused strength rather than looking to God for the help he so lovingly longs to provide.

Give It Away

So to know and understand God's Word, we read it through, we think it clear, we write it down, we pray it in, we live it out, and then, finally, we *give it away.*

Truly, you can only give to others what you yourself possess. Once you write God's Word on your heart, you will find yourself reflexively incorporating scriptural truth into conversation. You won't necessarily try to do this, you understand; it will simply pour forth from your heart. Wisdom, encouragement, and truth will be so embedded in your thoughts that you will become the wisest, most encouraging, most truthful version of yourself there has ever been. Really! Give this a try and see if you don't find it to be true: As you find yourself in conversation with friends, family members, co-workers, and neighbors, talk about the themes and truths you're learning from God's Word. The more Scripture you commit to memory, the more Scripture you will speak to friends and family. And the more Scripture you speak out, the more valuable your words will become.

Listen, the last thing this world needs is more opinions, more perspectives, and more flawed viewpoints on this or that. Human words drastically pale in contrast to the *real, relevant,* and *reliable* Word of God. Take seriously the goal of writing Scripture on your heart, and all the peace, all the promises, all the provision, all the guidance, all the wisdom and beauty and life—all that God's Word has in store for its reader will be bound up inside of *you.*

Soon after my cancer diagnosis, my wife, Deb, spoke a verse over my situation that sustained me throughout that entire unsettling season. Psalm 27:13 says, "I remain confident of this: I will see the goodness of the Lord in the land of the living" (NIV). During many months when my earthly prognosis was foggy, that promise appeared crystal clear. Nothing that Deb could have said in her own words would have held a candle to the beam of hope that psalm threw onto my mind and heart.

Satan's Ploys Against God's Word

Centuries ago, before the printing press had been invented, the primary means for carrying around a Bible was to memorize the stories, word for word. Young Jewish boys, for example, were not merely encouraged but rather expected to memorize the entire Pentateuch, which comprises the first five books of the Old Testament. This includes Leviticus, mind you, which isn't exactly light reading.

Later, after the printing press arrived on the scene, printed copies of the Bible were owned only by those who could afford to purchase them. Most people were not wealthy and therefore were left to rely on the verses they'd committed to memory.

Once the Book was available to millions, Satan was forced to up his game. And up his game, he did. In the words of theologian Donald Grey Barnhouse:

> The Bible was burned and banned, scorned and ridiculed. It was given lip service by those who denied the power of its truth. It was in the name of science built on false hypotheses that the great attack on the Bible and the Church came in the nineteenth century, and in our day psychology and psychiatry claim to duplicate the efficacy of the blood of Christ to break the power of sin in the life.[5]

Indeed, psychology and psychiatry play a role in our shrugged-shoulders response to God's Word these days, but I think the reason is far simpler: We're just plain lazy. The average North American family possesses *nine* copies of the Bible, and because of this ready access, this ridiculously abundant access, we slack off when it comes to writing God's Word on our hearts. And in the process, we make ourselves vulnerable to Satan's attacks. Let me explain what I mean.

Since the beginning of recorded time, Satan's primary attack against the people of God has centered on denying, disputing, debating, diluting, and ultimately defiling the Word of God. Genesis 3:1–4 bears out this point:

> Now the serpent was more crafty than any other beast of the field that the LORD God had made. He said to the woman, "Did God actually say, 'You shall not eat of any tree in the garden'?" And the woman said to the serpent, "We may eat of the fruit of the trees in the garden, but God said, 'You shall not eat of the fruit of the tree that is in the midst of the garden, neither shall you touch it, lest you die.'" But the serpent said to the woman, "You will not surely die."

Did you follow the pattern there? God gave explicit instructions, to which Satan came along and asked, "Did he *really* say that?"

God gave crystal-clear parameters, to which Satan said, "Nah, he didn't mean what he said."

God gave a hard-and-fast boundary, to which Satan said, "Let's redraw the line . . . *here*."

Satan sneakily inserted question marks where God himself had placed periods. And as a result, sin entered the world.

The devil knows that just as a man is as good as his word, God's goodness is reflected best in his infallible Word. Without God's Word, we have no revelation of him; without a clear and accurate understanding of God's precepts, principles, and promises, we do little more in this life than stumble our way through the dark. It is for this reason that you and I must insist on maintaining fidelity to the truth of God's written Word. To do that, we must know how to defeat Satan's ploys.

Satan Prohibits the Word of God

The first ploy to be aware of is this: Satan will try with all his might to keep the Word of God from penetrating your heart and mine. He will do whatever he can do to prevent God's wisdom from reaching into our lives and changing us for the better. And his schemes can be quite effective. In Luke 8, Jesus tells a parable to a great crowd of people from various towns who had gathered to hear him teach. In it, he proves it is possible for Satan to actually *snatch away* the Word of God from the lives of people who say they love him.

> A sower went out to sow his seed. And as he sowed, some fell
> along the path and was trampled underfoot, and the birds

of the air devoured it. And some fell on the rock, and as it grew up, it withered away, because it had no moisture. And some fell among thorns, and the thorns grew up with it and choked it. And some fell into good soil and grew and yielded a hundredfold.

vv. 5–8

Jesus continues by explaining the story he'd told to his disciples:

To you it has been given to know the secrets of the kingdom of God, but for others they are in parables, so that "seeing they may not see, and hearing they may not understand." Now the parable is this: The seed is the word of God. The ones along the path are those who have heard; then the devil comes and takes away the word from their hearts, so that they may not believe and be saved.

vv. 10–12

You'll notice that for those who are strolling along the path, unbelieving and unsaved, the Word of God resides at the shallowest of levels; it is easy for the devil to snatch it away before it ever penetrates the heart. Later, in 2 Corinthians 4:3–4, we find additional language to describe Satan's prohibitive ways:

And even if our gospel is veiled, it is veiled to those who are perishing. In their case the god of this world has blinded the minds of the unbelievers, to keep them from seeing the light of the gospel of the glory of Christ, who is the image of God.

The god of this age—Satan himself—blinds the minds of those who are already perishing, those already living far from God, so that they never will come to the place of belief in their lives, the place of full and heartfelt surrender to God.

② *Satan Perverts the Word of God*

A second strategy of Satan's is to pervert the Word of God. When he cannot keep Scripture from penetrating our hearts, he quickly works to distort what does find its way in. He is in the business of promoting not *rich relationship with God* but *empty religion,* and a key means to this end is planting emissaries in pulpits, people who preach a message not of God. Our enemy looks to deny Christ's deity, his virgin birth, his virtuous life, his victorious resurrection, and his imminent return. The devil wants to distort the idea that salvation is by grace alone, that there is a coming judgment, that there is a heaven, and also a hell. If he can transform himself into an angel of light, as 2 Corinthians 11:14 acknowledges, then surely he can show up on a Sunday morning in a clerical collar or a three-piece suit . . . or jeans, flip-flops, and an untucked shirt, for that matter.

Plenty of Scriptures confirm that in these "last days," we will find heresy running rampant. First John 4:1, for example, says, "Beloved, do not believe every spirit, but test the spirits to see whether they are from God, for many false prophets have gone out into the world."

First Timothy 4:1 says, "Now the Spirit expressly says that in later times some will depart from the faith by devoting themselves to deceitful spirits and teachings of demons," which ought to be a caution heeded by you and me both. Other Scriptures that warn against this kind of heresy include Matthew 7:15; 24:11, 24; and 2 Peter 2:1; 3:3.

We must arm ourselves with the sword of the Spirit, so that we can spot a fraud when we see one. Our only hope against darkness is light. Our only hope against error is *truth.*

One widely circulated example of what I'm talking about is the fact that when an aspiring agent of the United States Treasury is going to learn how to detect counterfeit money, he or she spends 100 percent of training hours evaluating not fake bills, but the real deal. If the would-be agent knows what the genuine article looks and feels and smells like, a counterfeit will be easy to spot. Certainly we're not to turn a blind eye to the world's goings-on, but there is credence in saturating ourselves so thoroughly in God's real-deal Word that when someone deviates from that Word and claims it as truth, we instinctively know to cry foul.

To this end, let's revisit the parable of the sower from Luke 8. If you'll recall, the story Jesus told cited four different types of soil that the seed of his Word fell onto: some seed fell onto the path, where it was quickly trampled underfoot and then devoured by birds; some fell on the rocks but withered away as it grew because of lack of moisture from the ground; some fell among thorns, which later wound up choking it; and some fell into *good soil* and grew and yielded a hundredfold.

Jesus, during his explanation to his disciples about the meaning of his story, said, "As for that in the good soil, they are those who, hearing the word, hold it fast in an honest and good heart, and bear fruit with patience" (Luke 8:15).

The encouragement I offer to you is this: It is possible to live as a fourth-soil person. It is possible to "hold fast" to God's Word, letting it protect and defend you, empower and embolden you, fully guard you—mind, body, and soul. You need do nothing more than to faithfully write God's Word on your heart.

Memorize the Word

Whenever I meet with new believers, I encourage them not only to *read* but to begin *memorizing* God's Word as soon as possible.

Typically I'm met with a glazed-over look. It's the look that says, "Maybe you pastor-types can commit that stuff to memory, but me? I can barely remember my phone number! Memorizing Scripture just isn't for me."

To which I typically say (with a loving smile, of course), "I hear you. And I totally understand. But I'm not buying a word you're saying."

I know an excuse when I see one, because I'm as guilty as the next guy at trotting out that same flimsy rationale! I balk when someone challenges me to memorize additional Scriptures, even as I commit new baseball stats to memory with barely any effort at all. The reality is that if I were to offer those I-can't-memorize-anything people ten bucks per verse, they'd suddenly become memorizing machines. The same is true for you and me. We don't lack the *capacity* to memorize God's Word; we simply lack the *motivation* to do so.

If you've never begun memorizing Scripture, you might get your hands on a copy of the Navigators' *Topical Memory System*, which features sixty key verses in eight different translations, arranged by topics that relate to everyday life. The verses fit into five categories that reflect the Christ-following journey: Live the New Life; Proclaim Christ; Rely on God's Resources; Be Christ's Disciple; and Grow in Christlikeness. Order the hard-copy memorization cards from Amazon, or download the app instead; either way, by adding the resource to your list of daily habits, you'll soon detect greater spiritual strength than you've previously known.

Someone has figured out that it takes exactly seventy-one hours to read the entire Bible aloud, at a regular speaking pace. Correct me if I'm wrong, but my calculations suggest that to read the sum of God's Word over the course of a full year would take just under twelve minutes per day. Twelve minutes! Who doesn't have twelve minutes to invest in getting the most powerful, precise words available embedded into our hearts and souls? Add to that another five minutes or so to memorize a verse or two, and for twenty minutes a day, we can thoroughly sharpen our swords. And in doing so, we'll be netting a win for every spiritual battle we're asked to fight.

Discussion Questions

1. When has the power of God's Word been made as "real" to you as it was for the character Christian in *The Pilgrim's Progress*, or for Jesus when he was tempted in the desert by Satan?

2. "It is God's Word that leads us to righteousness. It is God's Word that leads us to understanding. It is God's Word that keeps us from sinning, from taking the 'evil way.'" In your own life what, specifically, has God's Word led *you* to?

3. Regarding the six-part approach to Scripture introduced in this chapter—read it through, think it clear, write it down, pray it in, live it out, and give it away—where do you typically get "stuck," and why?

4. Still referring to those six parts, where would you like to see your greatest growth, and why?

5. A key strategy of Satan is to pervert the Word of God. How do you see this perversion occurring in our society at large today?

*Converting our unceasing thinking
into unceasing prayer moves us
from a self-centered monologue
to a God-centered dialogue.*

–Henri Nouwen

SEVEN
WARFARE PRAYER

An interesting phenomenon happened on the heels of September 11, 2001, the date that marks the worst terrorist attack ever sustained on United States soil. On that cloudless Tuesday morning, nineteen militants coordinated a series of four suicide missions in New York City and the Washington, D.C., area, taking down both towers of the World Trade Center; damaging the Pentagon in Arlington, Virginia; crashing into a field in Pennsylvania; and killing nearly three thousand people and injuring hundreds more. And while the aftershocks were tough to take—thousands of families suffering the loss of loved ones, air travelers fearful of flying, and the general sickening feeling that a group of radicals would prefer to have you dead—something beautiful emerged from those ashes, something that looked a lot like patriotism.

Recruiters serving all branches of our country's military reported wild upswings in enlistment during the days and months following 9/11. "As horrifying as they were to the nation's psyche, the 9/11 terrorist attacks in 2001 provided an impetus for bolstering the manpower within various branches of the U.S. military."[1] Evidently, people of all ages walked into one recruitment center or another and asked, "What do I need to do to sign up?" The visible signs of the war that had been waged against us compelled them to get involved. To date, since the attack, nearly 3.2 million Americans have entered military service.

Based on the utter devastation caused on September 11, 2001, this may be difficult to imagine, but we have an enemy whose power is far greater than that of even the darkest, deadliest terrorist. The threat is greater. The stakes are higher. The costs are more personal. But the first step in defeating Satan is the same first step required to defeat terrorism: *We must stay aware of the war.*

Staying Aware of the War

I know people who wake up every single morning and put on work-out clothes right after their feet hit the floor. Getting the attire on their body is the first step to actually making it to the gym. The simple act of putting on the right clothing reminds them that they are on a weight-loss journey and that they need to stay serious about exercising each day.

Most married people I know never leave home without their wedding band. For them the ring is a simple reminder that they are their beloved's and their beloved is theirs. The simple act of sliding that band onto the ring finger of their left hand focuses their attention on the seriousness of the covenant they made one day before God and before their mate.

Similarly, if you and I are faithful about putting on the armor of God each day, as the apostle Paul encourages us to do, we are far more likely to remember that spiritually speaking *we are at war.*

Paul himself couldn't help but remember that he was on the front lines of a bona fide war. As I've mentioned, he wrote the book of Ephesians from the cell of a Roman prison, where he was being held captive for preaching Christ. In Ephesians 3:1, he introduced himself as "Paul, a prisoner for Christ Jesus on behalf of you Gentiles." One chapter later, he referred to himself as "a prisoner for the Lord" (4:1). He was witnessing casualties left and right of others who chose to bear Jesus' name, and was all too aware of Satan's disdain for the church and his devastating work in the world.

Certainly we don't covet Paul's circumstances—none of us would wish to be imprisoned and bound in chains. But we would do well to possess his constant awareness of the battle that rages all around us all the time. Maybe we don't encounter tangible signs of the war—bullets flying through the sky, bloodied bodies, air-raid sirens blasting—but surely we recognize that life is not as God originally intended it to be. We face sleepless nights because our minds can't seem to calm down. We hesitate to open our email for fear of some relational strain or professional deadline catching us off guard. We refuse to let others see the real us for fear that we'll be judged or cast aside.

All is not right in the world. Indeed, we are at war.

For this reason, Paul closed his comments about the importance of donning spiritual armor by essentially saying, "Stay on guard! Stay awake! Don't be lulled to sleep!"

"Keep alert with all perseverance," are the exact words the apostle uses in Ephesians 6:18, an exhortation that proves to be a challenge even for devoted followers of Christ. For in a typical week, it's easy to find ourselves more concerned with the mundane—filling the gas tank, getting to work on time, helping with homework, feeding the dog, and padding the bank account—than with thinking for even a *moment* about spiritual warfare. But just because everything on our to-do lists gets done doesn't mean all is okay. Which is why we must "stay alert," stay calm, watch out. Nineteenth-century Anglican bishop J. C. Ryle notes:

> The saddest symptom about so many so-called Christians is the utter absence of anything like conflict and fight in their Christianity. They eat, they drink, they dress, they work, they amuse themselves, they get money, they spend money, they go through a scanty round of formal religious services once or twice a week, but the great spiritual warfare . . . its watchings and strugglings, its agonies and anxieties, its battles and contests . . . of all this, they appear to know nothing at all.[2]

Jesus warned against this same sort of spiritual sluggishness just before he was betrayed by one of his disciples, arrested by the very people he came to save, and crucified on a criminal's cross. Luke 21:34–36 says,

> But watch yourselves lest your hearts be weighed down with dissipation and drunkenness and cares of this life, and that day

come upon you suddenly like a trap. For it will come upon all who dwell on the face of the whole earth. But stay awake at all times, praying that you may have strength to escape all these things that are going to take place, and to stand before the Son of Man.

So yes, fine, keep an eye on your job, on your gas tank, on your kids, and on your bank account. But more important, keep an eye on *yourself.* Don't get bogged down with the fleeting cares of this life; *stay awake* to the war of eternal influence that is being waged all around you.

How Spiritual Battles Are Won

For several chapters now, we've been talking about the spiritual armor we are to put on, the various pieces of protection that will equip us for the fight. If this divine outfitting is the "what," then let's now turn our attention to the "how."

Immediately on the heels of Paul's reminder that we don the belt and the breastplate, the shoes of peace and the shield of faith, the helmet of salvation and the Spirit's sword, comes this helpful elaboration: "praying at all times in the Spirit, with all prayer and supplication" (Ephesians 6:18). The how of effective spiritual warfare, then, is *warfare prayer;* this battle is one we fight on our knees. Interesting to note is that between verses 17 and 18, there is no new thought introduced. Paul barely pauses between telling us to wear the armor (the "what") and telling us to pray at all times (the "how"). The verses are connected; in other words, it is by prayer *alone* that we are able to engage with and overcome the enemy of our souls.

Perhaps this prescription surprises you; you might think that Paul should have suggested something more . . . active. Or aggressive. Or tangible. We fight this fight through *prayer*? Could that possibly be enough? But Paul's words here are clear. In his view, it seems that prayer is the most engaging thing we can do.

It is by *prayer* that we stand firm.

It is by *prayer* that we live by truth.

It is by *prayer* that we practice righteousness.

It is by *prayer* that we exercise faith.

It is by *prayer* that we lean in to our salvation.

It is by *prayer* that we gain wisdom from God's Word.

It's no wonder that Jesus instructed his disciples of old—and us—to *pray* for deliverance from our enemy (see Matthew 6:13); he knew that such battles are won only in prayer.

The Nature of Warfare Prayer

Warfare prayer is different from "God is great, God is good, let us thank him for this food" and "Now I lay me down to sleep" prayers. Warfare prayer is militant praying, aimed solely at dispelling darkness with light, at overcoming evil with good, at advancing the causes of Christ in the world. We need more believers praying this way. We need them fighting from their knees.

We sorely need people who are willing to pray by *faith*: "Therefore I tell you, whatever you ask in prayer," Mark 11:24 says, "believe that you have received it, and it will be yours." We need people who will pray in *humility*: "If my people who are called by my name humble themselves, and pray and seek my face and turn from their wicked ways," promises 2 Chronicles 7:14, "then I will hear from heaven and will forgive their sin." We need people to pray with *pure and righteous hearts*, for "The sacrifice of the wicked is an abomination to the Lord, but the prayer of the upright is acceptable to him" (Proverbs 15:8). We need people who will come before the Father *consistently*, just as members of the early church were known to do. "All these with one accord were *devoting themselves to prayer*," Acts 1:14 reminds us (emphasis mine); we need that same sense of devotion today. Warfare prayer is not for the faint of heart; it is an act of worship, it is hard work, and it is outright war.

Warfare Prayer Is Worship

To understand warfare prayer is to understand, first and foremost, *worship*. For those of us who have surrendered our lives to Christ and long to relate intimately with God, prayer is the vehicle of choice. Warfare prayer is not a means for getting things *from* God; rather, it is the means of getting *to* God. One author says,

> Prayer is primarily a wartime walkie-talkie for the mission of the church as it advances against the powers of darkness and unbelief. It is not surprising that prayer malfunctions when we try to make it a domestic intercom to call upstairs for more comforts in the den. God has given us prayer as a wartime walkie-talkie so we can call headquarters for everything we need as the kingdom of God advances in this world.[3]

Warfare prayer is asking God to help us get on his plan, not begging him to get on ours. It is worshiping him for the love he lavished on us on that pivotal crucifixion day.

Throughout history, most wars have been tilted toward the victor by one single battle, an individual victory that eventually turned the tide. For example, in 1944, D-Day saw Allied troops invade the French coastline and take down Nazi Germany's forces on Normandy's beaches, which ensured the outcome of the Second World War. In 1863, the battle of Gettysburg tilted the Civil War toward a northern victory. Napoleon's forces swept across Europe in 1815 and occupied every country along the way, until they met their Waterloo in Belgium, where the British finally defeated them and landed a decisive coalition victory.

As the story goes, following his loss at Waterloo, Napoleon Bonaparte gathered his generals together to discuss their imminent defeat. His ambition had been to take over the entire world, but it was obvious that the goal would remain unmet. He unfurled a map of the world and pointed to a red spot that appeared beside the name *Waterloo*. Napoleon eyed his men and said, "Were it not for that red spot, I would have ruled the world!"

I can imagine Satan himself gathering the minions of hell around him, unfurling a map of the world, and pointing to a tiny corner of the earth located in Jerusalem. "Were it not for that red spot—that cross on Calvary's hill—I would have ruled the world!"

I don't know about you, but I praise God for that particular red spot! On that hill, our victory was won. On that hill, Satan's ultimate defeat was sure. Because of Jesus' selfless sacrifice, we have power that is greater than *all the power* in the world. As we pray in accordance with God's kingdom work in the world, we acknowledge his worthiness over all. We tell him once more that we honor him as Creator and Sustainer and Provider and King; we subject our will to *his* will, *his* ways, knowing his purposes and plans work for our good in the end.

Warfare Prayer Is Work

Even a cursory look at Ephesians 6:18 reveals just how much *work* warfare prayer requires: "praying at *all* times in the Spirit, with *all* prayer and supplication," it says, which leaves little room for *sometimes, half-hearted* praying. No, no, Paul says. We must pray at *all* times. We must pray in *all* ways. Warfare prayer must be our very *lives*.

We pray prayers of adoration. We pray prayers of confession. We pray prayers of thanksgiving. We pray prayers on others' behalf. We raise our arms, we bend our knees, we fold our hands, we lay our faces low. We sing prayer. We speak prayer. We write prayer. We think prayer. We allow all of life to be prayer, knowing that prayer is how battles are won.

Colossians 4:12 speaks of this type of effort, saying that as saints of God we must *struggle* or *agonize* or *wrestle* in prayer. So yes, prayer is work; it is a mental and spiritual discipline that demands attention, focus, heart. But no other investment is as satisfying as knitting ourselves to the very heart of God and joining him in his kingdom-building work. The prayers of saints do not return void.

Warfare Prayer Is War

Not only is prayer an act of *worship* and of *work* but also of *war*. Prayer is not preparation for battle; prayer *is* the battle. And it is in prayer, there in our one-on-one dialogue with God, that we find strength to face our foe. Samuel Chadwick, the great Christian of yesteryear, put it this way, referring to Satan: "He fears nothing from prayerless studies, prayerless work, and prayerless religion. He laughs at our toil and mocks our wisdom, but he *trembles* when we pray."[4] It is only when we pray that we set Satan back on his heels.

"Watch and pray" Jesus said in Mark 14:38, "that you may not enter into temptation. The spirit indeed is willing, but the flesh is weak." This is true in your life and is also true in mine. I have learned over the decades that any failure I've experienced was first a failure to pray. For example, there have been days when my attitude has been just north of atrocious. I was critical; I was angry; I was quick to use sarcasm instead of sincerity in my speech—whatever the manifestation, the source was a sour attitude fueled by an undeniable *lack of prayer*.

Taking into account two basic categories of sin—sins of dissipation and sins of disposition—I tend toward the latter every time. In other words, I am stellar about staying away from alcohol and drugs, and from sex with anyone but my wife. But tempt me with a negative, haughty, or judgmental spirit, and I'll take the bait almost every time. My attitude can just plain *stink* . . . unless I submit it to God through prayer.

I've noticed a frustrating trend in my life, which is that every single time I fly off the handle with a colleague, get agitated with Deb over something she has said or done, or respond poorly to well-placed criticism, I can always trace my inappropriate posture to the fact that I didn't pray about my attitude that day. *Every single time.* You'd think I'd learn my lesson, but nope. *Still*, I neglect to pray.

But here is the encouraging flip side: Whenever I am faithful to surrender my outlook to the lordship of Jesus Christ through prayer, I have a much sweeter spirit. I have a more God-centered walk when I choose to walk on my knees. That is the plain truth. Prayer changes things. It changes *me*. I know I'm not alone here; throughout the sum of human history, this has been true.

One of the great battles of the Old Testament took place when the children of Israel, led by Moses, came against a warrior named Amalek and his fierce fighting force. Knowing that a battle was imminent, Moses looked at his aide Joshua and said, "Choose for us men, and go out and fight with Amalek." He believed that all power rested in God's mighty hand, and so he added, "Tomorrow I will stand on the top of the hill with the staff of God in my hand" (Exodus 17:9).

In other words, Moses was saying, "You go put yourself in harm's way, and I'll just hang back here and pray."

I think if I were Joshua, I would have suggested a different tack. But ever-faithful Joshua did as he was told.

The next day, as the battle raged, Moses—along with his helpers, Aaron and Hur—went to the top of the hill. Whenever Moses raised his shepherd's staff, the battle swung in Joshua's favor, but the opposite also was true: When Moses' arms grew weary, and that staff of God fell to his side, Amalek prevailed. This went on for some time: Moses raising his arms to the heavens and Joshua gaining territory; Moses letting his tired limbs fall to his side, and the enemy having his way.

Eventually, the text says, an exhausted Moses had an inspired idea: He found a rock to sit on, and he recruited Aaron and Hur each to take an arm and to keep it held sky-high. "So his hands were steady until the going down of the sun," Exodus 17:12 says, speaking of Moses. "And Joshua overwhelmed Amalek and his people with the sword" (v. 13).

If you and I want to see the tide turn—in our world, in our country, in our workplace, in our schools, in our neighborhoods, in our families, in our marriages, in our own sometimes-faithless hearts—we will hold up holy hands in prayer. We will *commit* ourselves to prayer. It is only with spiritual weaponry that spiritual battles are won. Light overwhelms darkness in the prayer chambers you and I inhabit. "The secret prayer chamber is a bloody battleground," Lutheran pastor O. Hallesby wrote in his book *Prayer*. "Here violent and decisive battles are fought out. Here the fate for souls for time and eternity is determined, in quietude, in solitude, before God."[5]

The Benefits of Faithful Prayer

As I reflect on the quietude, the solitude before God I have enjoyed over the years, three by-products of warfare prayer bubble to the surface of my memory. If your tank is running low on power, on protection, on provision, consider forming a habit of pulling away from life's busyness and connecting with your Father through prayer. In his marvelous book *Wild Goose Chase*, my friend Mark Batterson wrote that when you change your place and you change your pace, your perspective can't help but also change.[6] I totally agree. When I slow down and separate myself from the busyness of the world around me, even for ten minutes, my entire viewpoint shifts.

If you don't know what to say, tell him so. If you don't know where to begin, allow his Spirit to instruct you. Remember, the Spirit intercedes with you as something of a prayer partner, so allow him to join you as you pray. If you find yourself distracted by the hum of the air-conditioner, the tilt of the dusty lampshade, or the dog barking at cars as they drive by, simply ask God to gently tug your thoughts back to him—his character, his kindness, his purposes in his world. And, refocused, begin again.

Don't take a pass on the profound benefits of prayer that can be yours: power, protection, unparalleled provision from God. Weak, vulnerable, and in need are terrible ways to live!

Prayer Yields Power

Jesus discloses an interesting by-product of prayer in John 14:12–14 (emphasis mine).

> Truly, truly, I say to you, whoever believes in me will also do the works that I do; and greater works than these will he do, because I am going to the Father. Whatever you ask in my name, this I will do, that the Father may be glorified in the Son. If you ask me anything in my name, *I will do it.*

There is real power to be had when we devote ourselves to prayer. Need to penetrate the darkness with light? There is power for that in Jesus' name. Need wisdom to know right from wrong? There is power for that in Jesus' name. Need strength to resist temptation? There is power for that in Jesus' name. Need authority to overcome evil? There is power for that in Jesus' name. Need release from breathtaking bondage? There is power for that in Jesus' name. Need victory on a day when all you can find is defeat? There is power for that in Jesus' name. *Whatever* it is that we suffer, we can know triumph in Jesus' name.

As I write, news headlines are dominated by unnerving themes: Unbelief in the God of the Bible is rampant; the name of Jesus is profaned; perversions are commonplace; demonic activity is on the rise. The family is attacked; the definition of marriage is revised; violence is the way to settle all disputes; babies are aborted; drunkenness and drug abuse elicit a so-what, to-each-his-own response. And that's just in North America. In other parts of the world, add to the list persecution on a *massive* scale.

In other words, warfare is very, very real.

But.

But we can pray in Jesus' name that the forces of evil will be restrained. We can call on *his* resources, on *his* merit, on *his* strength.

In Matthew 17, we read of Jesus' disciples' inability to heal a boy suffering from demon possession. The story picks up as Jesus and three followers descend the Mount of Transfiguration, where he had been communing with his Father and with Moses and Elijah, to find a crowd of people eager for the Messiah's attention. A man approaches Jesus, kneels before him, and says, "Lord, have mercy on my son, for he is an epileptic and he suffers terribly. For often he falls into the fire, and often into the water. And I brought him to your disciples, and they could not heal him" (vv. 15–16).

Jesus rebuked the demon and it came out of the boy, and instantly he was healed. Later, the disciples approached Jesus and asked why they had been unable to cast the demon out. Clearly, they were frustrated by their failure; they were Jesus' running buddies, for crying out loud. Why couldn't they accomplish such a straightforward spiritual task?

Jesus' reply is as instructive for you and me as it was for the disciples that day: "Because of your little faith," he explained. "For truly, I say to you, if you have faith like a grain of mustard seed, you will say to this mountain, 'Move from here to there,' and it will move, and nothing will be impossible for you" (vv. 20–21).

Just out of curiosity, do you have any mountains needing to be moved in your life today? A mountain of debt, maybe? A mountain of marital discord? A mountain of fear and anxiety? A mountain of addiction? A mountain of pain? Prayer alone moves mountains—faith-fueled, warfare prayer.

The early church knew this kind of warfare praying as well. In Acts 1:4–5, Jesus instructs his disciples to remain in Jerusalem and wait for the Holy Spirit, whose arrival his Father had promised. They were to stay there and pray, which they were faithful to do. And as a result of their commitment to prayer, thousands of people were brought into the kingdom of God days later as the church received the Spirit.

We read in Acts 2 that as the church became baptized in the Holy Spirit, they continued steadfastly in learning the Bible, enjoying the fellowship of the saints, and *prayer* (v. 42). Prayer wasn't just part of the agenda; it *was* the agenda. And it remains the agenda today. God, by his Spirit, brings people under his submission via the heartfelt prayers of his saints, people who pray in the unparalleled power of the name of the Lord Jesus Christ.

Prayer is what opens the doors in our lives that to this point have been closed. Warfare prayer, powerful prayer, prayed in Jesus' name. Indeed, one day, everyone will bow before Jesus Christ and confess him as Savior and Lord, to the glory of God the Father (see Philippians 2:10). Until then, you and I can get a head start, as we devote ourselves to prayer.

Prayer Yields Protection

Here's the plain truth: God flanks us on all sides at all times with his protective presence, as we are faithful to invite him in. Yes, Satan roams about like a roaring lion, seeking those he may destroy (1 Peter 5:8), but God's angelic host roams about too! And they seek not to destroy us, but to fit us for war.

We are so proud, aren't we? So self-sufficient, so dependent on nobody, so presumptuous that we've "got this," thank you very much. We struggle and scheme to live by our own strength, while God stands by with love in his gaze, thinking, *If only they'd come to me. . . .*

Our God is able to protect us from the trials and temptations we face, as 1 Corinthians 10:13 assures us. The question that remains is whether we will let him do what he is graciously willing to do.

Prayer Yields Provision

Most people know David as the man "after God's own heart," the man who committed grievous sin—yes—but who also was a great king, a great shepherd, and a great soldier. Like many other believers, I've long been intrigued by David's life. Where does one man find the faith, the boldness, the courage, the warrior's spirit to land so many victories in life?

If you've ever camped out in the book of Psalms, relishing its wisdom, its candor, its spunk, then you probably know where I'm going with this train of thought. David was given everything he needed to thrive in this thing called life—all the faith, all the boldness, all the courage, all the *provision*—during his long nights of devoted prayer. Whenever I read from Psalms, I receive it not merely as a book of worship—although it certainly is that—but as a series of reminders that we are provisioned for this journey by *prayer*. On countless occasions, we find the writer of a psalm begging God for insight, for resources, for relief, only to be followed four or five verses later with a declaration of God's goodness, his kindness, his faithfulness in serving as a refuge in our time of need. Perhaps nothing about the writer's actual circumstances changed between the petition and the provision; perhaps, like us, all he needed was a reminder that God knows, he sees, and he cares.

Why We Neglect to Pray

We have established that you and I are commanded in Scripture to pray—we are to put on the armor of God while "praying at all times in the Spirit, with all prayer and supplication" (Ephesians 6:18). We have also read stories from Scripture that inspire us to pray. We have declared that there are great benefits to be had, when we do pray. If you are like most believers, from time to time you even sense a *longing* to pray, believing that communication with the Almighty is actually possible. And yet if you are like most believers, you also often neglect to pray.

Based on the number of devotional books on prayer published each year, many Christ-followers are evidently less than satisfied with the quality or consistency of their prayer lives. Let's look at a few reasons why.

We Get Cynical

For many believers, the reason for their prevailing prayerlessness is that as a soldier in Christ's army, they have gone AWOL. The possible reasons for this are myriad: Perhaps they were hurt in the church of their youth; maybe they wearied of the "rules" of religion and simply needed a break, or perhaps they were discouraged by prayers that seemed to go unanswered. Could be they were just bored with Christianity and decided to put their energies elsewhere for a time.

Regardless of what has caused their absence, I contend that if they could only catch a glimpse of the mission God is asking them to serve—if they knew the heft of the challenge and the glory of the reward—they would be found joyously on their knees. In his fantastic book *The Weight of Glory*, C. S. Lewis likens these folks to the "child who is content to make mud pies in the slums, because he cannot imagine what it means to have a holiday at the beach."

If this describes you, I invite you to come back. Table your cynicism long enough to ask God to show you the delight of duty for his sake.

We Get Busy

Busyness is another possible reason for prayerlessness. In *A Praying Life*, author Paul Miller cites American culture as perhaps the most difficult place in the world to learn to pray:

> We are so busy that when we slow down to pray, we find it uncomfortable. We prize accomplishments, production. But prayer is nothing but talking to God. It feels useless, as if we are wasting time. Every bone in our bodies screams, "Get to work."[7]

My friend Bill Hybels wrote a book more than two decades ago titled *Too Busy Not to Pray*. In this instance, the name says it all.

We Get Tongue-Tied

Many believers don't pray because they simply don't know what to say. They carve out time to be alone with God, they read his Word, they bow their heads and close their eyes and with the sincerest of hearts try to begin. And then . . . *nothing*. They wonder, "Do I ask for something? Thank him for something? Talk about my mom, who is sick?" They stumble around for a few minutes before getting up to go about their day, defeated and despondent regarding prayer.

When I was a new believer, I came across a framework for prayer based on the acrostic ACTS. If ever you find yourself tongue-tied in prayer, consider following it for a time:

- Adoration. Praise God for who he is and for his faithfulness in your life.
- Confession. Express sorrow for the ways you have fallen short of God's perfect will for your life, and then claim his

forgiveness so that you can move forward with clean hands and a pure heart.

- Thanksgiving. Express gratitude for the specific ways you see God's presence, power, and provision at work in your life.

- Supplication. Ask God for what you need—healing for a family member, peace for a friend, hope for your own failing heart. Make your requests known to him, knowing he longs to meet your every need.

We Forget We Are at War

We have many reasons as to why we don't pray or why we have a hard time praying, but if I had to pinpoint what's behind them all, I'd point to the theme that began this chapter: *We simply forget we are at war.* The quality of our prayer lives is solely determined by our awareness of the invisible war.

Surely you have noticed this dynamic in your own life: The moment you find yourself unwittingly thrust into crisis mode—your spouse threatens to leave, you lose your job, unhappy creditors call—your prayer life kicks into high gear. Uncanny, isn't it?

Truly, we have no problem praying when the battle confronts us. Our problem is that when we don't see visible signs of that battle, we mistakenly believe that our lives are safe. In his classic book on prayer, E. M. Bounds writes:

It cannot be said too often that the life of a Christian is warfare, an intense conflict, a lifelong contest. It is a battle fought against invisible foes who are ever alert and seeking to entrap, deceive, and ruin the souls of men. The Bible calls men to life, not a picnic or holiday. It is no pastime or pleasure excursion.

163

It entails effort, wrestling, and struggling. It demands putting out the full energy of the spirit in order to frustrate the foe and to come out, at last, more than a conqueror. It is no primrose path, no rose-scented flirting. From start to finish, it is war.[8]

It's that last part that gets us, I think. The from-start-to-finish part. We may concede that *at times* we are at war. But to think that *every moment of every day* is shrouded by an unseen war? Honestly, we're not so sure.

When we stay aware of the war, we will engage in prayer. I know no simpler way to state this truth.

Coming Back to Prayer

If you have surrendered your life to the lordship of Jesus Christ, then it is true for you that God has placed you in specific places and near specific people so that you can play a strategic role in their lives. Largely, we should pray as a means of discovering what that role involves. So yes, while engaging in prayer often benefits us as the pray-ers in deeply personal and individual ways, it is also true that becoming effective warfare pray-ers also changes the *world around us* for good.

We pray to welcome God's work in the world. We pray to welcome our role in the battle. We pray to welcome the presence of peace. We pray to welcome assurance of salvation. We pray to welcome righteousness. We pray to welcome the Spirit's work, to welcome the unbounded joy he always brings. We pray to *welcome* these things so that we can bring these things to a world desperately in need. Look around you and see if you don't find a terrible void of peace and righteousness and joy. Of course you do! I do too. But crossing our fingers and wishing they would show up just isn't enough. We must come before the Father, who created these gifts and who longs to bestow them on us, and *ask him* to change our world.

Philippians 4 reminds us that it is not by hoping or wrestling, by struggling or resisting, that we find peace so pervasive that it simply passes our understanding; no, it is by prayer that this peace shows up in our lives. It is by *prayer* that we are refreshed in our understanding that the battle is actually the Lord's. I learned this lesson the hard way recently, on the heels of receiving my cancer diagnosis. I thought I could contrive a sense of peace for myself without leaning in to the power of prayer. Sadly, I was proved wrong.

For most of my career, I've employed a rather macho approach to ministry. I'm not proud of it, exactly, but I recognize it for what it is. I tend to try to wear a Superman cape, always wanting to be the tough guy, the strong one, the leader who remains vibrant for his church. You can imagine, then, how humbling it was when I received word from my doctor that I had prostate cancer and was in need of surgery. From the outset, my concern was not just for my own health, but also for the health of Prestonwood. I didn't want my disease to disrupt the church. I didn't want our focus as a congregation to be shifted from our ministry efforts. I didn't want our fellowship's young kids to be scared—was their pastor about to die? And so I decided to keep the diagnosis quiet, telling only my family and closest friends.

When it was time for my surgery, I admitted myself into the hospital under an assumed name, not wanting to risk having a news reporter who had scanned admittance records blow my cover.

Throughout the entire process—diagnosis, surgery, post-op recovery, chemotherapy, recovery from chemo, the whole works—I kept my news under wraps.

True to form, Jack "Superman" Graham was back in the pulpit preaching a mere eleven days after surgery. But the decision to "just jump back into things" nearly took me permanently out of the game. My body simply could not keep pace with my mind's wild ideals. Fortunately, the church's leadership had offered me a sabbatical around that time; even as I accepted it, I thought I could lie low for a few weeks and then hop right back into the full-time involvements I love. But that was not to be.

Not long into my sabbatical, I realized that I was not, in fact, going to be able to soar through the air like a bird, like a plane, like Superman. I was going to have to give myself some time to heal. Worse yet, I was going to have to spill my big secret to the church. And I was going to have to do it *now*.

The following weekend, I made the announcement before the loving, gracious people of Prestonwood, and sure enough, as soon as the news hit all the local media outlets, it felt to me as if everybody knew everything about my business. This was not the kind of press I desired. But beyond that, a deeper reality made me cringe: I had kept at arm's length a veritable *army* of pray-ers, whose petitions on my behalf could have saved me countless rounds of pain.

It goes down as the biggest mistake of my ministry career on a personal level—my decision *not* to be steadied by the prayers of the saints around me.

By the time my church knew the whole story, I felt it was too late. I can't say for certain how their early intercession would have helped me, but in my heart of hearts, I believe my recovery process would have been far easier had I been vulnerable from the start and invited others to pray.

We are encouraged by others' prayers. We are strengthened by others' prayers. We are changed by others' prayers. We are heartened as we invite the petitions of fellow sojourners in this thing called life.

Truly, there is not a person in our lives who is not facing some sort of battle. For this reason, God exhorts us to look to their interests before we look to our own (Philippians 2:4). "Lift them to my throne of grace!" God pleads with us, knowing that all people are safe in his grip. We pray for ourselves, placing our hearts, our souls, in his grasp. We ask faithful pray-ers to intercede on our behalf. And remembering Matthew 18:20, which says that where two or three are gathered in the name of Jesus, there he is among us, we pray for those needing fortitude for the fight. We do these things by way of acknowledgment that it is only by prayer that we stand.

Discussion Questions

1. Some people committed to healthful living have the habit of putting on their work-out clothes as soon as they get up in the morning, and married people committed to their spouses don't leave home without their wedding band. How do you practically live out your commitment to staying aware of the unseen war around you?

2. From this chapter we learn that it is by prayer that we stand firm, live by the truth, practice righteousness, exercise faith, lean in to our salvation, and gain wisdom from God's Word. What are some of the benefits prayer has yielded in *your* life?

3. What does the phrase *warfare prayer* mean to you? What relationships or experiences have influenced your definition?

4. Describe an experience when prayer has seemed like "work" to you. What resulted from your faithful labors?

5. In what ways can you relate to one or more of the common reasons cited in this chapter that we neglect to pray? We get cynical; we get busy; we get tongue-tied; we forget we are at war.

6. How did the author's story of neglecting to include a veritable *army* of pray-ers during his battle with cancer impact you regarding the importance of counting on the prayer and support of others?

Ordinary riches can be stolen,
real riches cannot. In your soul
are infinitely precious things
that cannot be taken from you.

–Oscar Wilde

EIGHT
THE SOULISH STAKES
OF WAR

Charlemagne, also known as Charles the Great, lived
in the eighth century and ruled the Carolingian Empire—considered the beginning of the Holy Roman
Empire—for nearly fifty years. His military conquests in and
throughout Western and Central Europe—roughly today's Germany, France, Belgium, the Netherlands, Northern Italy, Austria,
Switzerland, and Hungary—thrust him into such power that

by the time of his death he was known throughout the world as the Father of Europe.

Charlemagne avoided the advice of medical doctors his entire life, figuring his natural good health would see him through to the end. And the approach actually served him well until the age of seventy-two, when he fell gravely ill and died in a matter of days. Upon his untimely demise, his aides prepared him for burial, embalming him and draping him in purple regalia, as befitted a king. They placed a golden scepter in his hand, a bejeweled crown on his head, and a royal throne beneath him, and they encased him in a huge vault located in a grand German cathedral.

Oh, and they also placed a Bible in his lap.

Prior to his death, Charlemagne had strictly ordered his aides to see to it that the vault never be opened. Laden with gold and silver coins, the vault itself reflected the wealth of the kingdom—with its king sitting in state, no less—and Charles the Great wanted it to remain that way forever, with him ruling powerfully from the luxury of his throne.

But that's not how things would go down.

Centuries later, invaders entered Germany and eventually decided to pillage the emperor's regalia by opening Charlemagne's precious vault. Inside, they found the once-great conqueror, still seated atop his royal throne; still clad in his royal regalia; still bearing a gold-encrusted crown, there on his skeletal head. As the story goes, the invaders took a look at the Bible perched on old Charlemagne's lap, flipped to Mark 8:36, lifted the bony, disintegrated pointer finger of Charlemagne, and placed it over that verse, "For what does it profit a man to gain the whole world," it asks, "and forfeit his soul?"

Ignoring Our Souls

Interestingly, the same temptations that threatened Charlemagne centuries ago accost us still today. Based on input from the world's system—as well as the selfish longings of our own discontented hearts—we are encouraged to save ourselves, promote ourselves, have faith in ourselves, pull ourselves up by our own bootstraps, and carry on. "Look out for number one!" the mantra goes, and often we know nothing else to do but nod our heads in blind assent.

It's not that we don't think we have an inner life—a "soul," if you will. It's just that we tend to ignore it, assuming rather presumptuously that if we can make everything look good on the outside, then all must be fine on the inside too.

Case in point: In 2010, the total revenue for the United States weight-loss market reached $61 billion. A year prior, online dieting was estimated to be an $842 million market, with Weight-Watchers.com leading the charge with one million paid subscribers and revenues of $238 million.[1]

According to the International Health, Racquet and Sportsclub Association, United States health club membership reached 50.2 million members in 2010, with total revenues of $20.3 billion and the number of health club locations nearing thirty thousand.[2]

Based on records kept by the American Society of Aesthetic Plastic Surgery, in 2010 almost *ten million* surgical and non-surgical cosmetic procedures were performed in this country alone, representing a 155 percent increase since 1997 and costing patients $10.7 billion.[3] This is hardly the only thing consumers are spending exorbitantly on; at this writing, there are more than 600 million credit cards owned by residents of the United States, and the average credit card debt per household is $15,799.[4]

173

To be fair, there is nothing inherently wrong with working out, eating properly, watching our waistlines, or joining a gym. What does concern me is when we as a people settle for pretty, nipped-and-tucked bodies, while our souls sit in a state of disarray. What does it matter how much we can bench press or what size pants we can squeeze into if our souls are stagnating, if they're not reaching for and growing toward God? What does it matter how popular we are or what official title appears next to our names, if along the way we are losing our souls?

It is said that every man, every woman, has a price they would take in exchange for their soul. How much is *your* soul worth? What would it take to get you to sell?

Judas, one of Jesus' friends and disciples, sold out for thirty pieces of silver. Most likely, he's subsisting in hell today because he wasted his soul. And lest you mistakenly believe that he was an isolated case, that surely there are no "Judases" alive today, just have a look around. Think about your own sphere of influence, for starters. Who in your relational circle is living for the almighty buck? Who is killing themselves in order to have killer abs?

I see this kind of thing from time to time even at church. A twenty-something guy pulls into the parking lot here on our campus, steps out of his shiny black convertible, his muscles nearly bursting out of his shirt, and automatically I find myself thinking, *I wonder if his soul is in equally stellar shape.* . . .

Granted, it may be. But perhaps it is not. I simply want to pose the question: Are we as concerned about eternal things as we are about the temporal? Are *you*?

Am I?

I think it's worth a few moments of careful thought.

Here is what is true of me: I love baseball. You've probably gathered that by now. I love the Texas Rangers, and I love the fact that they're doing pretty well these days. I loved seeing them take the divisional title and contend for the championship. I know the players' names and positions and major stats. I know which teams threaten to impede our progress and which ones we'll likely blow away. I'm a little obsessed with it all, truth be told. But in my heart of hearts, here is what I also know: My Rangers could take the title this year, and next year a new champion will be crowned. Even my coveted high would be fleeting! The earthly achievements, applause, championships—in light of the permanence of eternity—*all go away.*

This perspective keeps me from living for this stuff. It keeps me from unwittingly selling my soul. (But still, I want those Rangers to win.)

You're probably familiar with Solomon, son of King David, who lived many millennia ago. Baseball wasn't his thing, but he tried plenty of other avenues to scratch the itch that persisted down deep in his soul. He looked to money. He looked to possessions. He looked to ambition. He looked to sex. He tried "everything under the sun" and *still,* he came up void. His assessment on the heels of his futile search was, "Vanity of vanities! All is vanity" (Ecclesiastes 1:2). In other words: *Nothing* satisfies.

Rulers and ragamuffins, despots and derelicts, leaders and laymen alike have wanted it all and worked to obtain it all, only to find in the end that the world, indeed, *is* passing away along with its desires (1 John 2:17). Power, prestige, position—yes, even a national championship for my beloved team—none of this is worth losing our souls, because none of it can truly satisfy.

You and I may lose our health, but we can recover. We may lose our jobs, but we can find new ones. But to lose one's soul? It will be gone forever. To exchange a soul for the lies of this world is to sign up for an eternal ache. And why would we want to do that? This is essentially the question Jesus is posing in that verse from Mark chapter 8: "For what does it profit a man to gain the whole world and forfeit his soul?" (v. 36).

Why would we give our lives for things that don't matter?

Why would we spend our souls on lesser things?

If our souls are going to live forever and ever, why on earth would we treat them like trash?

What does it profit a man to gain the whole world and forfeit his soul?

A man who had lived his life contentedly and now was enjoying the peacefulness of his sunset years came across a young man, an ambitious man, a man who was determined to have it all. The elder asked the younger what he would do with his life, to which the younger said, "I am going to be a great businessman." The elder replied, "Then what?"

"Then I will lead my own business!"

"Then what?"

"Then I will make a fortune and be rich, rich, rich!"

"Then what?"

"Then I will retire and live a life of luxury on a golf course somewhere."

"Then what?"

"Then I suppose I will die."

"Then what?"

Jesus' words in Mark 8 equate to the ultimate *Then what?* test. Whatever we think we just *have* to have had better stand up to the "then what" test. Striving for a smaller waistline?

Then what? Hoping for a job promotion? Then what? Desperate to finally get married? Then what? Paying a small fortune in order to conceive? Then what? Working eighty hours a week? Then what? Saving for that long-awaited trip to Hawaii? *Then what?*

Maybe these things are part of God's best plan for your life, but maybe they aren't. I dare you to come earnestly before the Father, asking for his perspective on the "then what" test. He just might hand you fresh consideration for how you're stewarding your one and only soul.

How *Not* to Forfeit Your Soul

Part of why Jesus' flesh-and-bones arrival on the scene was so disruptive for people was that his words, his actions, his attitude, his very person communicated a far different message than the one everyone had come to love. As we've established, humankind always has taken to the self-help bent, but as it relates to self, Jesus had only one thing to say: "*Deny yourself.*"

Huh?

Deny ourselves? Was Jesus serious?

How are we supposed to get ahead, make the cut, rise above, pass muster, blaze our trail in this big bad world?

Still, he stood firm with his claim: "If you are going to follow me, you *will* deny yourself."[5]

Incidentally, this claim came just before the forfeit-his-soul bit in Mark 8. By way of the fuller context, Jesus had called a crowd over that included his disciples and said these words to them:

If anyone would come after me, let him deny himself and take up his cross and follow me. For whoever would save his life will lose it, but whoever loses his life for my sake and the gospel's will save it. For what does it profit a man to gain the whole world and forfeit his soul? For what can a man give in return for his soul? For whoever is ashamed of me and my words in this adulterous and sinful generation, of him will the Son of Man be ashamed when he comes in the glory of his Father with the holy angels.

vv. 34–38

Clearly, in Jesus' mind, there is a connection between denying ourselves and not forfeiting our souls. Between denying ourselves and following Jesus Christ as Lord. There is a connection between denying ourselves and saving our very lives.

As I've mentioned, I've been a pastor for nearly four decades, and for that time I have been less than enthusiastic about the mercy ministry obligations of my role: hospital visits, deathbed prayers, homebound encouragements, and the like. When you're young and new, the implicit expectation is that you'll wear a thousand hats, but as I grew and aged and hired more and more staff, it became easier for me to wiggle out of such responsibilities. And wiggle I did.

But here is what I discovered on my way to becoming an outright pastoral slacker: When I actually swallowed my protests, humbled myself, and showed up ready to serve, I came away refreshed in my spirit. I came away lifted up. When I determined in my mind and heart to deny myself, God *blessed me* as a result.

And this is what Jesus is saying when he promises that it is by losing our lives that we save them; it is by laying ourselves down that we are lifted up. It is in our very denial that you and I are fulfilled.

The Soul Defined

For those who want to be followers, let them deny themselves, Jesus exhorts in this passage. But what exactly is meant by *themselves*? It's a curious concept, isn't it, this idea of your*self* and my*self*, our*selves* and them*selves*—what's actually involved in the *self*?

More than human beings living in a spiritual world, you and I are *spiritual* beings living in a *human* world. Yes, we have "human" effects—arms and legs, eyes and ears, heart and lungs—but there is an inner world we cannot deny, and I daresay it's the more important of the two.

Furthermore, while on this earth we remain inseparable from the body, it is actually the soul that experiences the sum of life. It is the *soul* that thinks, desires, evaluates, feels, decides, judges, and acts. It is the *soul* that reflects the real inner person. It is the *soul* that proves we are not merely highly evolved animals but intricate creations of God. It is your *soul* that serves as the part of you that makes you *you*, my soul that makes me *me*.

Scottish novelist and minister of the late nineteenth century George MacDonald was a major influence on some of history's greatest spiritual thinkers—Oswald Chambers and C. S. Lewis among them. He noticed that we talk as though the soul is something *we have* (think: an iPhone, a winter coat, a haircut) rather than *who we are*.

And here let me interrupt the conversation to remark upon the great mistake of teaching children that they have souls. The consequence is that they think of their souls as something which is not themselves. For what a man has cannot be himself.

Hence, when they are told that their souls go to heaven, they think of their selves as lying in the grave. They ought to be

179

taught that they have bodies; and that their bodies die; while they themselves live on. Then they will not think . . . that they will be laid in the grave. It is making altogether too much of the body, and is indicative of an evil tendency to materialism, that we talk as if we possessed souls, instead of being souls. We should teach our children to think no more of their bodies when dead than they do of their hair when it is cut off or of their old clothes when they have done with them.[6]

MacDonald's train of thought likely found its origin in the Old Testament, where we see David talking about his soul—his inner man—"thirsting" for God (Psalm 42:2) and later in the same psalm, talking to his soul as though it were himself: "Why are you cast down, O my soul?" (v. 5).

And if the soul is *who we are* (not something we have), then the soul reflects the *imago Dei*, the very image of God.

The Value of a Soul

In the midst of the calling forth and forming and shaping that occurred in the early chapters of the book of Genesis, we find God taking his likeness, his character, and fashioning his most magnificent masterpiece—man. Author Cindy West describes the scene as God surveyed his creation and prepared to add humankind to it:

Artist looked at His canvas, taking note of everything in its proper place, except that which would be His finest masterpiece. For now, a blank spot dead-center interrupted the flow of beautiful formation, but soon—very soon—the middle of Artist's canvas would be occupied by the crown of all creation.

Artist stirred the dust of the ground with the warmth of His breath until suddenly, stunningly, spiritually, a torso emerged.

A head, a face, two eyes, two ears, a nose, a mouth, two arms, two legs. The work of art lay perfectly still, ever so quiet, ever so brilliant.

Spectacular!

The triune Artist shared a sigh of astonishment. Man! We have created . . . man.

Artist peered inside this ultimate creation and patiently, confidently confirmed His design. Two-hundred and six bones. Ribs. Liver. Veins. Brain. Emotions. Creativity. And then, there was the heart—the most magnificent of centerpieces. He had shaped it after His own and secured deep within it a seat of longing—an insatiable craving, expanding over time, satisfied only by relating with Him.

All was as it should be, and Artist bent low, placing His mouth over man's mouth, breathing gentle, passionate puffs of life into man's lungs until at once, fingers and toes wiggled and writhed, eyes jittered under lids, nose twitched and sneezed and with that . . . the first exhale of human life.

The man coughed and sputtered and pulled himself up to his right-side elbow, looking all around to get his bearings, mentally reaching for the sense of it all. He came to his knees, determined to rise, to move, to go somewhere, but his immediacy was stilled by the presence of God.

Artist looked full-faced toward His masterpiece, and the art could only remain facedown.[7]

Loving breath yielded living souls—it was true for Adam and Eve, and also for you and me. We were made "a little lower than the angels," Psalm 8:5 says, "and crowned . . . with glory and honor" (NCV). The God of the universe created us all, declaring us in that instant sacred beings—an ultimate substantiation of the idea that you can always tell the value of something by looking to the one who made it.

For the past few years, with some degree of frequency, I have received a handmade picture from my grandson, Ian, who is now in the second grade. The bottom drawer of my home-office desk is stuffed nearly to overflowing with these crayoned works of art, works I deem priceless, not because of their street value, but because of the value of the little boy who created them. I don't love them because they're valuable; rather, they are valuable because the one who drew them is worth so much to me. Similarly, in the words of the great sixteenth-century priest Martin Luther, God doesn't love us because we're valuable; but we are valuable *because God loves us*. Our value is in him alone, and it is value of inestimable worth.

You could add up the mountains, the oceans, the tallest buildings, the monies from every bank account in the world, and *still* you would not scratch the surface of your intrinsic worth, or of mine. Jesus did not willingly endure the cross, suffering pain and spilling blood, for the birds of the air or the flowers of the field or the sunsets that stretch majestically across the sky. He died for *us*, for the sake of human souls.

The Soul Has Unlimited Potential

Because of the immense value God places on the human soul, we as those living souls are blessed with unlimited potential. The Bible promises that those who surrender their lives to Christ are destined *in* Christ to become like him. First Peter 1:14–16 calls us to this staggering potential:

> As obedient children, do not be conformed to the passions of your former ignorance, but as he who called you is holy, you also be holy in all your conduct, since it is written, "You shall be holy, for I am holy."

First John 3:7 reminds us of the training process we're undergoing as lovers of the Lord Jesus: "Little children, let no one deceive you. Whoever practices righteousness is righteous, as he [Jesus] is righteous."

In 1 Corinthians 1:30, we find assurance of the believing soul's truest identity: "And because of him you are in Christ Jesus, who became to us wisdom from God, righteousness and sanctification and redemption."

In Ephesians 1:3–4, we're given further hope about who we can be:

> Blessed be the God and Father of our Lord Jesus Christ, who has blessed us in Christ with every spiritual blessing in the heavenly places, even as he chose us in him before the foundation of the world, that we should be *holy and blameless* before him (emphasis mine).

This commitment to our purification is echoed in Ephesians 5:27, when the apostle Paul writes that we as the church will one day be presented to Jesus "in splendor, without spot or wrinkle or any such thing," *so that* we "might be holy and without blemish."

Whatever you do to nourish your soul—a topic we will cover later in this chapter—rest assured that your efforts are not in vain. We honor God's divine imprint on our lives when we pursue every inch of spiritual potential we possess.

The Soul Will Live Forever

Your soul is the only part of you that will live forever; as such, attention to soulful living is always well placed. Truly, long after your body and my body and the bodies of every once-living being have disintegrated, the soul alone will remain.

183

At this writing, our nation is mere weeks away from another presidential election, and for the past several days, at every opportunity, I've been making my position known regarding whose platform Christ-followers ought to support. This isn't a matter of partisanship; rather, there are some subjects in Scripture that outrank all other considerations. So yes, while we ought to educate ourselves toward an informed perspective on key issues such as taxes, energy, defense, and the training we're providing our children both at home and at school, we must elevate to the top of that list the issue of *protecting all human life*.

People are not mere products of conception; people are souls—souls created in the image of God. Souls that are *valuable* to God. When we support the practice of killing babies, we simultaneously endorse the wounding of souls. Based on what I know to be true of the soul, I simply can't vote for that. The soul is the aspect of humankind that is made solely for God. When we destroy a human being, we destroy his or her ability to pursue godliness, which is life's premiere worthwhile pursuit. And while we ourselves can choose—even if unwisely—to neglect the pursuit of God, to step into another's life and make that choice for him or her is a special sort of wrong.

The Soul Longs Only for God

What do we make of this longing we feel, this longing for our soul's sole desire? Well, when we choose to go God's way with our lives, we absorb the full implications of God's grace—of his forgiving our sin and bridging the gap to his perfect and holy presence through the selfless sacrifice of Jesus Christ—and come away with the most natural of inclinations, the yearning to *come near to God*. But then most people panic and stop short of nearness, unsure that intimacy with the Almighty is something they really want to allow.

Maybe there is another way to get the longing satisfied, we think. Maybe we'd better exhaust other options before doing something we might regret.

So we pave the path to our supposed fulfillment in a thousand other ways. We try entertainment and amusement and gaming our hours away. We try relationships. We try job changes. We try witty comebacks, we try nature hikes . . . we try *stuff*.

Oh, how we hope "stuff" will work. Last week, my wife had me cleaning out every last closet in our home in an attempt to clear away the things that over the decades we just *had* to have. As I lugged yet one more box full of useless trinkets and too-tight clothes downstairs, I thought about how ridiculous it is to let accumulation be life's goal. We want it all! But then we don't know where to put it. Truly, there is no room for *stuff* in the soul.

No, our souls were designed to find fulfillment only in God. Author Valerie Bell notes:

> My soul was created to be a God-fit. I am incomplete without him, frustrated and dissatisfied with other substitutes. God is the goal of the soul; all other hungers are symptomatic of the soul's longing to connect to its soul mate—God.[8]

If it is the soul that is purchased by Christ's death and the soul that will live forever—with him or apart from him—then is there any wiser endeavor than to push aside every other allegiance but this singularly eternal one?

We've come full circle, back to the admonition of Christ to deny yourself. To be guided by our own will is to be led by that which will one day cease to exist; it is only by inviting *God's* will, *God's* ways that eternal satisfaction is ours. It is only by laying our own lives down that we pick up the abundance we so desperately crave.

The Soulish Stakes of War

Satan, of course, doesn't want this for us; he's determined to make our souls *his*. And thus the unseen battle rages on. You and I—ourselves, our souls—*we* are the prize to be won.

Surrender Your Soul

In fact, we—the prize—already belong to God. He paid for us, if you'll recall. "You are not your own," 1 Corinthians 6 says, "for you were bought with a price" (vv. 19–20). We ensure Christ's sacrifice was not in vain when we receive his redemption with grateful hearts. And *receiving* is all that's required; the Bible is marvelously clear on this point. "So everyone who acknowledges me before men, I also will acknowledge before my Father who is in heaven," says Matthew 10:32. "Believe in the Lord Jesus, and you will be saved" (Acts 16:31). "He saved us," Titus 3:5 says, "not because of works done by us in righteousness, but according to his own mercy, by the washing of regeneration and renewal of the Holy Spirit." Acknowledge, believe, *receive*—the key here is that nothing we "do" will magically make us heaven-bound. It's simply by determining in our hearts and confessing with our mouths that Jesus is Lord that we enter permanent fellowship with him.

As unpopular an assertion as it is, every person will in fact face a day of judgment: "It is appointed for man to die once, and after that comes judgment," Hebrews 9:27 says. And so the charge is this: *Give your soul to Christ.* "We do not control the earth of Russia or Great Britain or the United States," Barnhouse confirms, but "we do control that bit of earth of which we are made."[9] As the apostle Paul said in 1 Corinthians 9:27, *we* are the ones responsible for keeping ourselves disciplined, and for joyfully subjecting our bodies to God.

Protect Your Soul

In surrendering our souls to Jesus' rule and reign, we also pick up the responsibility for *stewarding our souls well* each day. But this isn't what most of us want to do. People living far from God, and believers alike, tend to care more for their health than their souls. We tend to our wealth. We tend to the well-being of family and friends. Of course, these things are not *bad* pursuits, in and of themselves. But trumping them all must be the idea of tending the "inner man," of *expanding*, not shrinking, the soul.

Soul Shrinkers. To shrink your soul is to engage in something that causes you to feel apathetic toward God. In Luke 12:16–21, Jesus tells a story to a crowd that had gathered to hear him preach:

> The land of a rich man produced plentifully, and he thought to himself, "What shall I do, for I have nowhere to store my crops?" And he said, "I will do this: I will tear down my barns and build larger ones, and there I will store all my grain and my goods. And I will say to my soul, 'Soul, you have ample goods laid up for many years; relax, eat, drink, be merry.'" But God said to him, "Fool! This night your soul is required of you, and the things you have prepared, whose will they be?" So is the one who lays up treasure for himself and is not rich toward God.

soul shrinkers

Soul expanders

The choices we make every moment of every day lead us either to *richness* toward God or *apathy* toward God. They lead us to expansiveness of soul or to a soul that's been shrunk. From this parable, we glean two of the fastest tracks to a shrunken state of the soul: self-centeredness and shortsightedness. The rich man could not see beyond himself, as evidenced by the plentiful *I* and *my* pronouns; and he could not see beyond this temporal world—indeed, if this world is all there is, we might as well eat, drink, and be merry too.

Accumulation is another soul-shrinker. Too much television can do it too. Ditto for too much technology—really, now, how life-giving is it for you to stare at a computer screen for hours on end?

An inordinate amount of energy spent caring about what other people think of us, how we look, whether we're as rich/successful/powerful/popular as they are—these are soul-shrinkers as well. Spend a few years living this way, and spiritual burnout will soon be yours.

For me, being around negative people makes my insides feel constricted and sour. Being lazy can cause the same reaction, unless my Rangers are on TV. Anyway, you get the idea.

Soul Expanders. The flip side of the soul-care coin is far more encouraging. In the same way that we can make choices that suck the life out of our fragile souls, we also can choose to expand them. Yes, our outer selves may be wasting away, as Paul attests in 2 Corinthians 4:16, but our inner selves can be renewed day by day.

So how does this renewal take place? Let me offer up five biblical ideas:

1. Start and end each day with this earnest pursuit, from Matthew 22:37: "Love the Lord your God with all your heart and with all your soul and with all your mind." You

and I won't be perfect at this at every turn, but if we can at least make this our goal on a regular basis, we'll see our batting average start to improve.

2. Worship with a group of believers consistently, as we're encouraged to do in Hebrews 10:25. Live video streaming certainly has its usefulness, but to truly expand your soul, do whatever you need to do to gather and sing and read the Scriptures and pray *firsthand*—live and in person—at church.

3. Muster the energy and courage to initiate deep conversations with people you meet. Sure, ask about their day or mention the weather as a starting point, but don't let things stay superficial. Take the risk to ask a follow-up question as a means of "bearing one another's burdens" (Galatians 6:2). For example, if you ask how the clerk at the grocery store is doing, and he says, "Hanging in there, I guess," invest the few seconds it would take to find out what is making his week especially tough.

4. Absorb people's faith stories as often as you can. Read books, listen to podcasts, and pay attention to conversations that center on how other people have practiced "expanding" their souls. And then implement in your own life the wisdom that you find. If all believers practiced this idea, we would be fulfilling Romans 1:12, which says "that we may be mutually encouraged by each other's faith."

5. Read God's Word slowly, intentionally, and *daily*. Matthew 11:28–30 says, "Come to me, all who labor and are heavy laden, and I will give you rest. Take my yoke upon you, and learn from me, for I am gentle and lowly in heart, and you will find rest for your souls. For my yoke is easy, and my burden is light." What is not

soul-expanding about divinely offered insight and rest? You will never regret a moment of time invested in the Word of God.

There are countless other ways to "lose your life" for the sake of Jesus Christ, for the sake of his gospel of grace, but none of them will help to expand the soul unless you actually determine to practice them. Charge ahead confidently into your soul-expanding habits, because this is where life is truly found.

A final thought as it relates to tending your soul: Whenever I face decisions—both monumental and mundane—it helps me to pose the question "How will this affect my soul?"

Whether the consideration centers on how to spend a paycheck, invest a weekend, steward a talent, grow a business, discipline a child, or relate with another person, pausing long enough to ask yourself this question before God, and then waiting for an honest response, will serve you well.

See Others Not Only as People, but as Souls

Christ-followers are committed to global and local evangelization—sharing the gospel with people who don't know Christ—because as we grow in intimacy with our Savior, we begin to see others not only as people, but as souls in need of deep care. This is the context of the passage in Mark 8 we've been covering in this chapter. Just before Jesus explained what it would cost his disciples to follow him, he posed a question. Let's revisit the text (vv. 27–29):

> And Jesus went on with his disciples to the villages of Caesarea Philippi. And on the way he asked his disciples, "Who do people

say that I am?" And they told him, "John the Baptist; and others say, Elijah; and others, one of the prophets." And he asked them, "But who do you say that I am?" Peter answered him, "You are the Christ."

We *confess* Christ as Lord, then *deny* ourselves in order to follow him. We see *all* souls as souls for whom Jesus died, and we understand that the reason for our very existence here on earth is to help point others toward faith in Christ. "Whoever captures souls," Proverbs 11:30 tells us, "is *wise*." And the word there is, in fact, *souls*. We aren't looking to sway the hearts and minds of people as much as we're working to tend to their *souls*.

So in your marriage and parenting, you can be careful to tend to your spouse's soul and the souls of your children. In your vocation, you can tend to your colleagues' souls. And in your community, you can tend to the souls of your neighbors and merchants. The same is true in your church, in your friendships, at the gym, during your travels, and more. Begin seeing people as *souls* who are precious to our heavenly Father, and it will change the way you interact with them.

I still have the newspaper clippings from the week after my father died tucked away in a file in my desk drawer. The man who murdered my dad was only twenty-four years old and was already on his fifth felony. In the eyes of the state he was a hardened criminal, but I saw him as a broken and burdened soul in need of care.

Certainly, I wanted justice to be served—Romans 13 makes provision for that. But in terms of the person behind the crime, God gave me spiritual eyes to see him for who he really was. In my own strength, I would have felt nothing but anger and hatred toward the man; but by God's power living in me, I felt nothing toward him but *grace*. This is the Spirit's transformative work in our lives, which births beauty from ashes and promise from unparalleled pain.

I never had the opportunity to look into the eyes of the person who ended my dad's life too soon, to offer my forgiveness firsthand and to tell him that restoration for his soul is possible, regardless of the mistakes he had made. But I like to think that as I invest myself in the lives of countless others—talking with them about the Scriptures, walking with them through life's valleys, praying over their needs—I am staying refreshed in the idea that *all* souls matter to God. And because of that, all souls matter to me.

Discussion Questions

1. In what ways can you relate to the Charlemagne-like temptation to "save ourselves, promote ourselves, have faith in ourselves, pull ourselves up by our own bootstraps, and carry on"?

2. Describe a season of your life when you were able to successfully shift your focus from the temporal to the eternal. What factors played a role in your ability to train your attention on what really matters?

3. What characteristics do you see in Jesus' life that allowed him to always pass the "then-what" test described in this chapter? If you could more frequently manifest just one of those characteristics in your own life, which would you choose, and why?

4. How might it help you and other Christ-followers you know to consider your soul not as something you *possess* but rather who you *are*?

5. Who do you know in your own life who lives with a right view of the soul? What valuable lessons does his or her life teach?

NINE
AN APPOINTMENT WE CANNOT BREAK

I t was a beautiful fall afternoon in the Dallas-Fort Worth area when I headed to the Rangers Ballpark in Arlington for what was to be a dynamite match-up between my Texas Rangers and the Oakland Athletics. The year was 2004, game time was one o'clock, and as always, I got there early. Partly cloudy skies, eighty-six degrees, twenty-three thousand excited fans, nothing on my agenda except baseball—it was shaping up to be a perfect afternoon.

The A's were favored, but Texas had put together some promising trends; we were still in the pennant race in late September, which was more than we could say most years. Anyway, I had high hopes as things got underway.

The score was tied at two going into the sixth inning, but the A's quickly pulled ahead by one run. Then my cell phone rang. Things were just getting good when I answered the call and learned that my daughter-in-law was going into labor to deliver my first grandchild. While it's true that the Rangers can pull me away from all sorts of activities and obligations, this was one occasion I wasn't about to miss. I quickly left the ballpark, jumped into my car, and raced across town to the hospital.

I'd later learn that four of the five top plays of the game would happen after I left, and that the Rangers would come from behind in the bottom of the ninth to pull out a win. But still, I knew I'd made the right choice. There is nothing better than cradling a grandbaby in your arms immediately after he is born.

In most areas of my life, I have all kinds of control over where I go, what I do, whom I see, and how I spend my time. I can accept invitations or decline them. I can agree to a lunch meeting or say no. I can ask a colleague to work with me on a project one afternoon, or I can blow off work, buy a ticket to the Rangers game, and hole away with a hot dog for a few hours. I can even blow off *that* engagement, choosing instead to watch my son become a dad.

But there are two appointments I have zero control over, two occasions ordained for me that I can neither schedule nor cancel at will. They are the date of my arrival on this planet and the date when I'm due to depart. Ecclesiastes 3:2 says there is "a time to be born, and a time to die," and in the same way I had no say in the date of my birth, apart from taking drastic, irreversible action, I'll have no say in the date of my death. Regardless of a person's individual worldview, spiritual bent, or philosophy on life, these two dates are widely accepted as factors outside our control. What is debated is what exactly happens after that second appointment. Every person has questions about what's next, what's *after* life.

Several years ago, Jack Nicholson and Morgan Freeman starred in a movie called *The Bucket List,* in which they played two terminally ill cancer-ward escapees who head off on a road trip to check off a list of things they want to do before they die. It was a fascinating movie that spawned all sorts of discussion among friends and families about what would be on their bucket lists— and also about what they believed about death and the afterlife.

As part of the promotional package announcing the movie's release, *Parade* magazine interviewed Jack Nicholson about his own beliefs on life and the afterlife, on death and what comes next. He said,

> I used to live so freely. The mantra for my generation was "be your own man." I always said, "Hey, you have whatever rules you want. I'm going to have my rules. I'll accept the guilt. I'll pay the tab. I'll do the time. And I'll choose my own way." That was my philosophy well into my fifties, but as I've gotten older I've had to adjust. . . .
>
> We all want to go on forever, don't we? We fear the unknown. Everyone goes to that wall, but nobody wants to know what's on the other side. That's why we fear death. And, yes, *everyone* fears death.[1]

Certainly, you and I and Jack Nicholson aren't the only ones to wonder what comes after this life. In the oldest book of the

Bible, the book of Job, a man described as "blameless" and "upright"—as one who "feared God" (Job 1:1)—is found asking the very same thing. "A man dies and is laid low," Job 14:10 says; "man breathes his last, and where is he?" In other words, *what happens after we die?*

Indeed, myths and misconceptions and miscommunications abound regarding this thing called life after death. And errant information is damaging to us *all*, because *all* of us are facing death. The young and the old, the rich and the poor, the known and the unknown, the president and the peasant—*everyone* living will one day die; everyone will cease to exist. And most likely we're closer to death than we care to think.

Knocking on Death's Door

My friend Tony Evans once said it to me this way: "We are all marching toward a cemetery, whether we like it or not," and while the prospect may sound grim to you, factually, it's spot-on. "Teach us to number our days," Psalm 90:12 says, "that we may get a heart of wisdom." This is such good advice for all of us, who a hundred years from now will be long gone.

Life is a frailty; death is a certainty. It is true what the apostle Paul says in 2 Corinthians 4:16: "Our outer self is wasting away." This earthly tent is aging, and you and I both are knocking on death's door.

I saw a television commercial recently that showed in fast-frame a baby being born and then graduating from high school and then getting married and then having a child and then running for president of the United States, and I thought, "That's exactly how life feels!" You snap your fingers, and *poof,* it has utterly passed you by.

198

Baby Boomers are turning sixty-five, and it's a transition none of us ever expected. After all, we were the self-proclaimed "forever young." As much as we hate to admit it, the forever young are getting old. The great Bob Dylan wrote the classic song by that title, and just look at him! Old, old, old. I can only pick on him because I find myself in the very same boat. It seems like yesterday when I was graduating from college and launching my ministry career and teaching my boys to play ball. And literally yesterday, I was pitching to my grandson, thinking, *Man, time really does fly.*

Last week, Deb and I were driving home from one of Ian's baseball games, and in an approach that in my view lacked subtlety, she said, "You remember that next week is when we meet with our estate planner, right?"

I think my exact response was *"Huh?"*

Did she know something I didn't know?

It's sobering to know that death will be my reality someday. As it will be yours. And that day could dawn sooner than either of us expects; across the globe, a quarter of a million people die *every day*. "You do not know what tomorrow will bring," James 4:14 says. "What is your life? For you are a mist that appears for a little time and then vanishes."

That about sums it up.

Yes, death is a certainty. And yes, life is a frailty. But there is a third truth to consider: *Eternity is a reality.*

Eternity in Our Hearts

I saw a religious pamphlet the other day titled "How to Live Forever" and was intrigued enough to pick it up. I scanned the content, and while it was worthwhile, the title of the piece was misleading. The fact is, you and I don't have to do *anything* to live forever; we *are* going to live forever, regardless of what we do. In the same way that birth ushers us into time, death ushers us into timelessness.

Part of God's design for humankind was placing eternity in our hearts. The question is where we will spend that eternity. The Bible explains that both a *real place* called heaven and a *real place* called hell exist, and that based on what we do with the person of Jesus Christ, we get to pick where we go. Will we receive him or reject him? Our answer here matters a great deal. Before we look at the specifics of these two destinations, let's first explore what is involved in death.

Physical Death

The Bible speaks of three distinct forms of death, the first being *physical death*, in which the body is separated from the soul. As we saw in chapter 8, the soul is that part of us that lives on forever, but clearly, based on your empirical evidence and mine, the body does not.

God's Word says that death won't always be part of the scheme. The apostle Paul refers to death in 1 Corinthians 15:26 as the "last enemy" to be destroyed, a conquest that will occur, based on that same chapter of Scripture, upon Jesus Christ's return. At that time, "death is swallowed up in victory" (v. 54), a subject we'll explore further in chapter 12. But until then, *we all will die.* It must be noted here that physical death should not be considered punishment for our sin; Jesus Christ absorbed *all* our sin and the wrath of our sin at the cross.

Interestingly, while death is counted an enemy, for the believer, it also is counted a friend. The apostle Paul wrote in Philippians 1:21–23:

> For to me to live is Christ, and to die is gain. If I am to live in the flesh, that means fruitful labor for me. Yet which I shall choose I cannot tell. I am hard pressed between the two. My desire is to depart and be with Christ, for that is far better.

Furthermore, death for the believer is described as "sleep" in 1 Thessalonians 4:13–17. We are told in 2 Corinthians 5:8 (NCV) to "have courage" when facing death because "we really want to be away from this body and be at home with the Lord." The apostle John calls those who "die in the Lord" blessed (Revelation 14:13).

The Second Death

To face the "second death" (Revelation 2:11) is to die and yet never die; it is the term used in Scripture to describe the terrible prospect of an eternity spent apart from God, by annihilation, by fire, or by some other ultimately destructive means, depending on one's theology. In contrast to the concept of "life after death," spoken of often in Christian circles, the second death is "death after life." It is death upon death.

This subject necessitates a fuller treatment than what I've provided here, which is why I devote the entirety of chapter 10 to the topic of *real* death, aka, *hell*. But let me just say this: In the same way that we see the spiritual life cycle at a first birth, or physical birth, and at a second birth, which occurs when a person surrenders his or her life to Jesus Christ, there is a first death, or physical death, but also a second death, in which the soul is permanently separated from God.

Many believers have committed to memory Ephesians 2:8–10:

> For by grace you have been saved through faith. And this is not your own doing; it is the gift of God, not a result of works, so that no one may boast. For we are his workmanship, created in Christ Jesus for good works, which God prepared beforehand, that we should walk in them.

Truly, they are magnificent verses. But equally magnificent is their context: The reason grace is so crucial to us, the reason our being God's workmanship is such an utter relief, is that this divine rescue and divine purposing is what brought us from spiritual death to life. Here is what the preceding verses in that same chapter say:

> You *were dead* in the trespasses and sins in which you once walked, following the course of this world, following the prince of the power of the air, the spirit that is now at work in the sons of disobedience—among whom *we all once lived* in the passions of our flesh, carrying out the desires of the body and the mind, and were by nature children of wrath, like the rest of mankind.
>
> But God, being rich in mercy, because of the great love with which he loved us, even when we were dead in our trespasses, *made us alive* together with Christ—by grace you have been saved—and raised us up with him and seated us with him in the heavenly places in Christ Jesus, so that in the coming ages he might show the immeasurable riches of his grace in kindness toward us in Christ Jesus.

EPHESIANS 2:1–7 (EMPHASIS MINE)

We first see spiritual death as a result of Adam and Eve's sin in the garden of Eden, way back in Genesis 3. Here, in response to his sin and rebellion, God tells Adam, "By the sweat of your face you shall eat bread, till you return to the ground, for out of it you were taken; for you are dust, and to dust you shall return" (v. 19). When sin arrived, spiritual death set in. An infectious, mortal disease thereby afflicted the human race; in Adam, *all* of us die, because "the wages of sin is death" (Romans 6:23). Romans 5:12 elaborates on this idea: "Just as sin came into the world through one man, and death through sin, and so death spread to all men because all sinned."

I heard a statement years ago that stuck with me: "If you are born once, you will die twice; if you are born twice, you will die once." If you are born physically and die physically, then you ultimately also will face the "second death," which Scripture calls the lake of fire. Again, more on this topic in the next chapter.

But if you are born twice—physically and then spiritually, of God—then you will face only a physical death. Spiritually, you will live forever; spiritually, *you will not face death*.

Now, regarding this idea of spiritual birth, Jesus explains: "You must be born again" (John 3:7), which at face value seems quite odd. People in Jesus' day were perplexed by the concept too. In fact, the context of this verse in John is that a great Jewish leader named Nicodemus came to Jesus in the middle of the night, compelled to know what Jesus knew about God and the kingdom of God. He could tell by Jesus' teaching and his miracles and by his sturdiness, steadiness, and smarts, that he wasn't from this part of town; he was somehow heaven-sent. But still, how could Jesus know what seemingly was unknowable? And how could Nicodemus understand these spiritual things too?

Jesus' reply was "You must be born again." Spiritual things only make sense to spiritual people; as we learned in chapter 1, the kingdom of God may only be seen by those who have become citizens within its gates.

This confused the leader, who thought Jesus' advice somehow suggested a return to his mother's womb. Jesus corrected his thinking: "No, no. I'm not talking about re-doing your *fleshly* birth; I'm talking about being born by the waters of baptism and by the power of the Holy Spirit."[2] You and I are "born again" as we lay down our lives in Jesus and pick up life that is fueled solely by him—his will, his wants, his ways, his whys.

Certainly not all religions believe these ideas about death to be true. For example, some Eastern religions posit that rather than facing death and then life, you and I actually face life after life after life—otherwise known as reincarnation. Some believe that there is an intermediate state, wherein the soul falls asleep until the "last days," a topic we'll come back to in chapter 11. Still others believe that while the physical body dies and the spirit lives on, at some point in the future, body and spirit will be reunited and never separated again.

Opinions abound, but to believe biblical Christianity is to believe that death is both unavoidable and irrevocable, and that once we cross the line into death, we never may return to life—at least in the way we know physical, earthbound life today. But this is where the news gets really good. Because in the same way that this present existence can lead to eternal death and thus eternal separation from God, it also can lead to eternal *life*, and eternity spent in the presence of God.

Life That Is Truly Life

We have established that God has placed eternity in our hearts and that we will either live forever in the misery that is spiritual death, or else we will live forever in God's presence, in the joy that is spiritual life. It is to the realities of this latter option that I will turn now. What exactly happens, when the earthbound life of a Christ-follower ends? What really happens when we die?

We Continue to Live

First, the Scriptures are clear that although we will die, we also will continue to live. Second Corinthians 5 contains some of the best language of the entire Bible on this subject. We looked at parts of this passage previously, but let me give it to you here, in amplified form. Verses 1 through 10 say this:

> For we know that if the tent that is our earthly home [our body] is destroyed, we have a building from God, a house not made with hands, eternal in the heavens [our resurrected body]. For in this tent we groan, longing to put on our heavenly dwelling, if indeed by putting it on we may not be found naked [as a soul without the resurrected body]. For while we are still in this tent, we groan, being burdened—not that we would be unclothed, but that we would be further clothed [in our resurrected body], so that what is mortal may be swallowed up by life.
>
> He who has prepared us for this very thing is God, who has given us the Spirit as a guarantee. So we are always of good courage. We know that while we are at home in the body we are away from the Lord, for we walk by faith, not by sight. Yes, we are of good courage, and we would rather be away from the body and at home with the Lord [absent from the body and present with the Lord]. So whether we are at home or away, we make it our aim to please him. For we must all appear before the judgment seat of Christ, so that each one may receive what is due for what he has done in the body, whether good or evil.

Did you catch the line partway through, about our mortality being swallowed up by life? Interesting phrasing, isn't it? We who have placed our trust in the Lord Jesus die so that we might live. So that *forever*, we might live.

Our Souls Are Immediately With Christ

Second, we understand from Scripture that as soon as we perish, our souls enter the eternal presence of Christ. To the thief on the cross next to Jesus who asked to be remembered, Jesus clearly stated that he would be with him that very day. "Truly, I say to you, today you will be with me in Paradise" (Luke 23:43).

The apostle Paul spoke of his confidence that death would bring him into the presence of Christ, and that reality would be "far better" than life on earth. (See Philippians 1:21–23.)

You'll recall that in 2 Corinthians 5:6, Paul said that to be "at home in the body" was to be "away from the Lord." He preferred to be away from the body and in the presence of the Lord. I happen to feel the very same way.

So when we as believers die, we are ushered into the presence of Christ, where we await the "final resurrection," the physical return of Christ, when our resurrection bodies—our new bodies—are reunited with our souls, which are already with Christ. This is precisely the teaching of 1 Corinthians 15:40, which says, "There are heavenly bodies and earthly bodies, but the glory of the heavenly is of one kind, and the glory of the earthly is of another." Two verses later, we read this:

> So is it with the resurrection of the dead. What is sown is perishable; what is raised is imperishable. It is sown in dishonor; it is raised in glory. It is sown in weakness; it is raised in power. It

is sown a natural body; it is raised a spiritual body. If there is a natural body, there is also a spiritual body.

vv. 42–44

And further, in the same chapter:

I tell you this, brothers: flesh and blood cannot inherit the kingdom of God, nor does the perishable inherit the imperishable. Behold! I tell you a mystery. We shall not all sleep, but we shall all be changed, in a moment, in the twinkling of an eye, at the last trumpet. For the trumpet will sound, and the dead will be raised imperishable, and we shall be changed. For this perishable body must put on the imperishable, and this mortal body must put on immortality. When the perishable puts on the imperishable, and the mortal puts on immortality, then shall come to pass the saying that is written: 'Death is swallowed up in victory. O death, where is your victory? O death, where is your sting?' The sting of death is sin, and the power of sin is the law. But thanks be to God, who gives us the victory through our Lord Jesus Christ.

vv. 50–57

The perishable *really will* put on the imperishable. I can barely type those words without exhilaration absolutely taking over my thoughts. So much about this life is beautiful, but what comes *after* this life makes me shake my head in anticipatory awe.

The Coming Age Begins

There is a third expectation posited in Scripture, regarding what happens to us when we die, which is that time ceases to exist and eternity at Jesus' side begins. Ephesians 2:4–7 says:

207

But God, being rich in mercy, because of the great love with which he loved us, even when we were dead in our trespasses, made us alive together with Christ—by grace you have been saved—and raised us up with him and seated us with him in the heavenly places in Christ Jesus, so that in the *coming ages* [read: a very, very long time] he might show the immeasurable riches of his grace in kindness toward us in Christ Jesus.

Certainly, you and I don't understand all that is involved here, since the Bible leaves much of the detail veiled for now. But of this much, we can be sure: When we die, the permanent eclipses the temporal, and the sum of our earthly existence becomes an incidental drop in the bucket.

Judgment

Finally, we read in God's Word that upon death for the believer, *judgment will take place*. Some believe we will face three different types of judgment, while others hold to just one. Either way, Hebrews 9:27 assures us that "just as it is appointed for man to die once . . . after that comes judgment." The passage from 2 Corinthians we looked at previously echoes this sentiment: "For we must all appear before the judgment seat of Christ," it says, "so that each one may receive what is due for what he has done in the body, whether good or evil" (5:10). *2 with -*

So yes, you and I will face judgment, but this is not a judgment of sin. That judgment is made during this earthly life, when we decide whether we will place our trust and faith in Jesus Christ and thereby consign our souls eternally either to heaven or to hell.

This judgment is when an account is given for everything we have done in life. Varying opinions place the time of this accounting either before the final resurrection or at the final resurrection; personally, I find plenty of scriptural evidence to support the idea that the judgment will actually take place after the physical return of Christ. But regardless of the time frame, judgment *will* occur. You and I will be asked to account for how we managed our relationships, served the Lord, handled our finances, led our families, ran our businesses, loved our neighbors, treated our colleagues, and so forth. "I tell you," Jesus says in Matthew 12:36, "on the day of judgment people will give account for every careless word they speak."

The words we speak, the motivations of our hearts, the actions we choose to take or avoid—everything will be "brought to light" in order that we might receive commendation from God.

> Therefore do not pronounce judgment before the time, before the Lord comes, who will bring to light the things now hidden in darkness and will disclose the purposes of the heart. Then each one will receive his commendation from God.
>
> 1 CORINTHIANS 4:5

Did you catch that last line? *Each of us* will walk through this process, on our own, with nobody there to lean on. We will stand individually—before God. Paul quotes Christ in Romans 14:11–12, saying, "'As I live, says the Lord, every knee shall bow to me, and every tongue shall confess to God.' So then *each of us* will give an account of himself to God" (emphasis mine). You will stand before a holy God and before him assess how you stewarded the gifts, the talents, the resources he blessed you with. And so will I. And the truth of our lives will be revealed. Paul tells us in 1 Corinthians 3:13–15:

Each one's work will become manifest, for the Day will disclose it, because it will be revealed by fire, and the fire will test what sort of work each one has done. If the work that anyone has built on the foundation survives, he will receive a reward. If anyone's work is burned up, he will suffer loss, though he himself will be saved, but only as through fire.

Here is how I sum up that passage: "Let the coming judgment motivate you to live a holy life." That's it! Live according to the standard of holiness, and you'll have no regrets on judgment day. Love God; serve others; die to self. Engage in missions and in evangelism. Treat life as the gift that it is. Enjoy your days. Enjoy your spouse, your kids, your friends, your church, your job. Jesus is coming soon, Revelation 22:12 says, and is bringing his recompense with him, "to repay each one for what he has done."

So here is the invitation: Lay up for yourself treasures in heaven, refusing to live for the temporal, spending your energies and monies on pleasures that will disappear this side of eternity. Live a *holy life,* and that day of repayment will be the day of greatest joy you've ever known.

The Choice That Is Ours to Make

To speak of the gifts of God in the lives of humankind is to dive headlong into lavish grace, unconditional love, ultimate justice, indefatigable patience, unrelenting pursuit. But perhaps the most astounding of his gifts in our lives is that of a *free will.* To think that God possesses in his person all that we need for life and happiness and yet refuses to force it on us is a staggering thought, isn't it? He waits for us to open the door of our heart to him (see Revelation 3:20). He refuses to barge on in without an invitation.

And so a choice remains. We will either go it alone in life, trusting our own winsomeness and wit to save us, or else we will surrender the sum of who we are to Jesus, and ask him to escort us right into an eternity of life and love. And that's exactly the promise Christ offers: "I am the resurrection and the life," he says in John 11:25–26. "Whoever believes in me, though he die, yet shall he live, and everyone who lives and believes in me shall never die."

Interestingly, in the context of this passage, Jesus closes his comments with a question, posed to the sister of Lazarus, his friend who had died three days prior: "Do you believe this?"

I have the same question for you. *Do you believe this?* Do you believe that Jesus is the resurrection and the life, and that we gain access to the Father, and to eternity with him, through Jesus, and only through him?

We can "*know* that [we] have eternal life," 1 John 5:13 promises. We can know that our souls are redeemed from the power of the grave (Psalm 49:15). We can commit our spirit for all time and eternity into the grip of God (Luke 23:46). We can remain in the perfect company of Jesus forever, who is "the way and the truth and the life" (John 14:6).

There really is no mystery here; all these things can be *known*.

Many people think of death as some mysterious, unknowable transition, but in Christ, death is no longer a mystery; it is a *miracle*, an *eternal interruption* of all the limitations and all the liabilities of this earthly life; the decisive end of all the frustrations and failures, foibles and sins that have plagued us for so long. At last our struggle will be in the past, and our future *perfect* in Christ.

It is no wonder that the psalmist David wrote, "Even though I walk through the valley of the shadow of death, I will fear no evil, for you are with me" (Psalm 23:4). Death is but a shadow, and whenever there is a shadow, the sun is shining somewhere. Only in this case, it's the Son, our Great Shepherd, Jesus.

We surrender to him. We live for him. We eagerly anticipate his return. And until he arrives, we joyfully express his love to a troubled, tortured world.

Steve Jobs, the legendary co-founder, chairman, and CEO of Apple Inc., and according to many the "Father of the Digital Revolution," died in 2011 from an aggressive form of pancreatic cancer. His biographer, Walter Isaacson, released his book on Jobs—a self-declared Zen Buddhist—shortly after the genius's death, and in the final paragraph of the last chapter, quoted Jobs' beliefs on the plausibility of an afterlife:

> Sometimes I believe in God. But sometimes I don't. I think it's fifty-fifty, maybe. But ever since I've had cancer, I've been thinking about it more. And I find myself believing a bit more. I kind of . . . maybe it's because I want to believe in an afterlife, that when you die it doesn't all just disappear. The wisdom you've accumulated . . . somehow it lives on.

Jobs paused with Isaacson before going on. "Yeah," he then continued, "but sometimes I think it's just like an on-off switch. *Click,* and you're gone. Maybe that's why I didn't like putting on-off switches on any Apple devices."[3]

You and I will have to determine where we stand on this issue. We can't ignore the question of whether an afterlife exists. Life is short. And eternity is a very long time to be wrong.

Discussion Questions

1. What are your thoughts about Jack Nicholson's assertion that "*everyone* fears death"? Is this true for you? Why or why not?

2. How do you practice the Psalm 90:12 exhortation to "number our days"? In what ways might numbering our days yield "a heart of wisdom," as the psalm implies?

3. What do you think about the statement "If you are born once, you will die twice; if you are born twice, you will die once"? Had you thought about it that way before?

4. In what ways does the "coming judgment" motivate you to live a holy life today?

5. What is the significance of a cultural icon such as Steve Jobs giving God (and the possibility of an eternity spent with him) only a fifty-fifty shot at being real?

The safest road to Hell
is the gradual one—the gentle slope,
soft underfoot, without sudden turnings,
without milestones, without signposts.

−C. S. Lewis

TEN
WHERE GOODNESS GOES TO DIE

The Salvation Army is an international charity movement operating in 120 countries that began in the mid-1800s. Its founder, William Booth, was a British Methodist preacher whose work to help impoverished people began as a mission to convert souls to faith in Jesus Christ. As part of his regular training program for new officers in his organization, Booth taught course work in personal evangelism, just as tens of thousands of churches—Prestonwood included—continue to do today around the globe.

One of his courses was sixteen or seventeen weeks long, and during the concluding class, he reportedly looked at the faces of his officers and said, "I want to apologize that this course took so long. If I could just take you to hell for five minutes, you wouldn't need any of this training."

Later, Booth explained what he meant:

If they could see the flames and smell the smoke and feel the heat and hear the cries of the damned, they would go out to preach what they had seen and heard. They would then preach like dying men to dying people.[1]

I suspect Booth is right; if you or I were to spend any amount of time in hell, the experience likely would motivate us to share the love of Jesus Christ with the boldness and conviction we've never known.

In 2006, author Bill Wiese said he did spend time in hell. Twenty-three minutes, to be exact. His book of the same name—*23 Minutes in Hell*—soared to *The New York Times* bestseller list as millions of readers flocked to one man's account of descending into the place of torment most everyone tries to avoid.

Eight years prior, on November 22, 1998, Wiese says he was awakened at three in the morning, was catapulted from his bed, where his wife was still sleeping, and was thrust into a sort of barren holding cell in an inferno he soon discovered was the literal pit of hell. Fully awake and fully aware of what was happening, he then looked up from the cold floor of the prison cell to find that he was not alone; two thirteen-foot-tall asymmetrical reptilian creatures with sunken eyes, razor-like

Hell ✗

claws, and sharp fins stood before him, "hungry predators staring at their prey."[2]

As the creatures spewed blasphemies against God, Wiese felt the urge to run, to somehow escape—but had no strength to do so. He was a sitting duck—naked and vulnerable and weak. One of the creatures hoisted Wiese into the air, pressed the helpless man to his chest, and ripped his flesh into ribbons that did not bleed. "Death penetrated me," Wiese writes, "but eluded me."[3]

Wiese pleaded for mercy, but there was no mercy to be had. "There is never any peace of mind," he wrote of hell's dark dungeon. "No rest from the torments, the screams, the fear, the thirst, the lack of breath . . . the stench, the heat, the hopelessness, and the isolation from people."[4]

Frankly, I don't know what Mr. Wiese experienced or did not experience that night, although I have no reason to question his account. My point is that on this and all other weighty matters, we can look to God's Word to sort fact from fiction. We can trust God's Word to tell us the truth. And according to God's Word, hell is, as Mr. Wiese attests, *real*.

✗ Real people really will be made silent in darkness (1 Samuel 2:9 NIV).

Real people really will be laid in the lowest pit (Psalm 88:6 NIV).

Real people really will be cast into outer darkness (Matthew 8:12 KJV).

Real people really will be reserved for the day of doom (Job 21:30 NKJV).

Real people really will wail and gnash their teeth (Matthew 13:42 KJV).

217

Real people really will perish (Luke 13:3).

Real people really will spend eternity separated from God (2 Thessalonians 1:9).

Real people really will be paraded before the king of terrors (Job 18:14 NKJV).

Real people really will be cast into everlasting fire (Matthew 18:8 KJV).

Real people really will seek peace but be unable to find it (Ezekiel 7:25 NLT).

Real people really will have their names covered with darkness (Ecclesiastes 6:4).

Real people really will have no rest, day or night (Revelation 14:11).

Real people really will be gathered together and shut up in prison (Isaiah 24:22).

Real people really will have worms feed sweetly on them (Job 24:20).

But this is not what most "real people" believe.

Hesitating on Hell

A recent poll by The Barna Group reveals that while 71 percent of North Americans believe there is a literal place called *hell*, only one-half of 1 percent believes *they will actually go there.*[5] Staggering, isn't it? "Okay, okay," the majority of us evidently would say to God, "if you must have a hell, fine. Just be sure you don't make real people endure it."

Clearly, there is controversy regarding hell, further evidenced by the books being written today by popular authors who deny the literal reality of hell, the idea that hell actually will be populated by real people, and the capacity of a God who describes himself as the author and creator of love to be the one who sends them there. The objections tend to land in one of three categories.

Good People Deserve Better Than Hell

A common objection to believing in a literal hell is that lots and lots of people who don't profess to know and serve Jesus Christ are very kind, very generous, very moral people. Maybe it's a neighbor who comes over every Saturday with homemade blueberry muffins but who happens to be a practicing Muslim. "How can someone bearing blueberry muffins be consigned to an eternal pit of fire?" the argument goes. "Surely God won't send *nice* people to hell. Surely he'll give them a pass."

Uninformed People Deserve Better Than Hell

And then there are people who object to the idea of hell on behalf of those who have yet to hear the gospel. Their argument goes like this: "You mean to tell me that the poor woman sitting in a hut in a nearly deserted village in Zambia who has never heard of Jesus, never owned a Bible, and never set foot in a church—is going to go to *hell*?"

It's a valid question, isn't it? Let's see what the Bible has to say.

Romans 1 makes it abundantly clear that, yes, even old women without Bibles sitting in obscure villages in central Africa are "without excuse" on this issue:

For the wrath of God is revealed from heaven against all ungodliness and unrighteousness of men, who by their unrighteousness suppress the truth. *For what can be known about God is plain to them, because God has shown it to them.* For his invisible attributes, namely, his eternal power and divine nature, have been clearly perceived, ever since the creation of the world, in the things that have been made. So they are without excuse.

For although they knew God, they did not honor him as God or give thanks to him, but they became futile in their thinking, and their foolish hearts were darkened. Claiming to be wise, they became fools, and exchanged the glory of the immortal God for images resembling mortal man and birds and animals and creeping things.

VV. 18–23 (EMPHASIS MINE)

In other words, all men, all women, have the light of conscience, the light of creation, available to them. The heavens, indeed, declare the glory of God. It really is true that if you seek God, you will find him, as Jeremiah 29:13 promises. Take that woman in Zambia, for example: She looks up one evening and notices in the sky a blanket of stars, each glistening like a diamond, and something inside her cries out, "I want to know you, God!"

Where does that awareness come from? It comes, the Bible says, from eternity having been set in our hearts (see Ecclesiastes 3:11).

Hell Seems a Bit Harsh

Still others find the concept of hell so very . . . *harsh*. So *excessive*. So *unfair*. Outraged by the idea that God would exclude people from heaven, they simply modify the gospel to accommodate what they deem is a "better way." They deny hell altogether. Or they suggest that, while it may exist, nobody really *goes* there. Or they put forth the idea that while yes, hell exists, and yes, real people *could* go there, nobody, in fact, *will* go there, because before all is said and done, everyone everywhere will ultimately surrender their lives to Christ. (But they forget that the beautifully free will God has placed inside every human being cannot be forced to bow down to Christ and still exist in a context of love. You tell me: If my love demands that you love me in return, was my part of the equation ever true love?)

There are also some who say that hell as a location is utterly unnecessary, since people either will be saved and spend eternity with Jesus Christ, or else they will reject Christ and face annihilation in the end.

Yes, there is controversy regarding the subject. So much so that even fully devoted Christ-followers who in their heart of hearts concede the reality of hell—as well as the reality that real people will endure it—wrestle with how to then convey these beliefs in their nine-to-five everyday lives. They're almost embarrassed to admit their perspectives on judgment, retribution, and hell, fearing they'll be classified as bigoted, right-wing, Bible-thumping, hellfire-and-brimstone nut jobs.

What ultimately causes them to speak up, if in fact they do speak up, is that pestering little thought that chases through their mind like an itch that refuses to be scratched: *If there were no literal hell where flesh-and-bones people actually could go, then why did Jesus come to earth and die a criminal's death?* Why would God send his beloved Son on a mission of mercy for the purpose of seeking and saving the lost, asking him to suffer and suffocate on a Roman cross, bearing the weight of all sin—past, present, future—on his shoulders, if not to save those people from some significant and undesirable fate?

Why would God allow Jesus to lay it all down to rescue the crown of his creation from a hell that does not exist?

When on the cross Jesus cried out, "My God, my God, why have you forsaken me?" (Matthew 27:46), he bore the infinite weight of mankind's sin; in that moment, he walked the corridors of the condemned and baptized his soul in hell. On the cross he died for you and me so that we could thrive in everlasting life instead of enduring everlasting death. In one author's words, "[At the prospect of hell] we are meant to tremble and feel dread. We are meant to recoil from the reality. Not by denying it, but by fleeing from it into the arms of Jesus, who died to save us from it."[6]

Jesus did not die to save us from a nonexistent hell. He died to save us from our sins, understanding that the ultimate consequence of unconfessed sin is judgment, and that the ultimate judgment we can face is an eternity spent apart from God. He died to save us from *this*.

So we are left with an idea of hell that is utterly incomprehensible—and it is. It is also inconvenient, it is upsetting, and it is morose. It is about as enjoyable to think or talk about as debt, death, or secret sin. But according to the Word of God, it is *incontrovertibly true*. We have received the witness of Christ. We have heard—or at least seen in creation—the good news of the gospel. We have been given clear-cut instructions on how to avoid permanent torment, permanent pain. Therefore, any denial of hell is something we have to read *out* of the Bible, because it simply cannot be found *in* it.

J. C. Ryle wrote,

> If you would ever be a healthy and scriptural Christian, I entreat you to beware of any ministry which does not plainly teach the

reality and eternity of hell. Such a ministry may be soothing and pleasant, but it is far more likely to lull you to sleep than to lead you to Christ or build you up in the faith.

It is impossible to leave out any portion of God's truth without spoiling the whole. That preaching is sadly defective which dwells exclusively on the mercies of God and the joys of heaven, and never sets forth the terrors of the Lord and the miseries of hell. It may be popular but it is not scriptural. It may amuse and gratify, but it will not save. Give me the preaching which keeps back nothing that God has revealed![7]

Charles Hodge, a great theologian who taught at Princeton Seminary during the same era (when Princeton was not merely a university but also a Bible-believing seminary), concurred:

The doctrine of hell is a doctrine to which the heart submits only under the stress of authority. The church believes the doctrine of hell because it must believe it or renounce faith in the Bible and thereby give up all the hopes founded upon its promises.

In other words, if you believe the Bible, you believe in hell. And if you don't believe in hell, then you might as well throw away your Bible and all the other promises that the Scripture provides. For how can we believe in heaven if the Bible teaches that there is both a heaven and a hell, and yet we have determined that it was wrong on the latter point?

To be sure, the entire life, death, resurrection, and mission of Jesus Christ points to the truth of two literal, eternal destinations for our souls. Regardless of our preferences, regardless of our social opinions, regardless of what our friends may say, regardless of how we *wish things were,* the Bible teaches that there is a hell and that unrepentant sinners will spend eternity forever separated from God in this terrible, torturous place.

The Bible's Perspective on Hell

We left chapter 9 after a discussion on what happens to people after they die. We said that for the believer, incredible events transpire—we begin in God's eternal presence, we take up residence with Jesus Christ, and we receive divine commendation for the good that we did while on earth. Similarly, for those who are not followers of Christ, physical death awaits, eternal separation from God begins, and judgment shall be theirs. But it's a far different scenario, as shown by Jesus' warnings against hell. It has been said that 13 percent of the 1,850 verses in the New Testament that are ascribed to Jesus Christ center on this very subject. He spoke of hell twice as much as he spoke of heaven; the topic was important to him and therefore must be important to us.

"If your right eye causes you to sin," Jesus says, "tear it out and throw it away. For it is better that you lose one of your members than that your whole body be thrown into hell" (Matthew 5:29).

Then in Matthew 10:28: "And do not fear those who kill the body but cannot kill the soul. Rather fear him who can destroy both soul and body in hell."

Impressed by the great faith of a military man who asked Jesus to heal his servant, Jesus says:

> Truly, I tell you, with no one in Israel have I found such faith. I tell you, many will come from east and west and recline at table with Abraham, Isaac, and Jacob in the kingdom of heaven, while the sons of the kingdom will be thrown into the outer darkness. In that place there will be weeping and gnashing of teeth.
>
> MATTHEW 8:10–12

Just as a believer's soul is immortal and upon physical death goes to paradise—or the "intermediate heaven" as it is also known—the soul of the unbeliever is immortal and upon physical death goes to the intermediate place known as *Hades,* a term used to mean "a place of torment."

A few examples may help.

In Matthew 11:23, Jesus begins to reject and condemn cities that have not repented after seeing the works that Christ performed. He says, "And you, Capernaum, will you be exalted to heaven? You will be brought down to Hades. For if the mighty works done in you had been done in Sodom, it would have remained until this day."

Following Peter's confession of faith—"You are the Christ, the Son of the living God"—Jesus says, "You are Peter, and on this rock I will build my church, and the gates of hell shall not prevail against it" (Matthew 16:16, 18).

In Revelation 20:11–15, during John's vision from the isle of Patmos, we read this:

> Then I saw a great white throne and him who was seated on it. From his presence earth and sky fled away, and no place was found for them. And I saw the dead, great and small, standing before the throne, and books were opened. Then another book was opened, which is the book of life. And the dead were judged by what was written in the books, according to what they had done. And the sea gave up the dead who were in it, Death and Hades gave up the dead who were in them, and they were judged, each one of them, according to what they had done. Then Death and Hades were thrown into the lake of fire. This is the second death, the lake of fire. And if anyone's name was not found written in the book of life, he was thrown into the lake of fire.

You'll note that in this scenario, according to the text we've just read, unbelievers will be judged according to *what they had done*. And what had they done? They had denied the living Christ. They are people who chose to live apart from God, people who heard the message of grace and rejected it, people who wanted nothing and nobody to control their self-focused lives. In return, God will give them exactly what they have requested all along: an existence devoid of him.

What Is Hell Like?

In Luke 16, a story shows up that wraps detailed description around the actual experience of hell. There is some debate over whether this story told by Jesus is factual or parable; it does appear amid several other parables being delivered, but out of the nearly forty parables Jesus tells in Scripture, this would be the only one in which a person is referred to by name. Whichever it is—parable or real-life situation—the meaning remains the same.

Let's pick things up at verse 19.

> There was a rich man who was clothed in purple and fine linen and who feasted sumptuously every day. And at his gate was laid a poor man named Lazarus, covered with sores, who desired to be fed with what fell from the rich man's table. Moreover, even the dogs came and licked his sores. The poor man died and was carried by the angels to Abraham's side.
>
> The rich man also died and was buried, and in Hades, being in torment, he lifted up his eyes and saw Abraham far off and Lazarus at his side. And he called out, "Father Abraham, have mercy on me, and send Lazarus to dip the end of his finger in water and cool my tongue, for I am in anguish in this flame."
>
> But Abraham said, "Child, remember that you in your lifetime received your good things, and Lazarus in like manner bad things; but now he is comforted here, and you are in anguish.

And besides all this, between us and you a great chasm has been fixed, in order that those who would pass from here to you may not be able, and none may cross from there to us."

And he said, "Then I beg you, father, to send him to my father's house—for I have five brothers—so that he may warn them, lest they also come into this place of torment."

But Abraham said, "They have Moses and the Prophets; let them hear them." And he said, "No, father Abraham, but if someone goes to them from the dead, they will repent."

He said to him, "If they do not hear Moses and the Prophets, neither will they be convinced if someone should rise from the dead."

Luke 16:19–31

Hades is mentioned some eleven times in the New Testament and, as we've established, is translated as *hell*, the intermediate place reserved for those who have died without Christ. "Abraham's side," which we see in verse 22, was considered by Jews to mean heaven, or paradise. Abraham was the most important person of faith in their tradition, and to be placed "at Abraham's side" would have equaled the highest of honors. Lazarus may have been a diseased beggar while on earth, but in eternity, he was of utmost importance.

Hell is hot. We learn several things about hell from this story, first and foremost, that *hell is hot*. The rich man says, "I am in anguish in this flame" (16:24). In Matthew 5:22, Jesus says, "But I say to you that everyone who is angry with his brother will be liable to judgment; whoever insults his brother will be liable to the council; and whoever says, 'You fool!' will be liable to the hell of fire."

Furthermore, the primary New Testament word for eternal damnation is *Gehenna*—literally, the Valley (*Ge*) of Hinnom

227

(*henna*), an actual valley southwest of the city of Jerusalem, which in Jesus' day housed the city dump. In fact, when you visit Jerusalem today, tour guides point out this particular valley outside the city gates, noting that when the dump was operational, it reeked to high heaven of dead bodies and dead animals . . . and it smoldered constantly with fire.

Hell is lonely. Notice in this story of the rich man and Lazarus that upon death, there was a great distance separating the one in heaven and the one in hell. Regardless of how desperately we may crave fellowship, none is allowed for those who descend to hell.

I know crass people are prone to tossing around flippant sentiments to people who enrage them—"I'll see you in hell!"—but the reality is, they will see *nobody* in hell. Or take the immature frat boy who asserts, "Me and my buddies are gonna have a big party when we all get to hell!" Someone really ought to tell him that fun and games aren't all that feasible when you're sitting in solitary confinement in a smelly pit.

Hell is tortuous. Certainly, we see *physical* torment reflected in the Luke 16 passage. The rich man called out from hell for Abraham to have mercy on him, for him to send Lazarus to dip the end of his finger in water and cool his tongue, because he was in utter anguish. And it's understandable: Matthew 13:47–50 describes hell as a fiery furnace where there will be weeping and gnashing of teeth. Seven times in the New Testament, this phrase appears, "weeping and gnashing of teeth"—proof positive that hell is one place you and I don't want to be.

There is also *mental torment* to be found: Abraham told the rich man to "remember" his earthly life—his selfish focus on accumulation instead of service—which assumes the rich man *could* remember. And with all that time on his hands in isolation, I wonder exactly what memories he replayed. Every sermon he'd ever heard, maybe? Every instance while riding on his decked-out donkey when he thought, "There has got to be more to life than this . . ."? Every time he'd tried to answer the ache in his heart with possessions and pleasure and success and sex instead of turning to God?

Did he remember every sunrise declaring God's glory? Every sunset marvelously painted across the sky? The sound of a newborn baby cooing? The scent of rain as it fell?

The rich man is so tormented that he begs Abraham to send Lazarus as an emissary to warn the rich man's brothers about the perils of hell. The Salvation Army's William Booth had it right: Spend five minutes in hell, and you'd have all the motivation you'd need to warn everyone of irrevocable doom.

Hell is a place of "no more." No more comfort, no more fellowship, no more joy—if I were to sum up the nature of hell in two words, it would be these: *no more.*

No more beauty.

No more adventure.

No more laughter.

No more peace.

No more encouragement.

No more enthusiasm.

No more excitement.

No more relief.

But perhaps most devastatingly, in hell there will be no more repentance. This is what I believe all those references to the "gnashing of teeth" point to: In hell, sinners still will be blaming God for their sorry state, but even as repentance would solve their problems, repentance can never be theirs. It is *God's kindness* that leads to repentance, Romans 2:4 says, and we know that in hell, God's kindness is not present, only his wrath against sin.

As an aside, this is why I encourage Christ-followers never to make jokes about hell or even listen to jokes about hell. For some people, "hell" seems like a benign expletive, but I beg to differ. If we truly understood the reality and the tragedy of this awful place of "no more," we would be more circumspect in our use of the word.

Who Goes to Hell?

So then, who actually is given over to this place of torment? With some degree of frequency, I find myself on the receiving end of people's notions about who gets into heaven and who gets relegated to hell. "Well, surely prostitutes and porn producers and child molesters and mass murderers . . . they're all going to hell, right?" they surmise. "And televangelists who rob innocent people of their retirement funds . . ."

You get the idea.

In Matthew 7, Jesus puts an end to the speculation and answers this question once and for all. By way of context, Jesus is concluding what later would be known as the Sermon on the Mount—his longest teaching during his earthly ministry, as well as his most well-known teaching among contemporary Christians, since it contains both the Beatitudes and the Lord's Prayer. His parting words are startling ones to his disciples, and they ought to be startling to us as well. Beginning in verse 21, this is what he says:

> Not everyone who says to me, "Lord, Lord," will enter the king-dom of heaven, but the one who does the will of my Father who is in heaven. On that day many will say to me, "Lord, Lord, did we not prophesy in your name, and cast out demons in your name, and do many mighty works in your name?" And then

will I declare to them, "I never knew you; depart from me, you workers of lawlessness."

vv. 21–23

Sobering passage, isn't it?

Here are people who named the name of God, who worshiped God, who did great works for God's glory. They professed their faith and were religious to the core. *And yet.* And yet Jesus said to them, "I never knew you."

It's not bad people who go to hell; it's *all* people whose hearts don't belong to God. It's not irreligious people who go to hell; it's *all* people who rely on religion instead of relationship and thus forsake ever knowing Christ. The apostle Paul said in 2 Corinthians 13:5, "Examine yourselves, to see whether you are in the faith. Test yourselves." In other words, *be sure that you're saved.*

My friend James MacDonald, who pastors Harvest Bible Chapel outside of Chicago, led a men's meeting at our church recently on the subject of assurance of salvation. "It is the fruit that gives evidence that we belong to Christ," he reminded us. As we do the will of God the Father, we prove our allegiance to Jesus Christ. Certainly, we are not saved by good works; but the faith that saves us prompts us to work. And in the end, we are judged by that work.

Matthew 25 speaks of this final judgment, saying,

> When the Son of Man comes in his glory, and all the angels with him, then he will sit on his glorious throne. Before him will be gathered all the nations, and he will separate people one from another as a shepherd separates the sheep from the goats. And he will place the sheep on his right, but the goats on the left. Then the King will say to those on his right, "Come, you who are blessed by my Father, inherit the kingdom prepared for you

from the foundation of the world." . . . Then he will say to those on his left, "Depart from me, you cursed, into the eternal fire prepared for the devil and his angels."

vv. 31–34, 41

And who are these "cursed" that Christ speaks of? Paul explains, in 2 Thessalonians 1:5–9:

> This is evidence of the righteous judgment of God, that you may be considered worthy of the kingdom of God, for which you are also suffering—since indeed God considers it just to repay with affliction those who afflict you, and to grant relief to you who are afflicted as well as to us, when the Lord Jesus is revealed from heaven with his mighty angels in flaming fire, *inflicting vengeance on those who do not know God and on those who do not obey the gospel of our Lord Jesus.* They will suffer the punishment of eternal destruction, away from the presence of the Lord and from the glory of his might.

Hell was not created for humankind. But for those who reject God and refuse the gift of grace offered by way of his Son, hell is what they will endure.

How to Avoid Eternal Hell

There is, of course, a way to avoid hell, made possible by going God's way, and not ours. He has *lavish love* in store for us, love that can keep us eternally knitted to his side.

Acknowledge the Love of God

One of my favorite passages in all of Scripture is tucked inside a lament, a dirge, a gut-wrenching plea for divine help.

On the heels of taunts and bitterness, desolation and affliction, one man's beloved city utterly in ruins, comes this conclusion, from the Old Testament prophet Jeremiah:

> The steadfast love of the Lord never ceases; his mercies never come to an end; they are new every morning; great is your faithfulness. "The Lord is my portion," says my soul, "therefore I will hope in him."
>
> LAMENTATIONS 3:22–24

God's love is unceasing. It is persistent. It is unfathomable. It is great. And yet there is more to God than his extravagant love.

The same God who loves us with an everlasting love feels anything *but* love for wickedness and sin. The one who has wonderful plans for our lives also maintains a plan of wrath for those who reject him. He is angry with the wicked every day (Psalm 7:11 KJV), which is why it is a fearful thing to fall into the hands of the living God (Hebrews 10:31).

Granted, these are not popular sentiments in this day and age. Somewhere along the way, we as a society shifted from being sinners in the hands of an angry God, as fiery eighteenth-century preacher Jonathan Edwards noted, to relegating God to the hands of angry sinners. We want a kinder, gentler God, one who is a bit easier to control. But regardless of our wishes and whims, God's divinity demands that justice be served for sin. His holiness demands a hell.

But in the same breath, I remind you that according to 2 Peter 3:9, "The Lord . . . is not willing that *any* should perish, but that all should come to repentance" (KJV). Hell is not God's desire for anyone. And based on the profound wisdom of John 3:18, God does not consign a single soul to that terrible place.

"Whoever believes in him [Jesus Christ] is not condemned," that verse says, "but whoever does not believe is condemned already, because he has not believed in the name of the only Son of God."

 God does not "send people to hell"; people choose hell for themselves.

Accept the Love of God

Any person who goes to hell goes there as an intruder. Because for *human beings* to enter a place of wretchedness prepared solely for *the devil and his angels* (see Matthew 25:41), they would have to scale sky-high obstacles left and right. They'd have to climb over the grace and love of God, for starters. They'd have to climb over the faithful prayers of loved ones who intercede on their behalf. They'd have to climb over the witness of their friends. They'd have to climb over a pool of precious blood, poured out by Jesus Christ.

If you happen to be one of those "climbers" today, can I invite you to sit down and rest for a moment? Can I suggest that through the words on this page, God might be calling you to ditch that plan and simply accept his love instead? Can I remind you that there really is a day favorable for salvation, according to 2 Corinthians 6:2, and that that day is *today*?

"Today, if you hear his voice, do not harden your hearts," Hebrews 3:15 exhorts.

That is my straightforward plea to you.

A hard heart leads to fear and protectionism and defensiveness and pain. It leads to the shaking of fists and death without Jesus and an eternity spent far from God. But a tender heart? That is another matter entirely.

A tender heart leads to acceptance and repentance and deep breaths of relief. It leads to second chances and lavish love and unmerited grace and abundant life.

"I am the way, the truth, and the life," John quotes Jesus as saying, in John 14:6. "No one comes to the Father except through me." Or, in other words, "*Everyone* can come to the Father through me." Escape hatch! For one and all! Just imagine: the sum of humankind, hell-bound, condemned in our sin. Bound up without God and hopeless, desperate for some way of escape.

But then . . .

Jesus arrives on the scene and says, "Look! Over here! The path turns . . . you can walk this way!"

We do an about-face and take steps toward heaven, toward a future that is bright and secure.

God poured out 100 percent of his wrath on Christ, so that, believing in him, we never would experience hell. May we receive that truth as the gift that it is. And may we regift it to everyone we know.

Give God's Love Away

In Acts 20:27–28, the apostle Paul reminded the elders of the church in Ephesus that he "did not shrink from declaring to you the whole counsel of God" and encouraged them to follow suit. "Pay careful attention to yourselves and to all the flock, in which the Holy Spirit has made you overseers," he said, "to care for the church of God, which he obtained with his own blood."

It was a message not only to Ephesian elders but also to you and me. One of the ways we care for the church of God, the people of God, is to declare to them the entire counsel of God, even when some of that information is highly uncomfortable to hear.

We speak of hell because it is real. I think you'd agree that it is far crueler *not* to speak of hell to hell-bound people than to speak of it. The apostle Paul said that it is because we know the terror of the Lord that we persuade women and men to be reconciled to him (2 Corinthians 5:11). And so, we ask God for the passion to speak the truth. We ask him for divine appointments, both across the globe and across the street. We ask him for courage to engage in conversations that are timely, gracious, and brave.

Months ago, after reviewing my outline for this chapter, I wept over it. What I write here about the realities and agonies of hell, I do so with trembling fingers. And that is as it should be. Thankfully, Christians have migrated away from the turn-or-burn threats of old; but still, we must find a way to convey with dignity what is real. We should never delight in proclaiming the truth that hell exists and that real people will go there. But just as important, we should never *neglect* to proclaim it.

So be bold. Let God break your heart over this matter, and then let him empower you to reach people who don't yet know the truth.

In the days following one of the world's most devastating tsunamis to date, the one that struck Indonesia in late December 2004, I remember sitting slack-jawed in front of my television—like most of us in this country did—and watching as the death toll multiplied. The earthquake that set off the tsunami was the longest in duration ever recorded on a seismograph, lasting not one second or a few seconds, as do most recorded earthquakes, but between *500 and 600 seconds*.[8] In the end, nearly a quarter-million lives were lost. From *one* earthquake. Nobody could watch the footage without coming away changed; all that devastation and not a single soul had been warned. Or rather, none but a handful had been warned.

While there had long been a tsunami-warning system in place in the Pacific Ocean, where tsunamis are more common, no such system existed in the Indian Ocean. Interestingly, two weeks prior to the Boxing Day tsunami of 2004, a British schoolgirl named Tilly Smith had been taught all about tsunamis—how to spot them, what to do to protect yourself from one, and so forth—by her geography teacher at Danes Hill School.

Tilly and her family were touring Thailand when the earthquake shook. Soon thereafter, she saw the eerie symptoms she and her classmates had just studied—frothy bubbles on the surface of the sea, dramatically receding waters in a phenomenon known as "disappearing sea"—and immediately alerted her parents. They in turn alerted the staff at the beachfront hotel where they were staying, who alerted the more than one hundred other tourists who were playing and sunning on the beach. That beach was one of the few beaches across the region that reported no casualties as a result of the tsunami that did, in fact, overwhelm the area. And it was all because a little blond eleven-year-old chose to speak up when the stakes were high.

Later, Tilly Smith would be awarded a commendation from the UK's largest maritime charity, the Marine Society, which encourages young people to consider a career with the sea services. At a memorial service for the victims, Tilly said, "It wasn't devastation or death that won the day. It was humanity that triumphed. The shining victory of generosity, courage, and love."[9] Listen, as believers in Jesus, we are the warning system people need. The stakes don't get higher than an eternity spent in hell, but as long as we operate as Tilly did—with generosity, courage, and love—you and I can help plant people's feet on a far better path.

Discussion Questions

1. A Barna Group study revealed that while 71 percent of North Americans believe in a literal hell, only *one-half of 1 percent* of them believe they themselves will actually go there. What factors do you think contribute to this disparity?

2. In your own life, how has your understanding of hell evolved?

3. In what ways can you relate to the skeptics who say that "good people" and/or "uninformed people" deserve better than hell?

4. How do you reconcile in your own heart the truth that "God is love" with the truth that God, even though it is not his desire, allows some to perish in hell?

5. It is suggested that Christ-followers are the "warning system" people need in order to avoid eternity in hell. What is involved in being an effective warning system in the lives of those you meet?

Heaven wheels above you,
displaying to you her eternal glories,
and still your eyes are on the ground.

−Dante Alighieri

ELEVEN
PARADISE FOUND

John Milton's 1667 epic poem *Paradise Lost* is considered by most literature buffs to be one of the greatest literary works in the English language and has gone on to influence countless other poets, songwriters, screenplay writers, and authors, including C. S. Lewis and Frank Peretti. The two-pronged plot is fairly straightforward: Lucifer is banished from heaven's paradise, and Adam and Eve are banished from earth's.

Along the way, there is deception and manipulation, lust and lying, sin and outright war. There is rebellion and rhetoric, debate and defeat, nightmarish negligence, chaos and contempt.

Edicts are ignored. Freedom is abused. Knowledge is wasted. Vanity is revered.

And all the while, we as readers find ourselves thinking, *Something feels familiar here.* Indeed, you and I are part of the sin-scarred landscape Milton described hundreds of years ago. Still today, we don't have to look far to see the effects of paradise lost: Our hearts are burdened, our anxieties are weighty, our schedules are busy, and our waistlines are thick. Still there is rebellion. Still there is lust. Still there is chaos. Still there is outright war.

Some days, our only hope is that we know we're not home—eternally home—yet.

Pilgrims Headed to a Better Place

Jonathan Edwards once compared our present life to a pilgrimage, the goal of which is eventual eternal life with God in heaven. He wrote:

> God is the highest good of the reasonable creature, and the enjoyment of him is the only happiness with which our souls can be satisfied. To go to heaven, fully to enjoy God, is infinitely better than the most pleasant accommodations here. Fathers and mothers, husbands, wives, or children, or the company of earthly friends, are but shadows; but the enjoyment of God is the substance. These are but scattered beams; but God is the sun. These are but streams; but God is the fountain. These are but drops; but God is the ocean.
>
> Therefore it becomes us to spend this life only as a journey towards heaven, as it becomes us to make the seeking of our highest end and proper good, the whole work of our lives; to which we should subordinate all other concerns of life. Why

should we labour for, or set our hearts on, anything else, but that which is our proper end, and true happiness?[1]

Studies show that previous generations were far happier than we are today, and that one of the reasons for this phenomenon is that people from those previous generations were quicker to concede the fact that life isn't contained in the here and now. "A heavenly mind is a joyful mind," the great Puritan Richard Baxter once said, and these folks lived that idea out.

One in eight Americans today is being treated for depression of some sort, a percentage that is higher than at any other point in history—and astoundingly, mental-health professionals believe the number of those who should be treated based on symptoms alone is one in *five*.[2] I daresay this is not what Jesus intended when he promised abundance and peace and joy.

What Jesus intended was transcendence, and we see only fragments of it sometimes, fleeting moments we wish we could capture and bottle, the occasions of this temporal life we wish could somehow last forever. A breathtaking sunset, the gaze of a newborn baby, those magical first few moments after your girlfriend has agreed to become your wife—these and a thousand other shadows and beams and streams and drops bring beauty and magnificence to this earthly life by captivating our attention and warming our hearts. Randy Alcorn writes, "Whenever we see beauty in water, wind, flower, animal, man, woman, or child, we see just a sample of what Heaven will be like."[3] Indeed.

We weren't made for this world—this is the crux of my argument. "Our citizenship is in heaven," Philippians 3:20 reminds us; our names are written *there*.[4] We lay up treasures in *that* place, not here, where moths and rust destroy.[5] We eagerly anticipate that endless hallelujah, where paradise finally can be found.

Myths and Misunderstandings

Myths are in plentiful supply regarding the eternal destination known as heaven, and it's time they were exposed for what they are: *patently false*. For example, it's not uncommon in pop culture and in the media to see heaven portrayed as a puffy-clouded, ambiguous, oversentimentalized fog zone where inhabitants are lulled to sleep by a chubby cherub playing some stodgy, unsingable hymn on an out-of-tune seventeenth-century harp.

We ministry leaders sometimes don't make things any better. Take the well-meaning worship leader who, lost in a moment of inspiration, says to the congregation that the singing feels "like a foretaste of heaven." And in silent response, half the crowd has their greatest fear confirmed: *We really will be forced to sing "I Could Sing of Your Love Forever" forever!* While it is true that we will experience ceaseless worship, surely we will enjoy it far more without the distractions of a singer singing off-key, an overly warm worship auditorium, hunger pangs demanding lunch (now!), or any of a thousand other reasons that worship sometimes feels a little south of "heavenly."

We go to a friend's house for dinner and hear him describe heaven as constant reincarnation that leads, ultimately, to Nirvana, where he will be "one with the universe," and we come away baffled, even if a bit amused.

We go to funerals, and we hear that while the person has sadly died, her "spirit lives on in our hearts," and we wonder if that could actually be true.

We go to a sister-in-law's house for the holidays and listen incredulously as she describes heaven as merely a state of consciousness, "something we ourselves create."

We go to the movies— even *kids'* movies—and are told that heaven is actually becoming not one with the universe, but one with *nature*, and that the ultimate satisfaction in the afterlife will be our ability to communicate with the wind, the rain, the ground, and the trees.

We go to the bookstore and pick up the latest bestseller on heaven, figuring that nine hundred thousand discerning readers surely can't be wrong, and find these troubling words:

> Heaven is somewhere you believe in. It's a beautiful place where you can sit on soft clouds and talk to other people who are there. At night you can sit next to the stars which are the brightest of anywhere in the universe.[6]

Come on, now. Sitting on soft clouds next to bright stars in a place that exists only in our imagination? Is this really what we have to look forward to?

It would be easy to brush aside this author's comments with something of a hey-whatever-works-for-you posture, but what you and I believe about heaven *matters*. It matters that we get our facts straight, that we internalize only that which is truth.

Leaders in both business and ministry settings understand the principle that what we determine things to be like in the *future*—our "vision," if you will—powerfully affects how we live in the *present*. Former CEO of General Electric Jack Welch says, "Good business leaders create a vision, articulate the vision, passionately own the vision, and relentlessly drive it to completion."[7] Pastor Charles Swindoll says, "When you have vision, it affects your attitude. Your attitude is optimistic rather than pessimistic."[8]

Regarding our views on heaven in particular, Pastor John Piper writes,

When you know the truth about what happens to you after you die, and you believe it, and you are satisfied with all that God will be for you in the ages to come, that truth makes you free indeed. Free from the short, shallow, suicidal pleasures of sin, and free for the sacrifices of mission and ministry that cause people to give glory to our Father in heaven.[9]

How we look at the future affects how we live today.

So what can we know about heaven, on this side of the proverbial pearly gates?

What We Know About Heaven

Certainly there are unanswered questions about the size and the scope, the greatness and the grandeur, the rules and realities of heaven; in this regard, the Bible operates on something of a need-to-know basis. But not all things are left vague; there is much we can take from Scripture about our eternal dwelling place.

For many years now, I have made a habit of researching vacation and ministry-related travel destinations prior to trip departure, so that upon arrival I have a sense for the top sites to see, the best places to eat, and the secrets that will make my stay smooth. I scour the Internet, checking out the hotel where I'll be staying and looking for interesting entertainment near where I'll be; I consult a few applications on my phone that consolidate menus and ratings of local eateries; and I interrogate friends and family members, trolling for insights and information I didn't already learn online.

Take this most recent trip, for example. I'm writing this chapter from a hotel room on the lovely island of Oahu. I don't come here often; in fact, this is my first time here. I was invited to speak at a pastors' gathering, and I think I forgot to pray about my response. I've *always* wanted to come to Hawaii; how could I say no?

As soon as I agreed to make the trip, I started tapping away on my computer keyboard, hunting for what to eat, what to do, and where to go when one finds oneself in an island state of mind. I did all of this important research, mind you, before I gave my sermon even a passing thought. But so far, it has proven worthwhile. Even before my toes touched sand, I knew the beaches to visit, the rare birds to try to spot, the specific fish to taste—misoyaki butterfish is about the best seafood I've ever had—and where to sign up for surfing lessons, should someone from the little group of colleagues who also insisted on coming be so inclined. Oh, and where to get the best Puka Dog, which is essentially a Hawaiian feast stuffed inside a bun. I can tell you from firsthand experience that the only thing that could make that dog taste better is a baseball game on a sunny afternoon.

I also refreshed myself on the history of Pearl Harbor, knowing we'd make a visit there. Yesterday, as my wife and my colleagues and I walked through the museum and studied the names on the USS *Arizona* memorial just off Ford Island, I was overwhelmed by the reality of the place. I had read about Pearl Harbor. I had seen images of Pearl Harbor. I had even watched the Ben Affleck movie of the same name for the second time just to get an emotional sense for things. And yet actually *being* at Pearl Harbor was far more moving than I could have imagined.

I think this will be true of heaven. We can talk about it, read about it, envision what it will be like. But until we actually get there, we're scratching the surface, at best.

UNSEEN

The Second Heaven and the Eternal Heaven

From the first verse in Scripture, we find this idea of heaven taking shape. In Genesis 1:1, we read: "In the beginning, God created the heavens and the earth." In Psalm 8:3, the psalmist writes: "When I look at your heavens, the work of your fingers, the moon and the stars, which you have set in place . . ."

We see this term *heaven* being used to describe the sky that surrounds the earth in Psalm 104:12: "Beside them the birds of the heavens dwell; they sing among the branches."

At Jesus' baptism in Matthew 3:16, we read: "And when Jesus was baptized, immediately he went up from the water, and behold, the heavens were opened to him, and he saw the Spirit of God descending like a dove and coming to rest on him."

Peter once saw this vision: "[He] saw the heavens opened and something like a great sheet descending, being let down by its four corners upon the earth" (Acts 10:11).

So there is this type of heaven—referring to the sky that surrounds the earth, to outer space, to the sun and the moon and the stars; and then there is the other heaven, our eventual dwelling place, the place where we will live eternally with God.

Revelation 21:1 says there will be "a new heaven and a new earth, for the first heaven and the first earth had passed away," a topic we'll explore more fully in chapter 12. But to clarify John's point here in Revelation, the earth and its atmosphere are considered the "first heaven," and it will someday cease to exist. The temporary place where believers go between when they die and Christ returns to earth for his church is considered the "second heaven." Renowned author on the subject of heaven Randy Alcorn refers to this location as the "present heaven" and writes this:

This state is one of rest and peace with God, and is presumably disembodied since it precedes resurrection as a spirit-animated body (see 1 Corinthians 15:44). But no further details of it are given. When a Christian dies, he or she enters into what theologians call the intermediate state, a transitional period between our past lives on Earth and our future resurrection to life on the New Earth. Usually when we refer to "heaven," we mean the place that Christians go when they die.

Though it will be a wonderful place, the intermediate heaven is not the place we are made for—the place God promises to refashion for us to live in forever. God's children are destined for life as resurrected beings on a resurrected Earth. We must not lose sight of our true destination. If we do, we'll be confused and disoriented in our thinking about where, and in what form, we will spend eternity.[10]

It is critical to note that the "present heaven" or "second heaven" is *not* purgatory. In fact, there is no scriptural evidence to support the idea that a soul goes to a holding ground to be purified from sin until that person is somehow "fit" for heaven.

The intermediate state also is not what some call "soul sleep," or the idea that when we die, we slip into a state of unconscious existence or soulish annihilation. The Bible is clear that when we die, we enter the presence of Christ (in the "second heaven") and await our new bodies, and that we will be totally *alive* and *aware* of what is taking place around us.[11]

Our final home will be the new earth, or what some refer to as the "third heaven." The home you and I so desperately long for shows up not merely as life after death, but "life *after* life after death," to quote Bishop N. T. Wright.[12] This ultimate victory, this eternal resurrection life, is the fundamental building block of the hope of the Christian church.

So upon the closure of this present age, when the entire universe surrounding us—the heavens and earth and atmosphere—are no more, God will usher in a new heaven, a new earth, a brand-new reality in which we will live. The prophet Isaiah prophesied this very fact: "For behold, I create new heavens and a new earth, and the former things shall not be remembered or come into mind" (65:17). *Isaiah*

Frequently I am asked whether we will remember all that came before once we enter the reality of this new heaven and new earth. Indeed, at face value, the Isaiah verse cited above seems to indicate that we'll have no recollection of what happened while we experienced earthly life. As with so many aspects of eternity, God doesn't answer this issue forthrightly in his Word; but just as one could find credible substantiation for the idea that we won't have memory of this present life, one can support biblically the other side of the argument as well. For example, Revelation 6 speaks of martyrs in heaven who remember clearly their suffering and their death. In various places in Scripture, we learn that those in heaven receive perfect comfort; if there were no memories of painful experiences, why would such comfort be necessary?

Also, in Matthew 24:35, Jesus says that while heaven and earth indeed will pass away, "my words will not pass away." Some things certainly will live on. To this point, a plausible scenario involves not a wholesale replacement of this heaven and earth, but rather a *renewal*. One Bible commentator notes that the word for *new* in Revelation 21:1–2 means "emphasizing more qualitative newness than temporal newness."[13] That is, the word denotes the quality of the universe as renewed and pristine.

But this still leaves unanswered the question regarding how the old heaven and earth relate to the new heaven and earth.

While myriad experts have weighed in throughout the ages, wide diversity of thought still remains. Let me give you a couple of varying viewpoints.

Respected commentator G. K. Beale likens the old creation/new creation dynamic to that of Jesus' pre- and post-resurrection body. Even following the resurrection, Jesus maintained similar bodily features, crucifixion scars, and so forth:

> Despite the discontinuities, the new cosmos will be an identifiable counterpart to the old cosmos and a renewal of it, just as the body will be raised without losing its former identity . . . the new creation follows the pattern of Christ's resurrection.[14]

Writers of the *Dictionary for Theological Interpretation of the Bible* take the opposing side: "Christ says, 'Behold, I make all things new,'" the line of thinking goes, "not 'Behold, I make a new set of things.'"[15] More on this in chapter 12.

Let's move to an issue we *can* be sure of—namely, how the "passing away" will occur. Second Peter 3:7 says, "By the same word [the word of God, that formed the world during the Genesis account] the heavens and earth that now exist"—he is speaking here of our contemporary world—"are stored up for fire, being kept until the day of judgment and destruction of the ungodly."

In essence, then, the atoms that form every aspect of this current existence are filled with and fueled by fire. The keyboard I'm typing on is filled with fire. The chair I'm sitting on is filled with fire. The car I drive is filled with fire. The bed I sleep on is filled with fire. The clothing I wear, the food I eat, the table where I eat it: fire, fire, fire. And the same is true for you. Everything in our present reality is filled with and fueled by fire. *All* of life is a partially controlled chemical fire, which helps 2 Peter 3:10 begin to make sense. "But the day of the Lord will come like a thief," it says, "and then the heavens will pass away with a roar, and the heavenly bodies will be burned up and dissolved, and the earth and the works that are done on it will be exposed."

People mistakenly believe that the world began with a Big Bang; in reality, with a big bang is how it will *end*, as fire burns up and dissolves all we see.

Peter continues his train of thought:

> Since all these things are thus to be dissolved, what sort of people ought you to be in lives of holiness and godliness, waiting for and hastening the coming of the day of God, because of which the heavens will be set on fire and dissolved, and the heavenly bodies will melt as they burn! But according to his promise we are waiting for new heavens and a new earth in which righteousness dwells.
>
> 2 PETER 3:11–13

A new heaven and a new earth are forthcoming, my friend. We do well to hasten that day, defining our lives by that which is eternal instead of all that will be set on fire and ultimately dissolved.

In 2 Peter 3:5–7, the apostle explains what will happen on the last day of *this* heaven and *this* earth's existence. He writes:

> The heavens existed long ago, and the earth was formed out of water and through water by the word of God, and . . . by means of these the world that then existed was deluged with water and perished. *But by the same word the heavens and earth that now exist are stored up for fire, being kept until the day of judgment and destruction of the ungodly.*[16]

That last line is key: Unlike the heavens that one day will be destroyed, the heaven of God's permanent dwelling is imperishable, unchangeable, and established not for loss, but for *life*.[17] Indeed, heaven is *real*. It is *good*. And it is available to *all* people today.

Heaven Is Real

The Word of God lays out a handful of important themes about heaven, the first of which is that *heaven is real*. Heaven is *not* a figment of wishful thinking, as some skeptics would have us believe. Heaven, in fact, is real. (Or "for real," as child author Colton Burpo attests.) Heaven is a real place, a real destination, a real reality, according to Christ. And those of us who have surrendered our lives to Christ will live there with real bodies in a real existence, enjoying real fellowship with Jesus Christ. We will not spend eternity as disembodied spirits floating around in the universe somewhere; we will exist in real forms and figures, set free from all the ravages of sin. We will know neither death nor destruction, for we will have been made alive by the resurrection of Christ. Really.

Jesus said to his disciples in John 14:1–4:

> Let not your hearts be troubled. Believe in God; believe also in me. In my Father's house are many rooms. If it were not so, would I have told you that I go to prepare a place for you? And if I go and prepare a place for you, I will come again and take you to myself, that where I am there you may be also. And you know the way to where I am going.

Now, the context here is important, so let me give you the quick version before we move on. Jesus had been in the upper room with his disciples, washing their feet, distributing wine and bread at the first Lord's Supper, knowing that too soon, he would face the cross. He was distraught in spirit as he warned his disciples of his impending departure from them.

It's against this backdrop that he explained their eternal "place." And not surprisingly, they didn't get it. The text says that they were too busy fighting over who was going to have prominence and position in the government that Jesus eventually would set up to really hear what he was saying to them. But they did catch the part about his "departing" from them; this part got their attention, no doubt. And so he tried to reassure them.

Yes, Jesus would leave his disciples. Yes, he would suffer death on a cross. But after he was resurrected, after he ascended to heaven, he would return for them. He will return for us. He will come back to escort us to the "better country," as Hebrews 11:16 calls it, the "heavenly one" called home.

Heaven Is Good

Next, we see in Scripture that *heaven is supremely good.*

I think you'd agree that based on Scripture there is no greater track record in existence than that of Almighty God. His batting average is a thousand, every day, in every way. His innovativeness is unparalleled, his creativity is unmatched, his wisdom in decision-making is second to none. He is good, he is great, he is perfect. He is the Creator of the cosmos and the Creator of every good thing. He can do nothing but that which is awesome and grand. And it is this God who for the past two thousand years has been preparing a place *just for you.*

Yes, we will feel at home there. Yes, we'll be welcomed with open arms there. Yes, we'll be loved unconditionally there. Yes, we'll have a permanent home there. Yes, we'll wear comfortable clothing there—for this, I'm especially grateful. Yes, we'll laugh uproariously there. Yes, we will find ultimate fulfillment there, knowing all things "even as [we] have been fully known" (1 Corinthians 13:12).

Yes, to answer the question I get most often about heaven, we *will* see our loved ones there.[18] This is especially consoling to me. If there was any hope to be had on the heels of laying my father to rest way too early in his life, it was on the spiritual side. When Dad's life was still hanging in the balance, I knew enough of God, enough of the Bible's principles and promises, to know that if my father didn't live through the experience, he'd enter the presence of Jesus, where he would stay for all eternity.

My dad had trusted Christ with his life as a boy and had raised us Grahams to love and serve God as well. He wasn't the type of guy who was involved in church leadership as an elder or deacon or the like. But he led our family to church every Sunday, joyfully, with a grateful heart. Dad had only an eighth-grade education; he wasn't a Bible scholar by any stretch of the imagination. But he was an ethical man, a man of integrity, a man who always did the right thing. Most important, he had surrendered himself to Jesus; I knew we'd be reunited in absolute splendor someday.

Indeed, in *all* regards, heaven will defy our wildest imagination. It will overwhelm us with its perfection and peace. Allow me to prove my point: In 1 Corinthians 2:9–10, Paul writes, "'No eye has seen, nor ear heard, nor the heart of man imagined, what God has prepared for those who love him'—these things God has revealed to us through the Spirit."

It's as if Paul has no language that will do justice to our permanent home and has settled for "nor the heart of man imagined." It will be better than all we have seen thus far. It will be better than all we have heard. It will be better than all we could imagine. Heaven will be better than all this. And this makes sense, doesn't it? When the infinitely Good Shepherd who takes impeccable care of his sheep and constantly has their best interests in mind promises to prepare a place for us, we can rest assured that it will be the fulfillment of our truest, deepest desires. This is the purpose for which we were created, after all, to enjoy fellowship forever with the Lord Jesus.

We Can Choose Heaven Now

If there is another theme regarding heaven I glean from God's Word, it's this profound and yet simple one: *You and I can go there too.*

I find that refreshing.

In the midst of a life that is sometimes disappointing, often disillusioning, *always* less than perfect, you and I actually can make choices that position us for eternal bliss.

But did I mention there's a catch?

In John 14, one of the disciples—Thomas—asked, "Lord, we do not know where you are going. How can we know the way?" (v. 5).

You'll recall that Jesus had just told his most faithful followers that he was going to prepare a place for them and that they "know the way" to where he was going (v. 4). Thomas (*doubting* Thomas) wanted to be sure his GPS was set right.

"Lord, we do not know where you are going," he said. I can almost sense the terror in his voice. *What if Jesus bolts, and we're left here with nothing—no hope, no direction, no future?*

Jesus quickly addresses his concern in verse 6: "Jesus said to him, 'I am the way, and the truth, and the life. No one comes to the Father except through me.'"

In other words,

John 14:6

No one can make the ascent without [me], for [I am the] way, [the] truth, [the] life, [the] strength, [the] confidence, [the] reward. [I am] the way that receives [you], the truth that strengthens [you], the life that invigorates [you].[19]

AMBROSE, FOURTH-CENTURY BISHOP OF MILAN

In other words,

Follow thou me. I am the way and the truth and the life. Without the way there is no going; without the truth there is no knowing; without the life there is no living. I am the way which thou must follow; the truth which thou must believe; the life for which thou must hope. I am the inviolable way; the infallible truth, the never-ending life. I am the straightest way; the sovereign truth; life true, life blessed, life uncreated.[20]

THOMAS À KEMPIS, FIFTEENTH-CENTURY MONK
AND RENOWNED AUTHOR, *THE IMITATION OF CHRIST*

In other words,

If you want this place called heaven, I'm the guy you need.

JESUS

I know, I know, this line of thinking doesn't exactly square with popular culture these days, for the simple reason that people want more than one way. They want the way called *good works,* or the way called *meditation,* or the way called *nature,* or the way called *self-help.* It's all just a big mountain anyway, right? With multiple ways to the top? As long as we all desire heaven, who really cares how we get there?

Jesus does. He happens to *really* care. Essentially he says, "It is not a given that your desire alone will get you into heaven. You've got to enter by the narrow road."

I love how the King James Version renders Luke 16:16: "The law and the prophets were until John: since that time the kingdom of God is preached, and every man presseth into it." Isn't that rich imagery: *pressing in* to the kingdom of God?

We press in to Jesus.

We press in to our faith.

We press in to the destiny that is ours by following the Way.

Those of us who actually want what Christ is offering do these things anyway. Ultimately, not everyone will go to heaven because not everyone truly wants that which heaven is all about.

In John 3:19, Jesus refers to himself as light—*the* Light, to be clear. "This is the judgment," John writes: "the light has come into the world, and people loved the darkness rather than the light because their works were evil." John knew what we are sometimes slow to admit: Coming into the light is humbling and hard. Standing before the holy God of the universe, who knows the nuances of our inadequacy, rebellion, and sin without our having to say a single word, is not most people's idea of fun. By nature, we hate the light. We would much rather stay in the dark.

So, left with no other choice, God says, "If you don't want to be with me, you won't be." No one goes kicking and screaming into heaven; only those who actually wish to be there will, in fact, be there.

For Those Who Want to Come Home

If you are one who wants to be in heaven, and if you are desirous of walking Jesus' path in order to get there, then you can take steps toward home today.

Scripture provides us a simple ABCD framework: First, we *admit* our sin before God; second, we *believe* on the Lord Jesus Christ; next, we *confess* him as both Savior and King; and finally, we *demonstrate* our faith by openly following him for the rest of our days.

Admit

To admit our sin is simply to acknowledge the truths of Romans in our fragile and failing hearts. All really have sinned and come short of the glory of God (Romans 3:23). There really is none righteous, not even one (Romans 3:10). The wages of our sin really is death (Romans 6:23).

There are things we've done that we shouldn't have done, things we haven't done that we probably should have. In short, this is sin. Telling God that we see it as such is the first step toward coming home to him.

Believe

"You believe in God," Jesus said in John 14:1. "Believe also in me."

We "believe in the Lord Jesus" by assenting to his purity and perfection, his status as Son of God, fully God and fully man. And also by assenting to the fact that Jesus clothed himself in human flesh, came to this world, died on the cross as payment for our sin, rose from the grave, and lives even now, that we might have eternal life. But with that said, this assent is more than intellectual; even the devil can quote the Bible and acknowledge the truth of its claims. Rather, our belief is a wholesale trust in these claims. It is belief down to our toes.

Confess

Next, to secure an eternity spent with Jesus, we confess him as Savior and King. Romans 10:9 says, "If you confess with your mouth that Jesus is Lord and believe in your heart that God raised him from the dead, you will be saved." In Matthew 10:32, Jesus says, "Whosoever therefore shall confess me before men, him will I confess also before my Father which is in heaven" (KJV).

Demonstrate

Finally, we demonstrate our faith in Christ by openly following him, in the power of his Spirit, all our days.

Now, to be clear, while the first three elements—admit, believe, confess—are *required for* salvation, this fourth one is a *by-product of* salvation. We admit our need, we place our belief in Christ, we confess him before women and men, and then because of the transformation that takes place in our lives, we simply can't help but demonstrate the change we've undergone. In essence, *this* is how we come home.

With a fair amount of frequency, I come across people throughout the Dallas-Fort Worth area who are homeless, and when I look into their eyes, I typically see emptiness there. On street corners, underneath overpasses, crouched behind restaurants looking for food—regardless of where I find them, I see in their gaze the unmistakable sense that they just wish they could go home.

In Luke 15:11–32, Jesus tells the stunning story of a homeless man who did just that. Known as the "prodigal son," the young man demanded his share of his father's inheritance while his father was still alive. In a streak of ill-placed independence, he fled his father's house, squandered every penny of his wealth on wild living, and wound up eating pig slop because he couldn't afford a proper meal.

If I'd come across that man at this point in his life, I imagine I would have found emptiness in his eyes too.

But his story doesn't end there. For the text says that eventually he "came to himself" (Luke 15:17) and headed home.

He'd rehearsed his excuses, his apologies, his humble requests, and yet all he found upon returning was an open embrace, new clothes, new shoes, and unabashed *blessing* from the dad he had wronged.

We can get wrapped up in frameworks and formulas, ticking off ABCD to-do's, but at the core of Jesus' "requirements" for us is the painfully simple idea of *turning our hearts and our feet toward home.*

Heaven Starts Here

A final thought, as it relates to the usefulness of this emphasis on the destination and motivation of heaven. In the next chapter, we'll look more closely at what life will be like in our eternal dwelling place, but to whet your appetite, let me sum up that new reality by saying that you and I and everyone else who surrenders their life to Jesus Christ is headed for a place defined by a series of wonderful "no mores." We saw in chapter 9 that hell is a place of *no more*: no more beauty, no more fellowship, no more laughter, no more peace. Heaven is the opposite of all that. There, we will find the absence not of beauty, but of pain: no more suffering, no more mourning, no more crying, and no more death. No more heartache, no more hardship, no more destruction, no more grief (Revelation 21:4).

I read a list like that and can't help but be reminded that you and I, as citizens of heaven, can begin heavenly living *now*. In his book *After You Believe*, N. T. Wright says, "God's future is arriving in the present, in the person and work of Jesus, and you can practice, right now, the habits of life that will find their goal in that coming future."[21] In other words, the blessings of the Beatitudes Jesus cites in Matthew 5 can actually find their beginnings today, right now, through us.

Jesus promises eternal blessing for those who are at the end of their rope; when there is less of them, there is more of God, more of his divine rule.

He promises eternal blessing for those who have lost what is most dear to them; only then can they be embraced by the One most dear to them.

He promises eternal blessing for those who have learned to be content with who they are, no more and no less; that's the moment when they find themselves proud owners of everything that can't be bought.

He promises eternal blessing for those who have worked up a good appetite for God, knowing he's the best meal they'll ever eat.

He promises eternal blessing for those who care for others, knowing it's then that we ourselves receive care.

He promises eternal blessing for those who get their minds and hearts put right, so that they are able to see God in the world.

He promises eternal blessing for those who show people how to cooperate instead of how to compete and fight; that's when those people are able to discover who they really are, as well as their place in God's family.

He promises eternal blessing for those who take a strong stand for Jesus Christ; persecution always drives a person deeper into God's kingdom.[22]

Yes, these blessings will be fully realized in heaven's timeless realm, but you and I can actually serve as conduits to their being established now. We can help encourage those who are at the end of their rope. We can comfort those who have lost something dear to them. We can prompt people toward contentment, toward real fulfillment in Christ. We can teach our children to care for others, and our wayward colleagues to make righteousness their chief pursuit. We can be peacemakers in our corner of the world, giving away the grace we so gratefully received from God. We can speak up when the subject is Jesus, instead of sheepishly standing down.

Perhaps you've heard it said that some believers are so heavenly minded they are of no earthly good, but nothing could be further from the truth. Heaven-minded Christ-followers in fact do the *most* good, effecting the most impactful and necessary change.

Prolific author and past president of the Moody Bible Institute Joseph Stowell once reflected on the specific ways in which heaven-mindedness motivates us to greater earthly living:

Our *posture toward God improves* because we're no longer focused on the temporal. Our *perspective on possessions shifts*, because we're no longer self-absorbed. Our *perception of people assumes the best*, because our heart expands for the lonely, the broken, the abused, the lost. Our *perspective on pain adjusts* to accommodate suffering as part of our spiritual growth. The *pleasures of this earth are sweeter*, because we recognize them as a foretaste of what is to come. And our *pursuit of purity expands*, as we determine to live in holiness.[23]

The dream of heaven can be ours here and now. We prepare for an "eternal weight of glory beyond all comparison," 2 Corinthians 4:17–18 says, "as we look not to the things that are seen but to the things that are unseen. For the things that are seen are transient, but the things that are unseen are eternal." As we embrace the eternal reality that Jesus promised us and purchased for us, we become more secure in our future "uplook"—and immensely more Christlike in our outlook today.

Discussion Questions

1. What troubling situation in your present life demonstrates the idea that paradise, at least for now, has been lost?

2. On the flip side of the coin, describe a few moments of transcendence you have experienced along the way, fragments of beauty you wish you could capture and bottle. How do these flickers of grandeur inject hope into our imperfect reality?

3. What does it look like for a person to live from the understanding that "we weren't made for this world"?

4. What reality of heaven do you most crave today?

5. What lingering questions do you have about what heaven will be like?

For everyone who has been born of God overcomes the world.

—1 John 5:4

TWELVE
WE WIN

The 1997 film *Life Is Beautiful* tells the story of a Jewish-Italian man, his Italian wife, and their charming five-year-old son, all of whom are seized by Nazis in 1945, taken by train to a concentration camp, and made to withstand the horrors of internment until the war at last comes to an end. While in the camp, the father, Guido, crafts an intricate lie to explain to his young son, Giosuè, the real-life suffering unfolding all around them. Shortly after their arrival, as a German guard barks out restrictions to Guido, Giosuè, and their eighty or so bunkmates who are relegated to one of the camp's barracks, the father volunteers to translate into Italian what the guard is saying to the group, even though he doesn't speak a lick of German. Instead of relaying the real rules being delivered, Guido explains to the men—and to his son—that this whole experience is actually a great, big game that starts now, and that the winner of the game will win a tank. At this news, Giosuè's eyes light up. A tank! He *loves* tanks. Suddenly, he's all ears, as his father lays out the rules to the game.

There's a point system, the father continues, and the first person to reach a thousand points wins. But just as points can be given for good behavior, they can be taken away for whining about the conditions or complaining about being hungry or saying you want your mommy. He says that the reason the Nazi guards are so mean and loud is because they really, really want the tank for themselves. And then he tells the group not to even *think* about asking for a lollipop, because the guards get to play the role of the cranky guys who take all the candy for themselves.

Later, as children begin disappearing—in reality, because they are killed by Nazi guards—Guido tells his son it's because they're simply hiding; after all, quiet boys who sneakily hide from the officials get lots and lots of extra points. When the misery, sickness, and death begin to take a toll on young Giosuè and he begs his father to let him drop out of the "game," Guido encourages his son with a smile and convinces his boy that they are in the lead for the tank and need to wait only a short while before everything will be over and they can finally go home.

As you watch the movie, you can't help but be heartened by the father's deep care for his son and by the extravagant measures he is willing to take to let his son know that everything will be okay in the end. The son was going to see things and hear things and smell things and experience things that would be devastating to his fragile heart, but the father was aware of something the young boy couldn't yet know: Hard things are easier to stomach when eventual victory is assured.

In the last chapter, we looked at the state of bliss known as heaven that awaits us and explored the idea that once you know your future destiny, present dilemmas fit inside a larger context and somehow are easier to take. Even the worst circumstances get reframed when viewed in light of eternal happiness, security, and peace. Truly, when you and I choose to live from victory, we tap into a reservoir of hope the rest of the world doesn't know exists. We can endure humbling tragedy and still keep our heads on straight, for the sole reason that we know this life isn't all there is.

And we do *know* this to be true. In the final two chapters of the book of Revelation, which also are the final two chapters of the Bible, we find detailed and dramatic imagery on the subject of eternal life with God, given so that you and I may be sure of what our future holds. Our victory in Christ is secure. There, the apostle John is given a spectacular vision of heaven, the ability to see what previously had been unseen. And the facts that he relays ought to make every believer rejoice.

We looked at part of Revelation 21 earlier, but let me give you a fuller portion here. John writes:

> Then I saw a new heaven and a new earth, for the first heaven and the first earth had passed away, and the sea was no more. And I saw the holy city, new Jerusalem, coming down out of heaven

from God, prepared as a bride adorned for her husband. And I heard a loud voice from the throne saying, "Behold, the dwelling place of God is with man. He will dwell with them, and they will be his people, and God himself will be with them as their God. He will wipe away every tear from their eyes, and death shall be no more, neither shall there be mourning, nor crying, nor pain anymore, for the former things have passed away."

And he who was seated on the throne said, "Behold, I am making all things new." Also he said, "Write this down, for these words are trustworthy and true."

vv. 1–5

These words, the angel tells John, are not mere speculations of men, but rather *reliable truth from God*. So what exactly is true about the victorious reality that awaits us? At least seven things.

We Will Dwell Forever With God

The apostle Peter once wrote that the entire reason Jesus Christ suffered for our sins was *so that he might bring us to God* (see 1 Peter 3:18). And heaven—eternal heaven, the "third heaven," our final dwelling place—is where this will occur. Heaven will be wonderful not because of what we will have or what we will do, who we will be reunited with or the rewards we'll receive, but because God will be there, *Jesus* will be there, and his presence will be *known*. "And if I go and prepare a place for you, I will come again and will take you to myself," John 14:3 says, *"that where I am you may be also,"*[1] remember?

And it is this last point that is actually most important, for if a person does not first and foremost long to be with Christ, then he or she has no business going to heaven. Attaining heaven is not the same as attaining a merit badge or a reward for good deeds—these deeds are merely the outworking of Christ's activity in our lives. No, heaven is about fellowship, about intimacy, about being knit together with our Lord. Any other motivation for being there is something south of right.

For this reason, Colossians 3:2 (KJV) speaks of us as believers having "set [our] affection on things above, not on things on the earth." Isn't that beautiful language? More than that, it's a goal that can be ours. When you and I set our affections this way—longing to be with Jesus face-to-face, arm-in-arm, side-by-side—we build a different set of desires, desires that lead us nearer to, not farther from, Christ. We become like Paul, who said in Philippians 1:23, "My desire is to depart and be with Christ, for that is far better."

"Seek first the kingdom of God and his righteousness," Jesus tells us in Matthew 6:33. "Lay up for yourselves treasures in heaven. . . . For where your treasure is, there your heart will be also" (Matthew 6:20–21). Truly, what greater treasure exists than a never-ending encounter with Jesus Christ?

And so we strain against this fallen world while soaring on all the beauty we can find, but in the back of our minds, in the depth of our souls, we long for heaven each day.

I did some online research for this chapter and came across people's general beliefs about heaven. For the most part, believers and unbelievers alike weren't antagonistic toward the idea of a blissful, eternal dwelling place; if anything, they were quick to put in requests for what it should include: the best golf courses, the best shopping malls, the best restaurants, the best fishing, the best skiing, the best boating, the best sex. Really. I kid you not. Suffice it to say, I came away from my research a little dejected.

But it brought to mind an insightful question John Piper once posed: "If you could have heaven," he asked, "with no sickness, and with all the friends you ever had on earth, and all the food you ever liked, and all the leisure activities you ever enjoyed, and all the natural beauties you ever saw, all the physical pleasures you ever tasted, and no human conflict or any natural disasters, could you be satisfied with heaven, if Christ were not there?"[2]

If you could have it all, just as you want it, and yet Jesus was nowhere to be found, would you still want it all?

It's a good question to ask, a question that strikes at the heart of our eternal motivations.

Martin Luther is quoted as saying, "I'd rather be in hell with Christ than in heaven without him," which pretty much tells us where he stands. But I'm curious: Where do *you* stand? Pearly gates, streets of gold, premier golf courses, a butler ready to comply with your every demand?

Or Jesus.

Which one is it, for you?

Sinful people, invited by our holy God, to dwell with him in peace forever.

Amazing grace indeed.

I've often thought about the first few eye-opening moments[3] we'll spend in heaven, in this place where we'll be rubbing shoulders interminably with none other than Jesus Christ. No longer will we be squinting in a fog, peering through a mist, like we do down here on earth. Finally we will see things *clearly*, as they truly are.[4] And I think the first thing we'll see clearly is what life always was about. My bet is that for the vast majority of people—myself included—the first four words uttered in heaven will be, "Ooooh! I get it!" What we'll finally "get" is that the sum of life was never about making a name for ourselves, building a healthy portfolio, or acquiring more stuff; it was always about dwelling with God. The first question of the Westminster Shorter Catechism reflects on this very idea: "What is the chief end of man?" it asks. "Man's chief end is to glorify God," says the answer, "and to enjoy him forever."

There's a lot of truth to those words.

As we saw in the last chapter, heaven will be grand not because of what it will do for us, but simply because *God is there*. The hope of heaven is God's presence; *this* is the greatest source of pleasure we will know.

Throughout redemptive history, we see God acting on his deep desire to "be with" his people. In the garden, God walked with Adam and Eve in the cool of the day (Genesis 3:8). He chose to *dwell* with them.

Of Moses' relationship with God, the Bible says they spoke "face to face, as a man speaks to his friend" (Exodus 33:11). He chose to dwell with him.

God visited members of the twelve tribes of Israel in a tabernacle; they would pitch their tents so that they faced the tabernacle,[5] where God's glory would fill the place. He chose to *dwell* with them.

Speaking of Jesus experiencing the incarnation—the God-man, come to earth—John 1:14 says, "And the Word became flesh and dwelt among us, and we have seen his glory, glory as of the only Son from the Father, full of grace and truth." Throughout Jesus' earthly ministry, God chose to *dwell* with his people through his Son.

Ever since the arrival of the Holy Spirit in the hearts and lives of believers, we are the temple of God; we are where God now resides.[6]

But in the new reality, we will actually *dwell with God*—in person, in reality, face-to-face. We will walk with God; we will talk with God; we will see him for who he is.

So what will it be like to "dwell with God"? In other words, what will we *do* all day? I find in Scripture at least six activities that will occupy us—mind, heart, body, and soul.

We Will Worship God

Based on clear-cut evidence in God's Word, you and I are going to sing and praise God in heaven. Revelation 19:6–10 gives us a glimpse into this worshipful place:

> Then I heard what seemed to be the voice of a great multitude, like the roar of many waters and like the sound of mighty peals of thunder, crying out, "Hallelujah! For the Lord our God the Almighty reigns. Let us rejoice and exult and give him the glory, for the marriage of the Lamb has come, and his Bride has made herself ready; it was granted her to clothe herself with fine linen, bright and pure"—for the fine linen is the righteous deeds of the saints.

We will worship the one, true God—passionately, consistently, in an undistracted manner.

We Will Learn About God

In 1 Corinthians 13:12, the apostle Paul writes, "For now we see in a mirror dimly, but then face to face. Now I know in part; then I shall know fully, even as I have been fully known." And while certainly he did not mean that someday we will know *everything*—only God himself is omniscient; this is true today and will be true in eternity as well—it thrills me to know that

I am invited to continue learning about God himself forever. Regarding this same verse, theologian Wayne Grudem writes, "Rightly translated, [1 Corinthians 13:12] simply says that we will know in a fuller or more intensive way, 'even as we have been known,' that is, without any error or misconceptions in our knowledge."[7]

We Will Work

You and I won't *have* to work in heaven; we will *want* to work in heaven. Since the new heaven and new earth essentially are Eden fulfilled and expanded, we can expect to find work—or service to God—to be a pleasing means of contribution, just as Adam and Eve did, back in the garden. In other words, labor will be a joy.[8]

Furthermore, we can expect that the work we have done to God's glory while here on earth will be preserved and brought into eternity. Revelation 21:24–26 says, "The kings of the earth will bring their glory" into the New Jerusalem, which is an allusion to Isaiah 60, which says, "The wealth of the nations shall come to you" (the New Jerusalem). Randy Alcorn connects the idea of work to dominion, culture, art, and creative productivity. He notes,

> Some people expect the New Earth to be a return to Eden, with no technology or the accomplishments of civilization. But that doesn't fit the biblical picture of the great city, the New Jerusalem. Nor is it logical. Would we expect on the New Earth a literal reinvention of the wheel?[9]

Far more plausible is commentator Albert Wolters' restoration theory:

Life in the new creation will not be a repristination of all things—a going back to the way things were at the beginning. Rather, life in the new creation will be a restoration of all things—involving the removal of every sinful impurity and the retaining of all that is holy and good. Were the new creation to exclude the diversity of the nations and the glory of the kings of the earth, it would be impoverished rather than enriched, historically regressive and reactionary rather than progressive.[10]

To hold this view is to maintain that the music of Mozart, the painting of Rembrandt, the writing of Shakespeare, the discoveries of science, and the God-honoring work that you and I have produced will not be lost upon life in the new creation. When we die, we don't really die! Our influence lives on, as does our work. Works may not get us to heaven, but they certainly follow us there.

We Will Rest

If your schedule is as jam-packed as mine typically is, this news comes as a relief. Yes, we will work in heaven, but it is equally true that we will *rest*. Revelation 14:13 issues this as something of a promise: "Blessed are the dead who die in the Lord . . . that they may rest from their labors."

But before you start shopping for new bedding and pajamas, keep in mind that "rest" in heaven does not equate with sleeping that future age away. Far more likely is that rest in the future reality will be like that described by Jesus in Matthew 11:28: "Come to me, all who labor and are heavy laden," he says, "and I will give you rest." In this world, we are restless because of stress, pressure, striving, and struggle; it's all a by-product of the curse, the "fallenness" we are forced to endure. But in the new world, these things will not be present; in heaven, we will be at peace. Rather than wringing our hands in worry and fear, we will be *at rest*.

We Will Eat

The news just keeps getting better, doesn't it! Yes, there will be food in heaven, and yes, you and I get to *eat*. We read of a heavenly banquet in Matthew 8:11, Mark 14:25, Luke 14:15–24, and again in Luke 22:30. We read of a wedding feast, referring to the marriage supper of the Lamb, in Matthew 25:10 and also in Revelation 19:9. I can't tell you whether your favorite food will be present—please, Lord, let there be hot dogs!—but I can tell you that you'll enjoy the experience of dining with saints both old and new.

We Will Reign

The Bible tells us in Revelation 22:5 that we will "reign forever and ever," and while I don't know all the ins and outs of such a role, it is clear from Scripture that God will give us the authority to rule, govern, and judge the earth. (See 1 Corinthians 6:2–3.)

In this and many other ways, once we are part of the new world, we will be like God, the Scriptures say. Freed at last from the tethers of sin and selfishness, we will take on additional characteristics of God himself that today we simply cannot know.

We Will Live in a Holy Place

It stands to reason that those who love God will live forever in a holy place. God himself is holy; surely his dwelling place must be holy. And it is. According to John's vision in Revelation, what began in the Bible with a garden marred by degradation, disobedience, and deceit will end in a holy city, where impurity cannot exist. Eden has been restored here into a spotless place, which is a far cry from the cities of today.

Though I'm a city boy at heart, even I must admit that our world's cities are often the most unpleasant of places to be: There is overcrowding. There is dishonesty. There is crime. There is abuse. There is filth.

But if there is one thing John offers us in Revelation 21, it is a redemptive view of cities—namely, by comparing them to a beautiful *bride*. The new city of Jerusalem comes down from God "as a bride adorned for her husband" (v. 2), the text promises us, which to me conjures images of a very good day in my life. On the day I saw my bride, Deb, walk down the aisle to become my wife, I thought I might collapse from the magnitude of that moment in time. I wanted the sight of her to last forever, the sight of *that* woman taking steps toward *me*. Similarly, the apostle John ransacks his vocabulary to describe the splendor that is this new city and yet *still* comes up obviously short: "It's a *city*. It's a *new* city, a *pure* city. It's going to be as beautiful as a *bride*!"

Let's take a look at the implications of John's helpful—if feeble—attempts.

The City's Setting

Several marvelous features make this new city divinely distinct. Let me show you three.

The human and the natural are reconciled. In this city that John describes, humankind at last makes perfect peace with the natural world surrounding it. "The heavenly Jerusalem is no work of humankind standing over against an alien wilderness," one author notes. "Rather, John's portrayal of the city with a garden at its center [a renewed Eden once again open to humankind] reveals it as a divine city in which the human and the natural are reconciled."[11]

God's workmanship is eternally on display. We read in Hebrews 11:9–10 that believers as early as Abraham longed for such a place.

> By faith he went to live in the land of promise, as in a foreign land, living in tents with Isaac and Jacob, heirs with him of the same promise. For he was looking forward to the city that has foundations, whose designer and builder is God.

And what is there *not* to look forward to about a place prepared for us by God? Clearly man has built cities without God across the span of time, but in this case, it is *God* who is doing the building—a city not made by mortal hands, but by God himself.

The goal of everlasting community is achieved. It is important to see that the eternal state will not be enjoyed in solitude or individualism. A city is the symbol of people gathered together in harmony. One commentator writes, "A city is the realization of human community, the concrete living out of interdependence as the essential nature of human life . . . for the city as a whole is the community of believers, the temple in which God dwells."[12]

Truly, heaven is not merely a place, but also a *people*. Heaven's identity seems inextricably tied to those who inhabit it: Christ and his church, Old Testament and New Testament believers who by faith are forever joined.

The City's Size and Scope

For some reason, God takes pains to provide detailed facts about the grandeur of this "new place." Verses 15–16, again: "And the one who spoke with me had a measuring rod of gold to measure the city and its gates and walls. The city lies foursquare, its length the same as its width. And he measured the city with his rod, 12,000 stadia [or, 1,380 miles in every direction]. Its length and width and height are equal."

Now, I don't know the reasons God chose to convey this information, but I'm guessing that one thing is true: There's enough room in this new environment for most every Texan to have a ranch.

And yet most likely, this information is symbolic, since John has a propensity for metaphor. But as Jonathan Edwards said, the substance is always stronger than the shadow. Whatever will be is greater than that which is described.

The text goes on to say:

> The foundations of the wall of the city were adorned with every kind of jewel. . . . And the twelve gates were twelve pearls, [hence the "pearly gates"] each of the gates made of a single pearl, and the street of the city was pure gold, like transparent glass.
>
> REVELATION 21:19–21

What is most interesting to note here is that the first place we see such precious stones mentioned is way back in Genesis 2:

> A river flowed out of Eden to water the garden, and there it divided and became four rivers. The name of the first is the Pishon. It is the one that flowed around the whole land of Havilah, where

there is gold. And the gold of that land is good; bdellium and onyx stone are there.

vv. 10–12

Which leads us to the new city's *significance,* its link to the beginning of time.

The City's Significance

Interestingly, when scholars translated the Hebrew word *garden* in Genesis into the Greek language of the day, it was rendered *Paradise,* the only word they could come up with to describe the luxury, the pleasure, and the grandeur of the garden of God.

In Revelation 21, we find that the garden of Eden has been improved upon—renovated, if you will—and that God has served as the general contractor, diligently working to make all things new.

For example, in Genesis 1:1, God creates the heaven and the earth. In Revelation 21:1, God creates the new heaven and earth.

In Genesis 1:16, God creates the sun. In Revelation 21:23, there is no longer any need for it: "And the city has no need of sun or moon to shine on it," that verse says, "for the glory of God gives it light, and its lamp is the Lamb."

In Genesis 1:5, God establishes the night. In Revelation 22:5, night is "no more. They will need no light of lamp or sun, for the Lord God will be their light, and they will reign forever and ever."

In Genesis 1:10, God forms the sea and all that is in it. In Revelation 21:1, we read that "the sea was no more."

In Genesis 3:14–17, sin enters the world, followed by its curse on humankind of physical death and separation from God. In Revelation 22:3, the curse is lifted: "No longer will there be

279

anything accursed, but the throne of God and of the Lamb will be in it and his servants will worship him."

In Genesis 3:24, Adam and Eve are driven from the garden, effectively removed from Paradise. In Revelation 22:14, we are fully restored there, in a renovated Paradise made especially for us: "Blessed are those who wash their robes, so that they may have the right to the tree of life and that they may enter the city by the gates."

In Genesis chapters 1 and 2, we see the river and tree of life, and, sadly, the man and the woman being led away from it. In Revelation chapters 21 and 22, we see the river and tree of life again, providing food and perpetual health for restored humankind. We read in Revelation 22:1–2:

> Then the angel showed me the river of the water of life, bright as crystal, flowing from the throne of God and of the Lamb through the middle of the street of the city; also, on either side of the river, the tree of life with its twelve kinds of fruit, yielding its fruit each month. The leaves of the tree were for the healing of the nations.

As one commentator puts it, "Eden has not only been restored but has been elevated and expanded for the people of God in eternity."[13] Because of Jesus' life, his death, his resurrection, and his ascension, *all* of creation can be redeemed. What God originally formed and declared "good" (see Genesis 1–2) will be deemed good once again.

We Will Be Reunited With Those We Love

Some readers who enjoy the beach may be disappointed to learn that according to John, the sea is "no more" in the new heaven and earth (Revelation 21:1). But before you send me a scathing email enumerating the many soulish benefits of boating, surfing, sunbathing, and fishing, let me be quick to add that this language is likely more symbolic than literal.

By way of context, Jews in the day of John were not a seafaring people. In fact, they often feared the sea, viewing it not as a place of rest and relaxation, but as a place of chaos and corruption. "The beast came from the sea,"[14] one author notes, citing Revelation 13:1. "The great harlot sits on many waters,"[15] according to Revelation 17:1. Furthermore, evil is often pictured in the Bible as a sea monster: the *dragon* (Job 7:12; Psalm 74:13); *Leviathan* or *Behemoth* (Job 40:15–24; Psalm 74:13–14; 104:26; Isaiah 27:1); and the *serpent* (Job 26:13; Isaiah 27:1).[16]

On a practical level, I've always envisioned John sitting on that isle of exile, surrounded by nothing but water and yet utterly failing to see any sea. As he stared across those waters in the general direction of Ephesus, where he had spent his last year of freedom, I wonder if it struck him that the sea is what separated him from his friends, his family, and his life. No more sea, to John, therefore, meant no more separation, no more isolation, no more distance, no more divide. The absence of that vast expanse could there mean intimacy, familiarity, security—all things heaven promises to be. We will be reunited with beloved believers. We will spend eternity with other lovers of God.

We Will Know No More Suffering and Pain

There in Revelation 21, we learn not only that the first heaven and earth will pass away, that the sea will be no more, that a holy city will come down, and that humankind will dwell with God, but also that there will be no more death, mourning, crying, or pain (v. 4). And that conveys volumes, doesn't it? For most people, the tears we shed across a lifetime could fill scores of buckets to overflowing. Tears of wounding, tears of disappointment, tears of sorrow, tears of pain. This is a world utterly *filled* with tears.

I have friends who have children with special needs and perpetually live life overwhelmed, tired, and confused. They have shed many tears.

I have friends suffering even today with brain tumors and other forms of cancer. They have shed many tears.

I have friends who have had to bury their own children. They have shed many tears.

I have friends praying for prodigal kids who have yet to turn toward home. They have shed many tears.

I have friends whose spouses recently filed for a divorce they themselves don't want. They have shed many tears.

I have friends who have lost their homes and all their assets in this down economy and simply don't know where to turn. They have shed many tears.

When I was a young man, I never wanted to do anything but be a pastor. And after more than forty years in that role, I still can't believe I get to do what I do. It is a *joy* to serve Christ and to pastor a local church. But in ministry, the ups are tempered by the downs. Yes, there are good days when interactions are gratifying and sweet. But there also are tough days when I meet with people with tearstained faces, and I simply don't know how to help. There are tears that human hands cannot wipe away. There are broken hearts that I myself cannot mend.

I come to this part of John's vision, and I exhale a sigh of relief. There is coming a time when *every* tear will be wiped away—no more suffering, no more grief. I eagerly await that day.

And then we find that there will be no more death as well. This makes sense to us, doesn't it, because we understand that we were made to *live*. We were created for eternity, my friend! Death, then, is a most unnatural act, one that will not be with us in heaven. "The last enemy to be destroyed is death," 1 Corinthians 15:26 says, a verse we looked at in chapter 9. Death's days are numbered! This gives us cause to rejoice. No more losing battles with cancer. No more funeral services. No more processions to the graveside. No more dark, lonely nights spent by the loved ones left behind. No more tombstones declaring death had its way again. There are absolutely no cemeteries in heaven. Life will win, at last.

We Will Experience "All Things New"

I first met the great evangelist Billy Graham when I was a seminary student in Fort Worth, Texas, and one of my professors introduced us. I felt like I was meeting the president or royalty. I had grown up listening to Billy's *Hour of Decision* radio program and had watched my parents give their lives to Jesus Christ at a Billy Graham crusade in the 1950s. For my entire life, this man has been one of my personal heroes, and several years ago, I had the high honor of meeting with him at his home in Montreat, North Carolina.

Partway through our time together, Billy and I got to talking about his late wife, Ruth, whom he still misses dearly, and Billy told me a funny story about how her tombstone's epitaph came to be. Evidently one day Ruth was driving through the beautiful Smoky Mountains, when she came upon a series of signs warning drivers of upcoming construction. "Caution" . . . "Under Construction." Ruth kept seeing those signs.

Along that particular stretch of highway, Ruth slowed her speed and took the turns a bit more carefully than usual until at last she came to the end of the construction zone. And that's when she saw the sign that would have quite an impact on her. "End of construction," it read, "Thank you for your patience."

As Billy tells it, Ruth returned home with a big grin on her face, told her husband of the experience, and said, "That's *exactly* what I want on my tombstone." She wound up telling her entire family of her wishes, and they all chuckled in reply. But she was completely serious. And today, there on the grounds of the Billy Graham Memorial Library, where Ruth is buried and where Billy someday will be buried, her tombstone does indeed read: "End of construction. Thank you for your patience."

Ruth grasped a truth that would be helpful for all of us to grasp: As long as we exist in this present reality, we remain under construction at best. God has perfection in store for us, but not one of us is quite there yet! Which is what makes the promise of Revelation 21:5 so marvelous: "Behold," God tells us, "I am making *all things new*" (emphasis mine).

Indeed, God has long been in the business of making things new. He gave us a new birth (John 3) and new life (Colossians 3) and makes us new creations, when we submit our lives to Christ (2 Corinthians 5:17). Furthermore, in heaven, we will have new bodies. We will exist in a brand-new world. Our in-process state will be behind us; finally, we will be *done*!

This is what you and I both crave, if we're honest. We want the twists and turns of our lives to be made straight. We want the construction zone to end. Writes John Ortberg:

> We want more than more of the same. We want what's wrong to be put right. We want suffering to stop. We want clean air, meaningful work, honest politicians, clear consciences, ceaseless beauty, instant Internet connections, the end of loneliness and war. We want the whole enchilada. We want heaven.[17]

Thankfully, heaven is what we will get.

The War, at Last, Will End

I don't know about you, but I love happy endings. Whether we're talking about a movie, a book, a song, or the circumstances in my life, I like it when things all work out. We're predisposed to happy endings from the time we're little children, in fact. Pull together an armful of the most popular children's books ever written, and you'll find that six magical words conclude them all: "And they lived happily ever after. . . ."

Isn't that what we desire?

We come to the last two chapters of the Bible, God's inspired and infallible Word, and we find the ultimate in happy endings. The prophet Isaiah foretold the events that will unfold, saying:

> He will swallow up death forever; and the Lord God will wipe away tears from all faces, and the reproach of his people he will take away from all the earth, for the Lord has spoken. It will be

said on that day, "Behold, this is our God; we have waited for him, that he might save us. This is the Lord; we have waited for him; let us be glad and rejoice in his salvation.

ISAIAH 25:8–9

Death swallowed up forever! The God we've waited for, right by our side. This isn't merely what we long for; it's actually what we *need*. There is a phenomenon in neuropsychology known as "psychic numbing," which means that at a certain point, when you and I are exposed to too much trauma, too much devastation, too much pain, we will withdraw our attention and focus on something that is a bit cheerier, more manageable, more fun. Clearly, I am no psychologist, but I think we're nearing the "numb" stage now.

There are wars and rumors of wars. There is tragedy and grief and pain. There is abuse and addiction wreaking havoc on too many lives, and many of us have simply shut down. We just can't take the agony. We can't take the disease. We can't take the poverty. We can't take the unrest.

We see the evil ripple effects of sin running rampant in our world—suffering and disability and loneliness and fear and temptation and injustice and greed—and we just don't know where to *put* it all. We don't know how to respond. We're too overwhelmed by all the bad to be of any good.

We look at our own lives—even our own bodies—and realize that what doesn't hurt doesn't work, and we know nothing else to do but to throw up our hands to heaven and plead for a refuge, for rescue, for relief.

God's answer? *It is near.*

Let me give you just a glimpse.

In the new reality, we will be *unable* to sin—to add to the side of life's ledger that produces pain, grief, death—for two reasons, at least. First, we know that God cannot be in the presence of sin.[18] If we are to dwell forever with God, as Revelation 21 promises, then clearly our old vices—cowardice, sexual immorality, lying, idolatry, hatefulness, despondency, fear, addiction, avarice, ugliness of every kind—will not be welcomed there.

But there is a second reason, which is that we will have been entirely sanctified.[19] Think of it! We won't even want to sin. Bible teacher and fellow Texan Tom Nelson writes:

> The eternal state is marked by "entire sanctification." I asked one of my professors in seminary if we will have a will in the eternal state. He said we will have a glorified will. I asked him, "Can we sin?" He said we will not be able to sin because we will have both perfect wisdom and a perfect will. The concept is similar to asking a person, "Can you put your hand on a red hot burner on a stove?" The answer is "No." Does that mean you're not able to? No, you are able, but you cannot and will not. Your will is sealed in wisdom because you have been through the experience of being burned. In the same way, we will be sealed, unable to sin.[20]

This is near, God assures us. Really, truly, it is. The battle we've been fighting will soon come to a victorious end. We win! Like the little boy in the movie who survived the concentration camp, you and I are about to receive the tank.

Those who have been blind will see. Those who have been deaf will hear. Those who have been oppressed will be set free. Those who have been mute will shout for joy. Those who have been paralyzed will dance around God's throne. The wounded will be made whole. The downtrodden will be lifted up. *All* people will flourish in the new reality, in that place where war has ceased. What has been unseen at last will be *seen*. We will enter into life as it was meant to be lived.

We Will See That Which Has Been Unseen

And so we come to an invitation, just as John did at Revelation's end. I simply can't do this text justice without quoting it word for word. Revelation 22:16–20, then, verbatim:

> I, Jesus, have sent my angel to testify to you about these things for the churches. I am the root and the descendant of David, the bright morning star. The Spirit and the Bride say, "Come." And let the one who hears say, "Come." And let the one who is thirsty come; let the one who desires take the water of life without price.
>
> I warn everyone who hears the words of the prophecy of this book: if anyone adds to them, God will add to him the plagues described in this book, and if anyone takes away from the words of the book of this prophecy, God will take away his share in the tree of life and in the holy city, which are described in this book.
>
> He who testifies to these things says, "Surely I am coming soon." Amen. Come, Lord Jesus!

The apostle John's vision began with "I saw" and ends here with "Come, Lord Jesus!" This is about the best summary in existence on the goal of the Christ-following life—we strain to see as Jesus himself sees things, and we yearn to live with him all of our days.

We see when we ask God for spiritual eyes to take in the unseen war being waged all around us. We see when we evaluate our lives not only in terms of our titles and roles and accomplishments and dreams, but in terms of the honest state of our soul. We see when we invest valuable time contemplating what eternity without God would be like, and choosing eternity *with* him instead. We see when we stand guard over our perspective that life—real life, full life, the life that Jesus gives—is more than what we comprehend with our natural senses. We see when we are willing to acknowledge that regardless of the lies society feeds us, there is much to "real life" that exists in the supernatural realm.

What do *you* see, as you open spiritual eyes? How has God worked in your life in years past, drawing you into relationship with him? How is he working, even now, to cultivate deeper intimacy with you? What is he showing you about your future that you can cling to as a divine pledge?

We strain to see as Jesus sees things. And then, we yearn to live with him all of our days.

Throughout the Scriptures the people of God are characterized by anticipation. In the Old Testament, followers of his awaited the coming Messiah; when they lost their sense of anticipation, their faith became stale and they fell away from God.

In the New Testament, we see followers anticipating Christ's return, followed by the splendor of the new heaven and the new earth.

How is your anticipation level these days? For many people I meet, life is going pretty well—so well, in fact, that their primary aim in life is simply maintaining the status quo. They finally have made enough money to afford the car/house/boat/wardrobe/vacation destination they've always wanted, and now they just want a little time to enjoy it.

God looks at that type of shortsighted desire and says, "You still don't get it, do you? You just can't fathom what I have in store for those who love me. Please stop placing trust in the temporal. Please, would you give me your heart?"

With more tenderness and patience than we've ever experienced, God slips in beside us along this path called life and whispers into our ear, "I know you think that job promotion is going to quench the thirst you feel. I know you believe down to your toes that having children will somehow satisfy the hunger down deep in your soul. But it won't. It can't. That ache you feel can only be relieved by me."

"Are you thirsty?" the offer goes. *Then come.*

"Are you hungry?" *Then come.*

"Do you want to fight on the winning side?" *Then come.*

Start making heaven a habit of your heart, and watch the pain of this place fade away. The day is coming, says 1 John 3:2, when we will see God just as he is, when we will actually be *like him*, if you can imagine that truth. And until that grand appearance, we get to live gracious, meaningful, victorious lives. We get to fight as those who have already won.

Discussion Questions

1. A question is posed from John Piper: "If you could have heaven with no sickness, and with all the friends you ever had on earth, and all the food you ever liked, and all the leisure activities you ever enjoyed, and all the natural beauties you ever saw, all the physical pleasures you ever tasted, and no human conflict or any natural disasters, could you be satisfied with heaven, if Christ were not there?" Why is this question significant for people to consider? How would you answer it?

2. Which of the eternal realities mentioned in this chapter—that we will worship God, learn about God, work, rest, eat, and reign—most make you long for heaven, and why?

3. Another heavenly reality is that all things will be made new. When have you experienced a taste of this "divine newness" in your earthbound life? What did the experience teach you about God? About yourself?

4. Once we enter heaven's reality, our old vices at last will be shed. Which personal vice—cowardice, sexual immorality, lying, idolatry, hatefulness, despondency, fear, addiction, greed, something else—do you most look forward to leaving behind?

5. What occurs in your mind and heart when you read the promise that someday soon, we as Christ's followers will no longer even *want* to sin?

NOTES

Introduction

1. George Carlin, "Football or Baseball?" www.youtube.com/watch?v=qmXac L0Uny0; retrieved 12 October 2012.

2. Billy Graham, *Nearing Home: Life, Faith, and Finishing Well* (Nashville: Thomas Nelson, 2011), 2.

Chapter 1: Pressing Questions We Can't Help but Ask

1. Madeleine L'Engle, quoted in Lynn Anderson, *If I Really Believe, Why Do I Have All These Doubts?* (Minneapolis: Bethany House, 1992), 61.

2. "Most American Christians Do Not Believe that Satan or the Holy Spirit Exist," *Barna Group,* April 10, 2009, www.barna.org/barna-update/article/12-faithspirituality/260-most-american-christians-do-not-believe-that-satan-or-the-holy-spirit-exist; retrieved 1 August 2012.

3. Ibid.

4. Adapted from "To See and Not See," Oliver Sacks, *The New Yorker* archives, 10 May 1993.

Chapter 2: The Dark Angel

1. See Paul Harvey and Janet E. Heseltine, *The Oxford Companion to French Literature* (Oxford University Press, 1959) for more.

2. C. S. Lewis, *The Screwtape Letters* (New York: Simon & Schuster, 1961), 37.

3. See Ezekiel 28:13–15.

4. See Revelation 12:3–9, in which, according to most commentators, "a third of the stars of heaven" refers to the expelled angelic host.

5. Emphasis mine.

6. For a thoughtful and more thorough treatment of this topic, I encourage you to read Donald Grey Barnhouse's 1965 classic, *The Invisible War.*

7. Chip Ingram, *The Invisible War: What Every Believer Needs to Know about Satan, Demons, and Spiritual Warfare* (Grand Rapids, MI: Baker Books, 2006), 29.

8. E. M. Bounds, *The Complete Work of E. M. Bounds on Prayer: Experience the Wonder of God through Prayer* (Grand Rapids, MI: Baker Books, 1990), 134.

9. I first heard pastor and author John MacArthur reference this quote. You can read the full transcript at the website of Grace to You Ministries, "The Armor of God," www.gty.org/Resources/Sermons/90-364.

10. See Isaiah 54:17.

Chapter 3: Heaven's (Mostly) Unseen Warriors

1. Billy Graham, *Angels: God's Secret Agents* (Nashville: Thomas Nelson, 1975), 12–13.

2. See 1 Corinthians 13:1; Revelation 5:11–12; 2 Thessalonians 1:7; Psalm 103:20; and 2 Samuel 14:20.

3. See Psalm 104:4; Luke 20:36.

4. See Matthew 22:30.

5. For example, we see proof of intellect noted in Matthew 8:29, proof of emotion noted in Luke 2:13–14, and proof of their will noted in Jude 6.

6. For example, Michael is named an "archangel" or "chief angel" in Jude 9; in Daniel 10:13, he is called one of the "chief princes"; and further ranks are suggested in Ephesians 3:10, 6:12, and in 1 Peter 3:22.

7. The idea of a halo most likely comes from passages such as Luke 2:8–9, Matthew 28:3, Revelation 18:1, and Revelation 10:1.

8. See Colossians 1:16; Matthew 22:30; Matthew 28:3; and Mark 12:25.

9. See Luke 1:19; Daniel 10; Genesis 32:24–32; Hosea 12:3–6; and Exodus 3.

10. See Job 38:4–7; Matthew 24:31; and 1 Thessalonians 4:16–17.

11. Perhaps it goes without saying, but to be clear, we do not become angels when we leave this earthly existence. Some may claim that we aspire to be "as the angels," but in fact, there is no biblical substantiation for this line of thinking.

12. See Revelation 7:11.

13. See Revelation 5:9–13.

14. See Isaiah 6:3 (NCV).

15. See Revelation 19:9–10.

16. See Colossians 1:16 and Hebrews 1:14.

17. See Psalm 103:20–21.

18. See Psalm 34:7 and Luke 15:10.

19. Johnson Oatman Jr. and John R. Sweney, *Holy, Holy, Is What the Angels Sing*, 1894, public domain.
20. See, for example, Luke 16:22.
21. Billy Graham, *Angels: God's Secret Agents* (Nashville: Thomas Nelson, 1975), 7–8.
22. See Luke 2.

Chapter 4: Battle Gear

1. Commonly attributed to early twentieth-century theologian Adolphus Frederick Schauffler.
2. "10 Burning Questions for John Wooden," ESPN, http://espn.go.com/page2/s/questions/wooden.html; retrieved 20 January 2013.
3. In the early 1960s, author Herbert Lockyer wrote *All the Promises in the Bible* (Zondervan), in which he enumerates each one.

Chapter 5: Mind Matters

1. Josh Hamilton, as told to Tim Keown, "I'm Proof That Hope Is Never Lost," ESPN the Magazine, July 5, 2007, http://sports.espn.go.com/mlb/news/story?id=2926447.
2. Ibid.
3. Doug Bender and Dave Sterrett, *I Am Second: Real Stories. Changing Lives* (Nashville: Thomas Nelson, 2012), 25.
4. Things are better today. My shield of faith is up stronger than ever before, but still I wrestle. Unwittingly, I wasn't taking a stand against the devil's schemes, as Ephesians 6 puts it. I will never say that I'm fully "over" this fear, because I think Satan would use my declaration as an invitation to attack me again. But I'm better, yes. This much I know. This much, I will declare.
5. Pastor Mark Driscoll offers this helpful typology: *Demonic oppression* attacks from the outside and takes the form of accusations, impossible regrets, and lies about who we are in Christ; *demonic occupation* occurs when Satan has internal influence in the life of a Christian—we have given him a foothold and now our desires, in some area of life, are bent away from Christ and toward evil; *demonic possession* occurs only in non-Christians and refers to Satan obtaining control of a person and leading him or her at will. Mark Driscoll, "Spiritual Warfare, Part 3," Mars Hill Church, February 5, 2008, http://marshill.com/media/spiritual-warfare/christus-victor.
6. Chip Ingram, *The Invisible War: What Every Believer Needs to Know about Satan, Demons, and Spiritual Warfare* (Grand Rapids, MI: Baker Books, 2006), 133.
7. Rustøen, Tone PhD, RN; Cooper, Bruce A. PhD; Miaskowski, Christine PhD, RN, FAAN, "The Importance of Hope as a Mediator of Psychological Distress and Life Satisfaction in a Community Sample of Cancer Patients," Cancer Nursing, July/August 2010, Volume 33, Issue 4, 258–267, http://journals.lww.

com/cancernursingonline/Abstract/2010/07000/The_Importance_of_Hope_as_a_
Mediator_of.2.aspx; retrieved 1 August 2012.

8. C. S. Lewis, *The Great Divorce* (New York: HarperCollins, 1946), 108–110.

Chapter 6: More Than Conquerors

1. Adapted from John Bunyan, *The Pilgrim's Progress* (Uhrichsville, OH: The
Christian Library, Barbour), 59–63.

2. Psalm 119:9–11, author's paraphrase.

3. Eugene H. Peterson, *Eat This Book: A Conversation in the Art of Spiritual
Reading* (Grand Rapids, MI: Eerdmans, 2006), 3.

4. Ibid., 4.

5. Donald Grey Barnhouse, *The Invisible War: The Panorama of the Continuing
Conflict Between Good and Evil* (Grand Rapids, MI: Zondervan, 1965), 109–110.

Chapter 7: Warfare Prayer

1. Charles Winokoor, "Military enlistment got boost as result of 9/11 terror
attacks," *Taunton Daily Gazette*, September 4, 2011, www.tauntongazette.com/
news/x1638743381/INSPIRED-ACTION-9-11-tragedy-turns-to-drive-for-recruits;
retrieved 19 October 2012.

2. J. C. Ryle, "True Christianity Is a Fight!" *Standing for God*, www.standing
forgod.com/2012/02/true-christianity-is-a-fight; retrieved 28 January 2013.

3. From John Piper's talk, "The Weapon Serves the Wielding Power," available at
www.desiringgod.org/resource-library/sermons/the-weapon-serves-the-wielding-
power; retrieved 19 October 2012.

4. www.goodreads.com/author/quotes/1148687.Samuel_Chadwick, retrieved
21 January 2013.

5. O. Hallesby, *Prayer* (Minneapolis: Augsburg Fortress, 1994 reprint of 1930
edition), 99.

6. Author's adaptation of concept found in Mark Batterson's *Wild Goose
Chase: Reclaim the Adventure of Pursuing God* (Colorado Springs: Multnomah,
2008), 50.

7. Paul Miller, *A Praying Life* (Colorado Springs: NavPress, 2009), 15.

8. E. M. Bounds, *E. M. Bounds on Prayer* (New Kensington, PA: Whitaker,
1997), 167.

Chapter 8: The Soulish Stakes of War

1. "The U.S. Weight Loss & Diet Control Market (11th Edition)," Marketdata
Enterprises Inc., May 1, 2011, www.marketresearch.com/Marketdata-Enterprises-
Inc-v416/Weight-Loss-Diet-Control-11th-6314539/; retrieved 19 October 2012.

2. "U.S. Health Club Membership Exceeds 50 Million, Up 10.8%; Industry
Revenue Up 4% as New Members Fuel Growth," IHRSA, April 5, 2011, www.

ihrsa.org/media-center/2011/4/5/us-health-club-membership-exceeds-50-million-up-108-industry.html; retrieved 19 October 2012.

3. "Demand for Plastic Surgery Rebounds by Almost 9%," Plastic Surgery Research Info, April 4, 2011, www.cosmeticplasticsurgerystatistics.com/statistics. html; retrieved 19 October 2012.

4. Ben Woolsey and Matt Schulz, "Credit Card Statistics, Industry Facts, Debt Statistics," www.creditcards.com/credit-card-news/credit-card-industry-facts-personal-debt-statistics-1276.php; retrieved 19 October 2012.

5. Mark 8:34, author's paraphrase.

6. George MacDonald, *Annals of a Quiet Neighborhood* (Charleston: Nabu Press, 2010, reprint of 1923 edition), 481.

7. Cindy West, *Saying Yes: Accepting God's Amazing Invitation to Artists and the Church* (Colorado Springs: David C. Cook, 2008), 75–76. Copyright 2008 Cindy West. *Saying Yes* published by David C Cook. Publisher permission required to reproduce. All rights reserved.

8. Valerie Bell, *A Well-Tended Soul: Staying Beautiful for the Rest of Your Life* (Grand Rapids, MI: Zondervan, 1996), 71.

9. Donald Grey Barnhouse, *The Invisible War: The Panorama of the Continuing Conflict Between Good and Evil* (Grand Rapids, MI: Zondervan, 1965), 39.

Chapter 9: An Appointment We Cannot Break

1. "Interview With Jack Nicolson: 'I Wasn't Inhibited by Anything,'" *Parade* magazine, www.parade.com/celebrity/articles/071204-jack-nicholson.html; retrieved 21 January 2013.

2. John 3:5, author's paraphrase.

3. Walter Isaacson, *Steve Jobs* (New York: Simon & Schuster, 2011), 571.

Chapter 10: Where Goodness Goes to Die

1. Verbal Witness, http://verbalwitness.blogspot.com/2009_09_01_archive. html; retrieved 10 April 2013.

2. Bill Wiese, *23 Minutes in Hell: One Man's Story about What He Saw, Heard, and Felt in That Place of Torment* (Lake Mary, FL: Charisma House, 2006), 4.

3. Ibid., 6.

4. Ibid., 25.

5. "Americans Describe Their Views About Life After Death," *Barna Group,* October 21, 2003, www.barna.org/barna-update/article/5-barna-update/128-americans-describe-their-views-about-life-after-death; retrieved 19 October 2012.

6. John Piper, "Behold the Kindness and the Severity of God," a sermon delivered 14 June 1992, Bethlehem Baptist Church, available at www.soundofgrace.com.

7. J. C. Ryle Quotes, "Preach on Hell . . . Because It Is Scriptural," http://jcrylequotes.com/2011/08/23/preach-on-hell-because-it-is-scriptural/; retrieved 1 August 2012.

8. Marsha Walton, "Scientists: Sumatra Quake Longest Ever Recorded," CNN, May 20, 2005, http://edition.cnn.com/2005/TECH/science/05/19/sumatra.quake/index.html.

9. Based on BBC news reports: "Award for Tsunami Warning Pupil," September 9, 2005, http://news.bbc.co.uk/2/hi/uk_news/4229392.stm and "Britons Commemorate Tsunami Dead," December 26, 2005, http://news.bbc.co.uk/2/hi/uk_news/4561248.stm; retrieved 21 January 2013.

Chapter 11: Paradise Found

1. www.goodreads.com/author/quotes/75887.Jonathan_Edwards; retrieved 11 October 2012.

2. "More That 10 Percent of Americans Being Treated for Depression," Right Diagnosis, www.rightdiagnosis.com/news/more_that_10_percent_of_americans_being_treated_for_depression.htm; retrieved 19 October 2012.

3. Randy Alcorn, *Heaven for Kids* (Carol Stream, IL: Tyndale House Publishers, 2006), 62.

4. See Luke 10:20.

5. See Matthew 6:20.

6. Maria Shriver, *What's Heaven?* (New York: St. Martin's Press, 1999), 14.

7. http://thinkexist.com/quotation/good_business_leaders_create_a_vision-articulate/151585.html; retrieved 1 February 2013.

8. http://thinkexist.com/quotation/when_you_have_vision_it_affects_your_attitude/13030.html; retrieved 1 February 2013.

9. From John Piper's talk, "What Happens When You Die? Glorified and Free on the New Earth," available at www.desiringgod.org/resource-library/sermons/what-happens-when-you-die-glorified-and-free-on-the-new-earth; retrieved 19 October 2012.

10. Randy Alcorn, *Heaven* (Carol Stream, IL: Tyndale House, 2004), 42.

11. See Genesis 35:18; Luke 16:19–31; 23:43; John 11:25–26; 1 Peter 3:18–19; Revelation 6:9–10.

12. In David Van Biema, "Christians Wrong About Heaven, Says Bishop," *Time* magazine, February 7, 2008, www.time.com/time/world/article/0,8599,1710844,00.html.

13. Grant Osborne, *Revelation*, Baker Exegetical Commentary on the New Testament (Grand Rapids, MI: Baker Book House, 2002), 730.

14. G. K. Beale, *The Book of Revelation: A Commentary on the Greek Text*, New International Greek Testament Commentary (Grand Rapids, MI: Eerdmans, 1998), 1040.

15. Kevin J. Vanhoozer, *Dictionary for Theological Interpretation of the Bible* (Grand Rapids, MI: Baker Book House, 2005), 686–687.

16. Emphasis mine.

17. See 1 Corinthians 15:50.

18. See Matthew 17:1–8; 22:31–32; 1 Thessalonians 2:19–20; 2 Corinthians 1:14; 1 Corinthians 13:12.
19. Joel Elowsky, ed., *Ancient Christian Commentary on Scripture: John 11–21* (Downers Grove, IL: InterVarsity Press, 2007), 126.
20. D. A. Carson, *The Gospel According to John,* Pillar New Testament Commentary (Leicester, England: APOLLOS, an imprint of InterVarsity, 1991), 492.
21. N. T. Wright, *After You Believe: Why Christian Character Matters* (New York: HarperOne, 2010), 103.
22. Matthew 5:3–10, THE MESSAGE, author's paraphrase.
23. Dr. Joseph M. Stowell, *Eternity: Reclaiming a Passion for What Endures* (Chicago: Moody Publishers, 1995), 88–89, author's paraphrase.

Chapter 12: We Win

1. John 14:3, emphasis mine.
2. www.goodreads.com/quotes/143049-the-critical-question-for-our-generation -and-for-every-generation-is; retrieved 19 October 2012.
3. A common question I receive from people who are interested in what heaven will be like is, "Will there be time in heaven?" The jury is still out on this one, but I defer to Randy Alcorn—truly a modern-day heaven "expert"—who says this on the subject: "That there is time in Heaven is made clear many places in the Bible." He then cites Revelation 8:1, Luke 15:7, Revelation 6:10–11, and Revelation 5:9–13 to support his claim. He also references the various occurrences in Scripture that refer to the presence of musical instruments in heaven, noting that "Meter, tempo, and rests are all essential components of music, and each is time related." Randy Alcorn, *Heaven for Kids* (Carol Stream, IL: Tyndale House, 2006), 72–73.
4. See 1 Corinthians 13:12.
5. See Numbers 2:2.
6. See 1 Corinthians 6:19.
7. Wayne Grudem, *Systematic Theology: An Introduction to Biblical Doctrine* (Grand Rapids, MI: Zondervan, 1994), endnote, 1162.
8. See Revelation 22:3; 5:10.
9. Randy Alcorn, *Heaven* (Carol Stream, IL: Tyndale House Publishers, 2004), 242.
10. Albert M. Wolters, *Creation Regained: Biblical Basics for a Reformational Worldview* (Grand Rapids, MI: Eerdmans, 2005), 64.
11. Brian S. Rosner, et al., eds., *New Dictionary of Biblical Theology: Exploring the Unity and Diversity of Scripture* (Downers Grove, IL: InterVarsity Press, 2000), 435. See also 2 Corinthians 12:1–4; *paradise* here is literally translated "garden" or "park."
12. M. E. Boring, *Revelation: Interpretation: A Biblical Commentary for Teaching and Preaching* (Louisville, KY: Westminster John Knox, 1989), 219.

13. Grant R. Osborne, *Revelation, Baker Exegetical Commentary on the New Testament,* (Grand Rapids, MI: Baker Book House, 2002), 768.

14. Walter A. Elwell, *Evangelical Dictionary of Biblical Theology* (Grand Rapids, MI: Baker Book House, 1984), 563.

15. Ibid.

16. See Leland Ryken, James C. Wilhoit, and Tremper Longman III, eds., *Dictionary of Biblical Imagery* (Downers Grove, IL: InterVarsity Press, 1998), 38.

17. John Ortberg, *When the Game Is Over, It All Goes Back in the Box* (Grand Rapids, MI: Zondervan, 2007), 235.

18. Habakkuk 1:13 tells us that God is so pure he cannot even "*look* at wrong," let alone reside with it.

19. See Revelation 21:27.

20. Tom Nelson, *The Big Picture: From Eternity to Eternity* (Friendswood, TX: Baxter Press, 1996), 250.

JACK GRAHAM is pastor of Prestonwood Baptist Church, one of the nation's largest, most dynamic congregations. When Dr. Graham came to Prestonwood in 1989, the 8,000-member congregation responded enthusiastically to his straightforward message and powerful preaching style. He challenged the Prestonwood family with a vision for a larger outreach, and in 1999 the church moved from its North Dallas location to a new 7,500-seat auditorium in west Plano.

Thriving with more than 31,000 members, Prestonwood continues to grow with seven weekend worship services, four mid-week services, about three hundred Bible Fellowship classes for all ages, and multiple outreach and community ministries that reach thousands. In 2006 the church added a second location, the North Campus, in a burgeoning area twenty miles north of Plano. And in 2011 Prestonwood returned to its roots—beginning its third location, the Dallas campus, about two miles from its original location.

Dr. Graham has served two terms as president of the Southern Baptist Convention, the largest American Protestant denomination, with 16 million members, and as president of the SBC Pastor's Conference.

He is a noted author of numerous books, including *You Can Make a Difference, Lessons from the Heart, A Hope and a*

Future, Life According to Jesus, Are You Fit for Life? Powering Up, and *Courageous Parenting*, coauthored by his wife, Deb. Dr. Graham's passionate, biblical teaching is also seen and heard across the country and throughout the world on PowerPoint Ministries. Through broadcasts, online sermons, and email messages, he addresses relevant, everyday issues that are prevalent in our culture and that strike a chord with audiences worldwide.

Dr. Graham was ordained to the gospel ministry in 1970, and has a master of divinity degree with honors and a doctor of ministry degree in church and proclamation from Southwestern Baptist Theological Seminary.